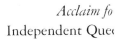

"This insightful, opinionated, and wide-ranging collection of interviews and reviews is the sort of book one can either devour in one sitting or nibble away at for days. Kramer captures the directors, actors, and films that made up a slice of early twenty-first century queer independent filmmaking and provides an invaluable resource for indie film junkies like me. *Independent Queer Cinema* makes me want to revisit films I've already seen and catch up with all the gems I've missed. Kramer's interviews are always intriguing and whether you agree or disagree with his critical opinions, his descriptions and analysis of films are thought-provoking, entertaining, and never snarky. *Independent Queer Cinema* is a vital contribution to film journalism that illuminates an all-too-often neglected area of independent film."

—Jim Tushinski
Director, *That Man: Peter Berlin*;
Author, *Van Allen's Ecstasy*

"I have known Gary for many years, and few gay writers today have such an intimate knowledge of queer cinema as he does. His new book will be the encyclopedia for lovers of queer cinema for years to come. The comprehensive book covers nearly a decade of groundbreaking gay cinema, along with insightful interviews with the stars and directors.

Each page was a step back in time, and a way to relive each of the films when I first saw them on screen. Yet, Gary seems to mention things I had never noticed, making me want to see many of them again. I am sure there will be a surge in DVD sales when this book comes out! As a travel writer who has visited many of the countries where some of the queer films originated, Gary also significantly explains the cultural backgrounds of what we see on screen, and what was in the directors' minds when they brought these stories to life. This is more than a compilation of Gary's wonderful columns, it's a historical record of the gay community and the images we present to the world on screen."

—Michael Luongo, MCRP
Collection Editor, *The Eyes of Caravaggio*;
Editor, *Between the Palms: A Collection of Gay Travel Erotica*

"Gary Kramer's *Independent Queer Cinema* is a scholarly film reference book that also takes a playful glimpse into the personal lives of some fascinating artists and personalities. Whether he's eyeballing Tilda Swinton's telling cufflinks or provoking Javier Bardem to elaborate on the actor's brief stint as a stripper, Kramer peppers this superior academic tome with the kind of dishy details that will keep readers turning the page.

Kramer skillfully addresses the political traps inherent in the subject matter, then offers an honest, witty exploration of cinema on the fringe. As with all good criticism, Kramer frames his insights within a cultural context—and he always considers the intent of the artist. Kramer's provocative work will not only delight connoisseurs of alternative cinema, it will prove equally rewarding for average filmgoers looking to expand their boundaries. *Indpendent Queer Cinema* is the essential film reference book about modern lesbian- and gay-themed cinema."

—Damion Dietz
Writer/director, *Beverly Kills* and *Love Life*

NOTES FOR PROFESSIONAL LIBRARIANS AND LIBRARY USERS

This is an original book title published by Southern Tier Editions™, Harrington Park Press®, an imprint of The Haworth Press, Inc. Unless otherwise noted in specific chapters with attribution, materials in this book have not been previously published elsewhere in any format or language.

CONSERVATION AND PRESERVATION NOTES

All books published by The Haworth Press, Inc., and its imprints are printed on certified pH neutral, acid-free book grade paper. This paper meets the minimum requirements of American National Standard for Information Sciences-Permanence of Paper for Printed Material, ANSI Z39.48-1984.

DIGITAL OBJECT IDENTIFIER (DOI) LINKING

The Haworth Press is participating in reference linking for elements of our original books. (For more information on reference linking initiatives, please consult the CrossRef Web site at www.crossref.org.) When citing an element of this book such as a chapter, include the element's Digital Object Identifier (DOI) as the last item of the reference. A Digital Object Identifier is a persistent, authoritative, and unique identifier that a publisher assigns to each element of a book. Because of its persistence, DOIs will enable The Haworth Press and other publishers to link to the element referenced, and the link will not break over time. This will be a great resource in scholarly research.

Independent
Queer Cinema
Reviews and Interviews

HARRINGTON PARK PRESS®
Southern Tier Editions™
New, recent, and forthcoming titles of related interest

The AIDS Movie: Representing a Pandemic in Film and Television by Kylo-Patrick R. Hart

The Spectacle of Isolation in Horror Films: Dark Parades by Carl Royer and Diana Royer

Queering Teen Culture: All-American Boys of Same-Sex Desire in Film and Television by Jeffery P. Dennis

Independent
Queer Cinema
Reviews and Interviews

Gary M. Kramer

Southern Tier Editions™
Harrington Park Press®
An Imprint of The Haworth Press, Inc.
New York • London • Oxford

For more information on this book or to order, visit
http://www.haworthpress.com/store/product.asp?sku=5482

or call 1-800-HAWORTH (800-429-6784) in the United States and Canada
or (607) 722-5857 outside the United States and Canada

or contact orders@HaworthPress.com

Published by

Southern Tier Editions™, Harrington Park Press®, an imprint of The Haworth Press, Inc., 10 Alice Street, Binghamton, NY 13904-1580.

PUBLISHER'S NOTE
The development, preparation, and publication of this work has been undertaken with great care. However, the Publisher, employees, editors, and agents of The Haworth Press are not responsible for any errors contained herein or for consequences that may ensue from use of materials or information contained in this work. The Haworth Press is committed to the dissemination of ideas and information according to the highest standards of intellectual freedom and the free exchange of ideas. Statements made and opinions expressed in this publication do not necessarily reflect the views of the Publisher, Directors, management, or staff of The Haworth Press, Inc., or an endorsement by them.

Cover photo credits: (top right) Photo from the João Pedro Rodrigues film *O Fantasma*. Image and poster art used by permission of Rosa Filmes and Picture This! Entertainment; (middle left) Cover artwork from the Michael Akers film *Gone, But Not Forgotten*, starring Matthew Montgomery and Aaron Orr. © 2003 United Gay Network; (middle right) Photo from the Lisa Knox-Nervig film *Wave Babes* by Michael Helms, courtesy of Wolfe Video; (bottom) Photo from the Everett Lewis film *Luster,* courtesy of TLA Releasing.

Cover design by Lora Wiggins.

Library of Congress Cataloging-in-Publication Data

Kramer, Gary M.
    Independent queer cinema : reviews and interviews / Gary M. Kramer.
       p. cm.
    Includes bibliographical references and index.
    ISBN-13: 978-1-56023-343-5 (soft : alk. paper)
    ISBN-10: 1-56023-343-5 (soft : alk. paper)
    1. Homosexuality in motion pictures. 2. Gays in motion pictures. 3. Motion pictures—Reviews. 4. Gay motion picture producers and directors—Interviews. 5. Independent filmmakers—Interviews. I. Title.

PN1995.9.H55K73 2006
791.43'653–dc22
                                       2005027587

For my father, Emmanuel, who read me,
and motivated me to write,
and to my mother, Judee, who listened,
and always gave the best advice.
And for Hank, Ben, and, of course, Mike.

ABOUT THE AUTHOR

Gary M. Kramer is a freelance writer and film critic. He is a contributing writer to *The Philadelphia Gay News*, *The San Francisco Bay Times*, *Gay City News*, *Frontiers*, and *Filmbill*. His writing and criticism also appear regularly in the magazines *Instinct*, *Out*, and *Film International*, and on the Web sites indieWIRE and AroundPhilly.com.

CONTENTS

Chapter 4. Fascinating Actors   67

Chapter 5. Promising Starts   85

Chapter 6. Not Their True Calling   101

PART II: FILM REVIEWS

Chapter 7. Hot and Sexy   115

Acknowledgments

I love books as much as I love movies. Since I was young, my dream has always been to write and publish my book. With the help of the following people, who have supported me, I have finally realized this dream.

First and foremost, Jay Quinn, for prompting me to write this book. Thank you! In addition, I want to express my appreciation for the various folks at The Haworth Press who helped me publish this work as well: Bill Palmer, Josh Ribakove, Margaret Tatich, Paul Deamer, Dawn Krisko, Kim Green, Jason Wint, Julie Ward, Marie Spencer, and my patient copy editor, Anissa Harper.

I want to also thank all of the newspaper editors who have given me the opportunity to write and have published me over the years: Patti Tihey, in particular, for her honesty, integrity, and professionalism, Kim Corsaro, Li Wang and Kawehi Haug, Steven Duchovnay, Kristin Detterline and Keith Scandone, Paul Schindler, Brian McCormick, and Aaron Krach, Wendy Mitchell and Eugene Hernanadez, Greg Montoya, Jaime Buerger, Kim McNabb, Molly English, John Sykes and Pam Zoslov, Alex Cho, Robbie Daw, and Mike Wood, Bruce Shenitz and Jeffrey Epstein, Lori Hill, Greg Salisbury, and Robert DiGiacomo. And special thanks to Ruth Russell, who started my career as a writer by giving me my first regular paying writing job.

In addition, I want to thank Beth Pinker and Patrick McHugh, along with Paula Moritz, Ann-Marie Nacchio, Frank Chile, Nick Tarnowski, Jesse Cute, Donna Baum, Andy Preis, Ray Murray, Corey Eubanks, Marcus Hu, Michael Berlin, and Doug Witkins, for getting me some great interviews over the years.

Independent Queer Cinema: Reviews and Interviews
© 2006 by The Haworth Press, Inc. All rights reserved.
doi:10.1300/5482_a

Thanks also to my early readers, Carol Reynolds, Harold Brown, Margaret Lacey, and the extended counseling I received from Herb Kaplan.

I owe a huge round of applause to Daniel O'Brien. Dan, it is so nice to thank *you* in a book for a change!

I also want to acknowledge the support I have received from Roberta (Bertie) Petusky and Ray Simon, Eleanor Pollak and Bruce Finkelstein, and Susan Dreher and Mark Wheeler from the Sunday Morning Breakfast Group, and my long-suffering moviegoing friends in the Cinema Salon, particularly Jennifer Steinberg, Claudine Richman, and Vicki Mager.

I should also acknowledge the writers, directors, actors, and producers who make independent queer cinema something to watch, think, and write about.

Of note to readers: The names, dates, and film titles in this book have been verified using various publicity materials, including press kits, news articles, databases, and Internet resources. However, any errors are my responsibility.

Finally, this book could not have been possible without the efforts of MKK, who woke me early on many mornings so I could write (and feed him); Emile—because I love you, you're my brother! And of course, Eoms, who gets all my *icky* love, always. And Mom.

Author's Note

The interviews and reviews in this book, with the exception of *Madame Satã, Burnt Money,* and *Gaudi Afternoon,* have been previously published in one or more of the following publications: *The Philadelphia Gay News, The San Francisco Bay Times, Gay City News, Filmbill, Honolulu Weekly, Las Vegas Weekly, The Cleveland Free Times, Out Front Colorado, Bay Windows, The Washington Blade, The Chicago Free Press, Syracuse New Times, Trade, Metroline,* and the Web sites aroundphilly.com and Indiewire.com.

Independent Queer Cinema: Reviews and Interviews
© 2006 by The Haworth Press, Inc. All rights reserved.
doi:10.1300/5482_b

Introduction:
There's No Accounting for Taste

Sometimes I like lemon on my fish, sometimes I don't.

Overheard at a seafood restaurant

I have always wanted to understand why people like the films they do. Since "there's no accounting for taste," what exactly shapes our tastes as moviegoers?

The films I watch and write about in this book represent images of men and women in contemporary independent and foreign queer cinema. As a gay man, I find that it is often difficult to find an adequate representation of myself on the screen. As gays (and lesbians) are woefully underrepresented—and often relegated to supporting roles in mainstream cinema—it has become increasingly important for me to uncover independent and foreign films that depict queer life, especially one I can identify with.

For years, gay men have not been portrayed in a positive light on screen; they have been suicidal, sexless, or flamboyant. Yet I firmly believe that bad exposure is better than none. Many of the films discussed in this book are positive representations of gay men—but not all. One of my favorite queer movies, *Burnt Money,* features gay guys behaving very, very badly.

What I hope to do in this book is to showcase the films and personalities that I think deserve attention, respect, and more success than they have earned thus far in their careers. With a few exceptions, the interview subjects will likely be mostly unfamiliar names. Most of the movies discussed have been theatrically released, albeit mainly in limited distribution, and some directly to video.

Independent Queer Cinema: Reviews and Interviews
© 2006 by The Haworth Press, Inc. All rights reserved.
doi:10.1300/5482_01

The 100 interviews and reviews contained in this collection are my way of calling attention to these people and their films. I admit some of the features discussed herein are not great. But even the less-than-stellar works are still of considerable interest, because they depict what I think is an important topic or issue of queer life in an unusual or original way. I am compelled to write about these films to prompt readers to discover them.

It is hard for me to select a favorite queer movie—however, *Come Undone* comes foremost to mind for its sensitive and complex portrait of gay youth. Some of my other personal favorites included in this book are *Luster,* an absolutely charming little low-budget romance, and *Madame Satā,* which impressed me for being not just visually striking, but also for featuring a powerhouse performance by Brazilian actor Lázaro Ramos.

My interest in writing about the films in this book stems from being wired a certain way. I have become highly aware of what I like to watch. Perhaps my ideal queer film would be a low-budget drama that has three sexy men in a room fucking or fighting. As a moviegoer, I have always gravitated toward independent, cult, and foreign films because I thought they all had the most interesting stories to tell—stories that would speak to me in ways a formulaic Hollywood blockbuster could not.

I should point out that I do not identify with every character or situation in the films discussed herein. I have never been to a circuit party, yet I have included interviews on a film about this subject. The reason for entries such as the ones on *Circuit* or *The Fluffer,* about the gay pornography industry, is that they allow me to understand these subcultures—even more so after talking with their filmmakers.

This book is arranged in two sections—interviews and film reviews. Each section is grouped thematically. All of the films being discussed have queer characters or content, or have been made by queer filmmakers or feature queer actors. There are a few exceptions. For example, in our conversation about *The Dancer Upstairs,* Javier Bardem discusses his queer role of Reinaldo Arenas, in *Before Night Falls.* I thought this interview was worthy of inclusion. Also, although it is only briefly suggested, *A Matter of Taste* does contain homoerotic tension between the two male characters, even though this is not mentioned in my lunch with Jean-Pierre Lorit.

The articles included herein are reprints of my work for various publications including *The Philadelphia Gay News*, *The San Francisco Bay Times, Gay City News*, and other alternative weekly newspapers. My criteria for inclusion is based on what makes the film discussed or the interview itself interesting. Some queer films I did not include here because I did not write about them when they were released; there are other queer films that I wrote about but chose not to include in this volume. My decision was based on what I thought made a good interview or good criticism.

The reviews in this book are mostly positive, to encourage the films to be seen. However, I have a section titled "Bad Taste" in which I review films I did not like, such as *Talk to Her*, which almost everyone enjoyed except me. As I said, there's no accounting for taste.

All of the pieces in this book were originally published between 1999 and 2004. Although I have made minor edits for clarification, for the most part the interviews are in their original format. This means that when someone mentions an "upcoming project," the film may have already been made and/or released by the time this book is published. Dates for all of the films discussed are included for chronology and reference. I have used the date of the film's production for consistency. (Some films may have been released years after being made.)

While looking back over the columns to include in this book I thought about what appeals to me as a cinephile. I still swoon over Stéphane Rideau in *Come Undone,* not only because he is incredibly sexy but also because his character's appeal comes from being wholly comfortable with his sexuality (especially in comparison with his suicidal co-star). I greatly admire the film *His Secret Life* for having the main gay character portrayed as a normal guy living a normal life with a set of unusual friends (who function as his family). And I also adore *Kissing Jessica Stein* for not insulting its audience, for being funny and touching and heartfelt. I also feel that the film's ending—which some people argue with—is wholly appropriate. To me, these films are remarkable movies, and ones that I strongly identify with. I know not everyone will agree.

And perhaps this best suggests why people like the films they do. We are what we watch. The silver screen is a mirror reflecting aspects of our life back to us. I was the teenager in *Come Undone* struggling with his sexuality; I try to be the gay man with supportive friends in *His Secret Life*; and I am the neurotic Jewish writer that is Jessica Stein. Yet I have my own identity as well.

As readers will see, I have filtered these films, filmmakers, and actors included in this book through my own queer perspective. I have sought these films, filmmakers, and actors out in an effort to shape my own life. Hopefully readers will use this guide and be encouraged to seek them out too.

PART I:
INTERVIEWS

Chapter 1
Intriguing Queer Filmmakers

The filmmakers discussed in this chapter operate outside the mainstream. Their films appeal to me because they tackle issues—sexuality, coming out, or finding one's place in the world—in provocative ways.

BILL CONDON: KINSEY

Kinsey (2004) is a great independent queer film. Made by the specialty arm of a larger studio, this biopic tackles issues that Hollywood would normally prefer to avoid.

Helmed by a gay man who is a master at depicting sexual longing, *Kinsey* was a provocative investigation into how people talk and think about sex. Condon himself spoke rather eloquently on the subject of sex—over breakfast, no less—and his frankness about films, and filmmaking, is refreshing.

Scaling Kinsey with Bill Condon

Where does openly gay Bill Condon—the writer-director of *Kinsey,* a biopic about the bisexual sexologist—fall on the Kinsey scale?

"The whole essence of those questions for Kinsey was complete confidentiality," the handsome filmmaker says over breakfast at the Four Seasons, adding slyly, "which means I *could* not answer."

But Condon, who won an Oscar for writing *Gods and Monsters* (1998), and was nominated again for adapting *Chicago* (2002), smiles and admits proudly, "I've been pretty much at the five to six end of the scale my whole life."

Independent Queer Cinema: Reviews and Interviews
© 2006 by The Haworth Press, Inc. All rights reserved.
doi:10.1300/5482_02

Like the characters in his impressive new film, Condon actually reveals much about his sexual history over the meal, something that most filmmakers in Hollywood would probably keep private.

"I figured out I was gay at such a young age. I went to an all-boys' high school, and had a wonderful romance in this extraordinary environment when I was fifteen. It was my first gay sexual experience, and it went on for a couple of years," says the filmmaker, whose current relationship is now in its eighth year.

Condon came out in high school, and he states that his father—who shares Kinsey's father's skittishness regarding any display or mention of sex—"was disappointed, but basically tolerant of [my homosexuality]. It was never really discussed again."

One gets the impression from Condon's candor that he thoroughly enjoyed exploring the topic of sex and Kinsey's sexual history during the year he spent doing research prior to filming.

"One of the things that I learned [making *Kinsey*] is how fluid sexuality is. Kinsey kept screaming out to everybody, 'you're individuals, be yourself!' and he thought that people were often sublimating their own individuality to fit into the group in some way."

Yet the talented writer-director is quick to note the irony of Kinsey being "somebody who is reducing human sexuality to data that fits in boxes on a piece of graph paper in order to prove that people can't be categorized and put into boxes."

Condon continues to talk passionately and at length about bisexuality, which is at the core of *Kinsey*. "I think it is one of those ideas that is hard for people to get their minds around. Do we tend to close ourselves down to certain things just because we so commited to an identity? Obviously, when you are gay, you tend to think of yourself as progressive. But I then found myself in the middle of my research coming up against my own biases that I had not been aware of. For example, I think a lot of us, because we know people who are closeted, tend to think of bisexuality as a kind of incipient homosexuality, or an undeclared homosexuality. But that really is not true."

His careful consideration of this topic, at 8:30 in the morning, suggests the energy and enthusiasm Condon used to present his portrait of Kinsey, a man who wrestles with both homosexual and heterosexual desires. The filmmaker describes his subject as "a mass of contradictions—a scientist who is asking people to be completely [open] and truthful about their sex lives, while he is being completely secretive about his own."

Condon explains that Kinsey waited until middle age to act on his gay impulses and, as such, the film has several suggestive, homoerotic scenes leading up to the notable moment in which Kinsey (Liam Neeson) is seduced in a hotel room by his nude research assistant, Clyde Martin (Peter Sarsgaard).

The director is pleased with how this critical queer love scene in the film has been received. "A lot of people tell me that the Peter scene is a real turn on," Condon says cheerily. And while he confesses to being attracted to many of the actors who have starred in his films, Condon says, "Nothing turns me on in this movie because I've been staring at it so long!"

This revelation actually reminds the writer-director of a shrewd comment Kinsey made in doing his work. "He always told his researchers what first might seem in some way exciting, will soon lose its allure." According to Condon, "it is true when you make a movie" as well.

Because of the strong sexual content, the filmmaker expects *Kinsey* to be "a litmus test for people's tolerance of discussions [about] sex."

When the MPAA called Condon to tell him they were rating the film "a hard R," he was pleased because they said, "It was a long debate, and we learned a lot. Thank you very much."

Audience response at festivals where the film has screened has run the gamut, with some viewers calling the film's depiction of sex "transgressive" while others find it to be "mild." One consensus is that audiences are calling the film both "relevant" and "funny."

The filmmaker applauds these reactions to his film. "To me, they just sum up what remains endlessly fascinating about the subject of sex. How connected it is to emotion, and how complicated it will always be."

What is more, Condon responds to this idea with the same rational and nonjudgmental attitude that his film's hero Kinsey developed. "I think it has to do with personal taste. It is a reflection of who those people are. I am hoping that people connect *Kinsey* to themselves in a personal way and ask 'What part of my own sexual makeup has made me feel uncomfortable?' and 'Where am I on that scale?'"

ROSE TROCHE: THE SAFETY OF OBJECTS

I missed *Go Fish* (1994), lesbian filmmaker Rose Troche's directorial debut, but I loved her underseen sophomore effort, the gay-tinged *Bedrooms and Hallways* (1998). Troche moved out of overtly queer territory with her third film, *The Safety of Objects* (2001), and I greatly admired this quartet of intertwined stories, even though the film has its detractors.

Touché, Troche

Lesbian filmmaker Rose Troche, looking lovely and quite hip in a gray sweater and jeans, sips a cosmopolitan in the Four Seasons Hotel where she is discussing her new film *The Safety of Objects*. An adaptation of A.M. Homes's short stories—the multitalented Troche wrote the screenplay in addition to directing—this astonishing drama chronicles the emotional trajectories of four suburban neighborhood families in an unnamed American town.

"The stories are about loss," Troche says about the project. "The thing we have to lose in order to move on with our lives."

The characters in the film, all of whom experience some kind of misfortune, are conflated from the book. The main players include Esther (Glenn Close), a mother coping with a comatose son and a despondent daughter; Jim (Dermot Mulroney), a lawyer who seeks meaning in his life; Helen (Mary Kay Place), a housewife searching for "the next best thing"; and Annette (Patricia Clarkson), a divorcée struggling to raise two children.

Although none of the episodes are particularly queer per se (though one storyline features a tomboy), the director explains that her lesbianism still has a very strong influence on her filmmaking in the sense of "where [I] put the camera, where it lingers."

But perhaps it is in her writing where Troche is best able to express herself and her sexuality. "I write my women like I like my women—they are strong, and say what they think. I know I became more that way when I came out," she declares, not one to mince her words, either.

The filmmaker also has great things to say about her extraordinary cast. Troche is thrilled to have had a chance to direct the "incredible" Glenn Close, and she gushes about Mary Kay Place. "She is like an icon to me," she says.

Likewise, Troche was pleased to showcase actresses Moira Kelly, Patricia Clarkson, and Kristen Stewart in the same film. As if to offer an explanation about what attracted such a fabulous cast to *The Safety of Objects,* the writer-director claims that the draw for the actors was the script.

"I'm not the kind of filmmaker that people say 'Ooh, that Rose Troche, once I get to work with her, my life will be . . .'," she deadpans as her thought trails off.

Yet Troche is becoming a pretty hot property. She shot the pilot for *The L Word,* the lesbian series Showtime picked up thirteen episodes for this summer, and she is currently on the writing team for the series.

One of the co-writers on *The L Word* is Guinevere Turner, who starred in Troche's debut film *Go Fish,* and has a significant voice-over role (as a doll) in *The Safety of Objects.* What is more, V.S. Brodie, who co-starred in *Go Fish,* was the person who brought *The Safety of Objects* to Troche with the suggestion to make it into a film.

Brodie gave Troche the book in 1994, but it took several years to get the film made because there were issues with optioning the material. (Homes started writing another book based on two of the characters from the *Objects* stories, which caused a conflict.) While the rights were being worked out, Troche made the gay romantic comedy *Bedrooms and Hallways.* However, "I could not get [*Objects*] out of my mind," she said. "I really wanted to do it."

Her persistence has paid off. This accomplished film expertly charts the parallel journeys of its characters, and raises Troche to a new level as a director. Furthermore, it appears that she will continue to work on exciting and challenging films. Describing her next cinematic project, *Lucinda's Changed,* Troche says that it is "a sequel to Mary

Shelley's *Frankenstein*. We're supposing that Victor Frankenstein made a female creature before he died."

Now dividing her time between New York and Canada (where she's working on *The L Word*), Troche has also found someone to share her life with. Troche talks lovingly about her girlfriend, a budding filmmaker.

"She's a writer/director. I have so much faith in her. She's much better than I was when I was at her level of experience. It's really inspiring and great."

With Troche getting all affectionate, the conversation shifts to discuss how she feel about objects, the precious items that the characters in her film sometimes cling to for strength and support.

"I try not to have objects define me," she boasts as if to prove she operates best without a safety net. "I have always been very afraid of caring for them."

Yet when pressed about her favorite possessions, Troche admits that there are two things she would hate to part with if her house was destroyed. "My books—but not really because I can replace them for the most part, except *Uncle Tom's Cabin*, which I have a really great edition of—and all the scripts with all the notes from all the drafts. It's a document of my progress."

With *The Safety of Objects*, Rose Troche is showing signs of amazing progress.

FERZAN OZPETEK: HIS SECRET LIFE

His Secret Life (2001) is a beautiful, bittersweet film about finding a new family. When a woman discovers her late husband was having an affair with another man, she seeks the guy out—and finds herself in the process. Maybe it is the self-assured gay male character played by the handsome Stefano Accorsi that makes *His Secret Life* so absorbing, but I find that Ozpetek's approach to telling this story makes it easy to get caught up in the characters and the rhythm of their lives.

Revealing Ozpetek's Secrets

"This movie appealed to the gay community because it broke a barrier—many [married] Italian men have secret lives with gay men," says director and co-writer Ferzan Ozpetek about his poignant new film *His Secret Life*. With this movie, Ozpetek explains, "Italian women saw for the first time what their husbands' 'hypothetical' lover looked like—what kind of life he had, what kind of people he hung around with, and what kind of meals they shared. I gave a face and a body to all those secret love affairs."

His Secret Life—titled *Fate Ignoranti (Ignorant Fairies)* in Italian— tells the story of a young woman named Antonia (Margherita Buy) whose husband Massimo is killed in a car accident. While grieving, the widow soon discovers that her husband was having an affair. Stunned by this news, she sets out to confront the other woman. However, Antonia gets an even bigger shock when she discovers that her husband's lover was in fact a man named Michele (Stefano Accorsi). As they cope with Massimo's untimely death, both Antonia and Michele's initial hostility toward each other soon forms a powerful bond.

Part of the film's success, the director believes, was based on the fact that "women could easily identify themselves with Antonia. Likewise, the gay characters had normal jobs, and normal lives. They were not stereotypes made to get laughs or pity. I wanted all the people who hung out at Michele's apartment to be considered as a family and not as individuals."

Many of the film's best scenes revolve around Michele's table, where the characters talk openly and honestly with—and about— each other. It is Antonia's participation in these meals with her husband's surrogate family that enable her to realize how to move on with her life.

"What appealed to me was having the characters grow, and as they grow, reaching a better and more profound understanding of themselves," says Ozpetek about how he developed the dramatic tension between the two main characters. "Antonia and Michele need one another."

The Turkish-born Italian citizen explains that such character arcs are very important to him. "I have always had to deal with finding and rediscovering myself. This process will never leave me."

This concept of self-reflection was prominent in Ozpetek's film *Steam: The Turkish Bath* (1997), which was released in the United States to great acclaim. One of *Steam*'s admirers in Italy was heart-throb Stefano Accorsi *(The Last Kiss,* 2001), who wanted to work with Ozpetek. After reading the script for *His Secret Life,* Accorsi liked the story and agreed to make the film.

Unlike American performers who might shy away from playing a gay role—especially one that involves a ménage à trois sequence—Accorsi, who is straight, "did not have any problems portraying a gay character," recalls Ozpetek. "Stefano never said anything about the kissing scenes in the screenplay. I did not tone down the gay content of the film for him, and he never asked me to. When we filmed the scene at the party in which he kissed two guys, or the 'ménage à trois' scene—in which they were totally nude—he did it without any problem and in a very professional way."

Ironically, Ozpetek says, "I was more nervous than him [about the love scenes] because I'm very prudish on the set." The part paid off handsomely for the actor, as Ozpetek says, "Stefano is now one of the most important leading men in Italy."

His Secret Life also boosted the director's profile in Italy. "I was amazed to see that the movie penetrated so deeply in to the movie crowd," said Ozpetek. "It really touched various kinds of moviegoers. From film buffs to housewives who never go to the movies but were dragged to the theaters by their daughters and gay sons."

And according to the director, his film "was a big success in Italy. It played in theaters nonstop for eight months because of word-of-mouth."

ÉMILE GAUDREAULT (WITH STEVE GALLUCCIO): MAMBO ITALIANO

Émile Gaudreault's *Mambo Italiano* (2003) is a fun piece of fluff, but it also makes serious points about negotiating gay and straight sexuality. For this reason, the Canadian filmmaker's amusing comedy deserves attention. And for those who identify with this kind of coming out story, screenwriter Steve Galluccio, who is interviewed with Gaudreault, shows the effects of art imitating life.

Émile and Steve Mambo

A hit play in Canada, *Mambo Italiano* was adapted for the screen by filmmaker Émile Gaudreault and playwright Steve Galluccio. The combined life experiences of these two gay men helped shape the film version of this very funny, very sweet romantic comedy about coming out of the closet and being true to one's self.

"It was a struggle, of course, when I first finally started to come out in my early twenties," says Galluccio, who based *Mambo Italiano* on his family and people he knew and grew up with in Canada. "The play was a huge part of my process."

For Gaudreault, accepting his sexuality was equally difficult. "I was twenty-four and I had been going out with a very well-known stage director for two years. I was convinced—narcissistically—that I would destroy my mother's life [if I told her I was gay]. I was lost. It ended up that my mother was very cool with it. She knew, and wanted me to tell her."

These kinds of coming out stories are universal, and the film deals head on with issues of parental approval.

Galluccio explains that while the Italian patriarch Gino Barberini's (Paul Sorvino) stunned reaction to his son Angelo's (Luke Kirby) revelation that he's gay may seem a bit overwrought, it was anything but. "Nothing was exaggerated," the screenwriter exclaims. "Trust me. In real life, it's much worse than that!"

Even Gaudreault, who speaks with a sexy French accent, identifies with the film's strong Italian emotions. "My father's side of the family was originally from Corsica. It was always very melodramatic—everyone screaming at each other."

Growing up Italian means dealing with larger-than-life people, Galluccio recalls. "Italians are great show people. They have grand entrances. Our Sunday get-togethers were insane!"

To get the tone of the film right, garish costumes and sets were used to create the proper ethnic feel. What is interesting (or downright scary, depending on one's perspective) is the fact that the gaudy wallpaper—which director Gaudreault describes as "chic kitsch"—is grounded in reality.

"We went to houses on location [in the Italian section of Montreal] and some of them were . . ." the director shakes his head instead of finishing his sentence. "We arranged it artfully, and exaggerated," he demurs.

If the designers of *Mambo Italiano* got the look of the film right, the outstanding cast of mostly Canadian actors perfected the film's characters. Ironically, the two leading men were neither gay nor Italian.

"First, I wanted only Italians, but it was tough to cast," Gaudreault remembers. "In finding the right actor for the part, I went for the best."

Galluccio concurs. "We saw as many Italians as we could, but it just didn't work out. We did a cross Canada search for all of the hot young actors, but there were not many that could do comedy. Luke Kirby was able to catch of the subtleties of the character."

And Angelo is a complex gay man. Teased as a child, he hesitates to acknowledge his sexuality as an adult. Although he wants to be out, he is ill at ease in Montreal's bars where men dance shirtless and are affectionate with each other in public. What is more, Angelo loves his boyfriend, Nino (Peter Miller), who is closeted—and wants to stay that way.

Gaudreault identifies with Angelo's character, and thinks audiences will as well. "I was teased as a kid, and I told myself it would never happen again. I went through long periods in my life where I wasn't comfortable in my own skin."

One of the ways the filmmaker dealt with his feelings was to work on a gay hotline. "I was a volunteer at a gay help line for two years. A therapist told me I was a 'natural active listener'," Gaudreault confides, before acknowledging, "This [skill] was very useful for directing a movie!"

The hotline sequences in the film were one of several changes from the original play. In addition, the story's ending was altered and made more upbeat for the screen.

Galluccio is proud that people who have seen both versions claim the film is "more gay than the play," despite the absence of male nudity and sex scenes that were shown on the stage. The screenwriter responds that these changes were a deliberate decision on his part and the director's.

The screenwriter continues, "We wanted to keep the soul of the play, but open up the characters. In the movie, we really wanted to explore the tenderness between Angelo and Nino. You didn't see that in the play. We wanted to make the story more palatable to small town America. We want them to see beyond the kissing, that Angelo and Nino are a real couple in love."

Gaudreault adds, "The main character is a gay man. He is not a caricature. He has a love life, he has tenderness with his partner, and he doesn't end up dead, or sick, or alone. I've never seen that in a mainstream movie. You think about all of the mainstream gay movies that have been done, *Philadelphia* (1993), *The Birdcage* (1996)—and I love those movies—but to make the audience comfortable, the characters have to be a little ridiculous. In *Mambo* the two guys are never ridiculous. Not all gay men are flamboyant—I didn't want to go there. The comedy comes out of something else."

That something else is a family so close that the ties that bind sometimes strangle. Angelo's quest is not so much for a partner as it is for self-acceptance as both an Italian and as a gay man.

The director is proud to have made a crowd-pleasing film that he claims does not play to stereotypes of gays or Italians. To its credit, *Mambo Italiano* wisely avoids both depictions of limp-wristed homosexuals and Mafioso references. "We got an amazing reaction from Italian and gay [audiences]. They were laughing from beginning to end," asserts Gaudreault. "It's not a niche movie."

He explains further. "It's a movie with gay content made for everybody to see. My sensibility is naturally mainstream. For me, there was no other approach."

MILES SWAIN (WITH LARRY SULLIVAN): THE TRIP

The Trip (2002) is one of those films that wears its good intentions on its sleeve. Writer-director Miles Swain makes his points about gay rights, political ideologies, and same-sex love, but with uneven results.

If Swain has yet to truly fulfill his promise as a filmmaker, *The Trip* is notable for showcasing the terrific performance by actor Larry Sullivan, who makes a great impression in the film's leading role.

Miles and Larry Make The Trip

Writer-director Miles Swain's film *The Trip* is an ambitious, personal, and—as audiences have proven—crowd pleasing film about the love/hate relationship between two very different gay men. Whereas Alan (Larry Sullivan) is a closeted Republican, Tommy (Steve Braun) is an openly gay activist. Over the course of this intimate epic, which takes place in a decade plus years starting in 1973, Swain has this odd couple meet, mate, and reunite.

The story was based on an "urban legend of two guys in Mexico trying to get to Texas," the handsome twenty-nine year-old filmmaker says. "I wrote their backstory, and added my personal experience to it. All of the people/characters in the film are based upon people that I know."

For Larry Sullivan, who stars in the film as Alan, the role was a fabulous acting opportunity. Discussing his character, the adorable up and coming actor says, "Alan is closer to myself because I am able to pull off the neurotic thing. That is a large part of who I am, being half-Jewish, half-Catholic, and a Virgo all at the same time." He pauses for a minute to laugh. Getting serious again, he says, "It would have been more of a challenge for me to play the outspoken one."

Sullivan, who is a trained dancer and gymnast, discussed getting in shape for *The Trip*, which involved having him do a comic striptease and a brief nude scene. "I was eating chicken and egg whites and going to the gym and doing cardio," he says, ironically munching on some french fries during the interview. While he is mostly unselfconscious about his trim body, he does suggest there are a few too many close-ups of him in his boxer shorts.

Swain, however, is very pleased with the film as a whole, and the palpable chemistry between the two performers in particular. "Larry was Alan," he says adamantly.

Likewise, Sullivan has nothing but praise for his hot co-star, Steve Braun, who made it very easy for him to form a couple in the film.

"He was okay with everything," Sullivan says, noting that a randy moment in which the characters grope each other in bed provided a love scene a sexy touch.

"That was something added," Sullivan admits about the undercover fondling. "We wanted to strengthen the relationship with some physicality and also with a little more kissing and touching, but we wanted to make sure it did not grow past a certain point of gratuitous."

Yet the film, which is an involving love story, does not contain a hot and heavy sex scene. This was a deliberate decision on Swain's part as a filmmaker. "In the beginning I would have something like that in there, in the end, it just didn't fit," he says. Then he adds (with a devious grin), "But I can be foul and perverted."

For Sullivan, who acknowledges that he "has a tendency to go towards the comedy," he enjoyed doing the film's dramatic and romantic parts. What appealed to him about the film "was that it was a couple of different films in one. There is the very serious love story, a whole history lesson, and there also is some campy—sometimes a little too over-the-top—fun."

For Swain, *The Trip* gave him the opportunity to both write and direct a feature film. Yet, he claims that it was more challenging to write the film than direct it. "In writing, the vision happens as you write it. It is not real until you write it out. As I was writing [the script] I could see the surroundings, hear the music, etc. I was [already] 'directing' it."

Not having lived through the 1970s, Swain says he relied on "research and reading" to get the period details right. Using archival footage and period music helped create the era, but it is the clothes that truly complete the picture.

Sullivan interjects at the mention of the costumes. "They are disgusting!" he says emphatically. "My contract did say I could keep clothes as long as they were not rentals from studios. But I'm in conservative sweater vests, or ridiculous stuff—green boxers, and jogging suits—things that I would never wear."

Still the experience was rewarding for both the actor and the director, who have been emboldened by the success of their film. While

Sullivan has had a recurring role on *Six Feet Under,* and hopes to do another indie film soon, Swain is working on his next feature.

Ultimately Swain says that regardless of the film's popularity, making *The Trip* has taught him to be "more patient in relationships." Adding that if he encountered the trials and tribulations of Alan and Tommy in his own relationship, "I would have taken [their] journey in a second."

VENTURA PONS: FOOD OF LOVE

Ventura Pons's *Food of Love* (2002) was a criminally neglected adaptation of a David Leavitt novel, and one that should have cemented his reputation as a world class filmmaker in America. Unfortunately, the opposite happened, and it is unlikely the Spanish filmmaker will make another "American" movie any time soon. Still, *Food of Love* is a worthwhile film, and one that should be appreciated for its sensitivity and grace.

Pons's Thoughtful Food

Catalan filmmaker Ventura Pons is not well-known in the United States. His films—*Beloved/Friend* (1999), *Caresses* (1998), and *To Die (Or Not)* (2000)—have not been shown theatrically in this country except in film festivals. (They are available on video.) Although Lincoln Center and The American Cinematheque (in Los Angeles) have hosted retrospectives of Pons's work, even the most jaded art film lover may draw a blank at the mention of his name. All that should change, however, with the release of *Food of Love*. [Alas, it didn't.]

In his meticulous adaptation of David Leavitt's novel *The Page Turner* for the screen, Pons has created a moving story about love and disappointment—one that is rife with tension, sexual and otherwise. What is more, the Spanish director filmed *Food of Love* in English and with an English cast. While Juliet Stevenson (*Truly, Madly, Deeply,* 1991) and gay actor Allan Corduner (*Topsy-Turvy,* 1999) are thoroughly convincing as Americans, lead actor Kevin Bishop (whose previous films include *Muppet Treasure Island,* 1996), masters his

American accent so well moviegoers may be stunned to learn he is British.

"I adore the British actors," said Pons about his film's casting. "They can play everything. I love to work with them. I talk and rehearse with the actors, and then I wait to see what they can bring to the action."

While *Food of Love* is a European co-production, the challenge, no—opportunity—to work in a foreign language appealed to the director. "I was thrilled about making my first film in English after so many ones in Catalan. I am very happy with this new experience. I hope from this film that the U.S. audience will know a little more about me and my way of filming."

This is not to say that shooting the English-language feature was trouble-free. "It was a difficult film from a production point of view—to organize between two continents and four different countries—but I think it was worthwhile," Pons says.

In *Food of Love*, Paul (Bishop), a piano student meets his idol Richard Kennington (Paul Rhys) at a concert in San Francisco. They later begin a passionate but clandestine relationship when they meet again in Barcelona. The film's second act takes place six months later when Paul is at Juilliard and is forced to come to terms with his career and his sexuality at critical junctures.

Pons, who has been a fan of Leavitt's since reading the author's *Family Dancing,* made very shrewd decisions in adapting the novel to the screen. Only a few minor characters were removed, and the nationalities of two characters in the book were changed. The most significant alteration, however, was the story's European setting. Whereas Leavitt set the story in Italy (where he has lived), Pons moved the action to Barcelona.

"I changed the action from Rome because, of course, I know my country much better and it was a far easier place to shoot," he enthused. "There was no betrayal to the story. The trip the characters take to Europe can happen in a lot of different places. Leavitt knew my town very well and he thought positively about it. And besides, Barcelona is so glamorous!"

Of course, Pons also retitled the film, perhaps to focus on the story's twin themes of music and love. He took the title from Orsino, the duke in *Twelfth Night*. Nevertheless, these changes will hardly anger the book's admirers.

Food of Love is extremely faithful to its source, and it is perfectly cast. Stevenson—who is probably the best-known of all the principal actors—gives a remarkable performance as Pamela, Paul's mother. While some viewers might find her shrill, Stevenson subtly conveys Pamela's transformation throughout the story. Pons has nothing but praise for her.

"Juliet is one of the best actresses I have ever worked with in my life. It was a pleasure to construct the character with her. From my point of view, her hysterical attitude towards her son is the key to understanding the story—otherwise you don't follow her son's reactions to life."

Likewise, the director is very supportive of Kevin Bishop who has to carry the film. "Kevin is a very talented actor and, because he is so young, he has a great future. I think he gives all the emotions and credibility to this young boy lost in the harsh world of the competitive Big Apple."

Yet the director also recognized the difficulties the role of Paul presented to Bishop, who is not gay, and was not initially at ease with the kissing and nude sex scenes required by the script. "The love scenes were a bit difficult for Kevin," Pons admits, "but I think that they work very well in the movie."

While there is an strong sexual bond between Paul and Richard, the director points out "the film's [sex] is as discreet as in the book. If I wanted to make an erotic movie, I would have chosen another story."

Bishop probably felt more comfortable in the piano scenes, perhaps because he had a double for the extended musical scenes. However, the actor and his co-star Paul Rhys were taught fingering by a tutor, and each tickle the ivories on screen during the film's concert sequences.

Continuing the discussion about the film's musical selections, Pons makes a point to compliment his longtime composer Carles Cases who provided the incidental music in *Food of Love*. "I think Carles is one of the best European film composers. He has written scores for nine of my movies. This music in this film was difficult because he had to mix it at the same time with all the best classical music. But he was really in state of grace. As always."

Food of Love also features a wonderful soundtrack of classic pieces by Chopin, Schubert, and Schumann. For the most part, Pons followed the selections mentioned in the book, but he also took the liberty of including some music that was more suited to his own taste. When asked what specific music he changed, Pons demurs and claims "not to remember" which ones.

And while the director is happy to discuss the contributions of actors, music, locations, and language that make his films special, he pinpoints the story as a successful film's key ingredient.

"This is something quite clear in all my movies," he says. "If you have a story as good as this one, it is much easier. *Food of Love* deals with emotions and real life. My sympathy is for Paul and Pamela, the losers who fight to find their place in this harsh society of ours. Their struggles are very interesting."

Chapter 2
Fierce Eroticism

This chapter contains interviews with a handful of filmmakers who are not afraid to explore gay male sexuality on screen. Their films range from the explicit to the tasteful, and yet each one makes a valid point about identity and sexuality. For this reason, these are notable films, even if viewers may question their merits.

JOÃO PEDRO RODRIGUES: O FANTASMA

Love it or hate it, *O Fantasma* (2000), João Pedro Rodrigues's feverish drama about a sexually active garbage collector, has an indelible imprint on anyone who has seen it. Rodrigues admits that the film—a fantasy—stems from both his reality and his desires, and his interview revealed a man who, like the others in this chapter, thinks seriously about the ways to express love and sex both on screen and off.

O João

"It's a film about solitude, the lonely side of Sergio's character," says Portuguese director João Pedro Rodrigues about his fiercely erotic drama *O Fantasma*. In this mesmerizing film, Sergio (Ricardo Meneses) is a garbage collector in Lisbon who becomes obsessed with a hunk he meets on his rounds. It is not long before he starts stalking the object of his affection, rummaging through the stranger's trash for fetish objects in an effort to satisfy his fantasies.

Sergio also has graphic sex with various men (and one woman), including a handcuffed cop, a guy who gives him a blow job in a men's room, and a few other strangers.

Independent Queer Cinema: Reviews and Interviews
© 2006 by The Haworth Press, Inc. All rights reserved.
doi:10.1300/5482_03

Rodrigues admits that his own fantasies inspired him to depict the intense sexual escapades in *O Fantasma*. "I was always attracted to rubbish collectors," he says.

From the aforementioned acts to autoerotic asphyxiation, the filmmaker does not shy away from showing explicit sex scenes. However, Rodrigues has a purpose for what he presents on screen. He says, "One of the questions I asked myself was how to film sex? I believe in cinema, it is always a question of what you show and what you keep hidden—from the writing of the script to the editing. When Sergio is being fucked [against a fence], the bars and the sound they make aren't much stronger than the penetration in itself."

While there is plenty of hard-edged realism in the film—audiences can practically smell the garbage on screen—Rodrigues includes elements of magical realism in the drama. "I tried to reveal 'hidden mysteries' in the film," he says. "I pursed a 'fantastic ambiance' through real palpable places and objects." The director achieves this through the use of fetishes, such as a skintight black latex suit Sergio wears off and on during the film.

What is more, *O Fantasma* contains many scenes that have little dialogue, most notably the film's final episode, a challenging, near-silent twenty-minute sequence.

"I tried to tell the story through pictures and sound. Sergio is alone most of the time. Being a garbage collector is one of the loneliest jobs there is. They are the phantoms of the city in the way that we see them but we don't pay attention; they are part of the urban landscape," Rodrigues reveals.

He continues, "Most people that live in Lisbon and have seen the film don't recognize the city they live in. It has another kind of geography, a fictitious geography. I got in touch with the garbage depot in my area, to know the people that work there and what their daily routine is. I followed them for four months and over that 'net of reality' I built the structure of my story."

While *O Fantasma* certainly has a dreamlike quality to it, it is helped immeasurably by the brave performance of nonprofessional actor Ricardo Meneses as Sergio.

"I was very lucky to find him. I think no one else could have played Sergio's part," Rodrigues says about his star, who was working in a gay bar when the director met him. "Even if he isn't the character, Ricardo became Sergio. He immediately understood his character's behaviors—playing a dog, fetishizing the objects/places. He has an intense physicality and sensuality. I think he had fun."

Yet the filmmaker acknowledges that had to ask his actor to do some rather rough stuff on screen. "Physically, there were very many difficult scenes, especially with the latex suit in the freezing dump at night. He suffered a lot. I believe we can actually see his pain on screen, and the sense of reality and tension we got could not be achieved if we faked the scenes in any way." As for the sex scenes, Meneses did not balk at performing any of them.

Nevertheless, the filmmaker waited until the end of the shoot to film these scenes "for obvious reasons," he explains.

And while *O Fantasma* will certainly have viewers engrossed in the action, some audience members may scratch their heads. "Either people like it or hate it," says Rodrigues about the response to his film. "It's been like that everywhere."

RICHARD GLATZER AND WASH WEST:
THE FLUFFER

I had seen Richard Glatzer's scrappy little film *Grief* (1993) before catching *The Fluffer* (2001), but I had never seen anything by his filmmaking (and life) partner Wash West. West's career was made in the adult film industry. This may explain why their film, set in the world of sex films, has affection for the industry but is more about identity and less about pornography.

Richard Glatzer and Wash West Get Fluffed Up

"The word 'fluffer' [which to the uninformed, is a person who helps a male porn star stay—ahem—filmable] stuck in my mind," Wash West said, indicating what might be the genesis of the film of the same name he wrote himself and co-directed with his partner Richard Glatzer.

West, a Brit from Leeds, arrived in Los Angeles to do research on the porn industry six years ago, and has since directed several adult features. When he met fellow cinephile Glatzer, who directed the indie film *Grief*, they bonded over *Rosemary's Baby* (1968), hoping one day to create a film like Polanski's masterpiece. However, their collaboration has instead yielded something entirely different, *The Fluffer*, a dark comedy-drama about the gay porn industry.

The film's story—which is much better and much less tawdry than it sounds—has Sean McGinnis (Michael Cunio) falling in unrequited love with the "gay-for-pay" porn star Johnny Rebel (Scott Gurney). Meanwhile, Johnny's self-destructive tendencies alienate him from his girlfriend Julie (Roxanne Day), who works as a stripper under the name Babylon.

"The idea of someone servicing someone was a metaphor for a lot of relationships," West says in a recent phone interview. Glatzer, on another receiver, agrees. He believes that this story about obsessive love "was an extreme form of romanticism—and there is nothing less romantic than a porn set."

Yet West found his subject matter quite stimulating: "The sex industry is potent, exciting, and erotic—in a twisted way. There are fascinating people . . . and I based some of the film's characters on observations I made from working in porn." Glatzer verifies the semi-autobiographical elements, deadpanning, "I'm much more Johnny Rebel than he is Sean McGinnis."

Actually, several people who make their living in the X-rated world, including Chi Chi La Rue and Cole Tucker, were given cameo roles, lending the film a certain authenticity. What is more, the filmmakers created a line of Johnny Rebel titles in all of the porn genres to "fluff up" the Rebel mythology.

Yet not all aspects of making *The Fluffer* were fun and games. Casting the film was a bit difficult, as many agents and actors were turned off by the title and subject matter. Ironically, West says, "There have been many films made about hustlers, but a film about a fluffer was much more scandalous." Nevertheless, people such as Debbie Harry were anxious to be involved, and the singer/actress took a supporting role as the manager of the strip club where Babylon works.

"With *The Fluffer*, we wanted to salute people in the sex industry," West said. "This film shows the glamour and excitement as well as the dark side. Porn can be a great source of money and fun, but it also can be a trap."

Glatzer concurs. "The sex industry is a minefield of emotions . . . . when sex becomes a job it gets very mechanical. We found something comical, or innately funny in that—and used humor as a way to disarm people."

It is obvious from the positive response to the film that Glatzer and West have done their job well. Claiming their working relationship is "an organic process"—West is the "immediate" one, concentrating on the details, while Glatzer "stepped back and looked at the big picture"—they make sure to work out their few disagreements on actors, camerawork, or storyboarding, in private.

And their efforts have paid off handsomely. *The Fluffer* is a winning film that has a singular, if somewhat cockeyed vision of love, sex, and pornography.

DIRK SHAFER: CIRCUIT

I first interviewed Dirk Shafer, the former *Playgirl* model turned moviemaker for his documentary *Man of the Year* (1995), about his experiences as a centerfold, and I was charmed by this good-looking guy with brains. When we spoke again about his feature *Circuit* (2001) I was even more impressed with him. Even though *Circuit* is flawed, Shafer proves himself to be a thoughtful filmmaker, and he gets a hell of a performance out of Paul Lekakis.

Shafer on the Circuit Subculture

"The music, the lights, the dancing, and the sex," answers Dirk Shafer when asked about what attracted him to write and direct *Circuit*, a cautionary tale about the "tribal" dance parties that are popular with gay men. "It's a hot button issue—people love it or hate it," he continues. "It's a subculture within a subculture. Every gay person has come in contact with it, either personally or through a friend. I was fascinated by the politics and sexiness of it."

While not a circuit boy himself, Shafer does admit to "experimenting" with the scene. While preparing for the film, Shafer relied on music—which is a critical element to the success of circuit parties—to guide him, listening to dance tunes almost nonstop. "I didn't know this music," he says about the soundtrack to the film, which includes circuit party staples Kim English, Deborah Cox, and Taylor Dayne. Instead, Shafer acknowledges his preference for soulful, folksy singer/songwriters such as Pete Yorn, John Mayer, and Norah Jones. "I picked out what I really liked for this or that sequence, and pictured scenes to certain music."

Visually, the film is a departure for Shafer as well. His previous credit as a filmmaker was *Man of the Year,* a clever mock documentary about his real life experiences as a *Playgirl* centerfold. With *Circuit,* Shafer was able to not only be more visual—using slow and speed motion photography, digital video, and other cinematic gimmicks—but also to tell the narrative using a 3/4 flashback structure. "It was my homage to *Funny Girl* (1968), which was one of my favorite and most influential movies," he explained.

Shafer, who co-write *Circuit* with novelist and screenwriter Gregory Hinton, said that one of the most important things he did as a writer/director was to film each character in a mirror. "That was a subtext in the movie. The characters are obsessed with their images/mirrors. Gay culture is obsessed with youth and beauty. The topics of aging and vanity are such a big part of gay men's lives that it becomes an addiction."

The ruggedly handsome Shafer then admits, "I never felt attractive. I did the [*Playgirl*] centerfold for validation as a model. You need to develop what's on the inside."

Circuit's ensemble cast includes several self-absorbed characters that need to learn this life lesson. The film's protagonist, John (Jonathan Wade-Drahos), is an ex-cop who comes to Los Angeles and gets seduced by the sex-and-drugs lifestyle from three very different men. They are his cousin Tad (Daniel Kucan), a wannabe documentary filmmaker; Hector (Andre Khabbazi), a hustler who resorts to injections to keep his youthful good looks; and Bobby (Paul Lekakis), a porn star/model.

When asked which character Shafer identifies with he replies, "All of them. I had the fantasy of being a dick dancer like Bobby; I have Hector's fear of aging, the naivete of John, and most of all Tad, the moviemaker who doesn't know who he is."

In fact, Shafer deliberately cast *Circuit* with unknown actors in the lead roles. He relied on performers such as Nancy Allen, William Katt, Bruce Vilanch, and Jim J. Bullock for supporting roles because he did not want audiences to have preconceived ideas about the actors in the lead roles. "We had an opportunity to go with someone famous [for the main character]," Shafer recalls, "but I thought John was better for the part." Not surprisingly, most "name" actors were afraid of the script's graphic sex scenes.

And speaking of the sex scenes, Shafer says that they were perhaps the most difficult scenes to shoot. "It was hard to choreograph them and stay professional. I coached the actors to go all out." As the finished film shows, they did.

The other important sequences were the circuit parties themselves. While the crew was able to shoot on location at the Red, Blue, and White parties, they also had to re-create some of these events at clubs with the cast. "After we shot at the White Party, I was so happy when we saw the footage. The lights and lasers held up in the DV format. It looked like we had shot them just for the film," Shafer says, enthusiastically.

Shafer is also pleased with the finished film. Perhaps his greatest pleasure after making the movie has been seeing how audiences have embraced *Circuit*. "Straight people find it edgy, shocking, and interesting. Gay people find it entertaining and disturbing. But circuit boys are the most important audience for me, and they thought it was accurate, which is all I ever really wanted."

FENTON BAILEY AND RANDY BARBATO: PARTY MONSTER

Fenton Bailey and Randy Barbato got my attention with their documentary *Party Monster* (1998) about club kid Michael Alig. When they made a feature on the same subject, also named *Party Monster* (2003),

I appreciated their ability to rework the same story a new way. Even though the feature is not nearly as chilling as the nonfiction version of the story, Bailey and Barbato show their moxie as filmmakers.

Monsters, *Inc: Randy Barbato and Fenton Bailey*

When you have a story as fascinating as the case of Michael Alig—the 1980s Club Kid who was famous for throwing outlandish outlaw parties, before he become more famous for murdering Angel Melendez—a film version is inevitable. In fact, directors Fenton Bailey and Randy Barbato were so interested in this story they actually made two films about Alig, both titled *Party Monster*.

The first version they did was a documentary made in 1998, which contains interviews with Alig (from prison) as well as testimonies from many of the original club kids. The second version, a feature, stars Macaulay Culkin as Alig, and Seth Green as his friend and mentor, James St. James, author of the book *Disco Bloodbath* about the time and the crime.

Bailey suggests that audiences should see both films, because they give "two perspectives on the same story." He recommends the doc first to understand the scene—and then the feature, which fleshes out the emotional issues between the characters. Significantly, there is very little overlap between the two versions, so the process of viewing both movies provides an enhanced, rather than repetitious, experience.

"Michael's rise was phenomenal," Bailey says about Alig's celebrity. "He transformed himself from someone that no one would give the time of day to the most fabulous person on the scene. He was very clever. It was an amazing act of self-invention."

The filmmakers knew Alig from their years DJ-ing at Danceteria, where Alig worked as a busboy when he first came to New York. They had even attended some of his parties. But as Bailey admits, "His antics did appall us."

The research Bailey and Barbato did on the documentary informed the feature, and the filmmakers made certain to be honest in the presentation of the events in the movie. "The film is as accurate as it could possibly be," Bailey explains. "It is more accurate than the doc in some respects. In the film we were able to maneuver sources and stories to get at the greater truth. Everything is something someone said or someone did."

Bailey describes the source materials he consulted to create the script. "We used Alig's unpublished manuscript *Aligula* and James St. James's book, Michael Musto's *Village Voice* column, and [co-conspirator] Freez's confession."

Yet in terms of presenting the facts of the murder, Bailey says that "there are many, many, many different versions of the murder, [several] coming from Alig himself. We don't know for sure what actually happened. I'm not sure even Michael and Freez know. They were addled by drugs." The interpretation the filmmakers use in *Party Monster* is wonderfully surreal, and suitable within the context of the film.

Yet in telling the story for the feature, Bailey explains that he "took out things, even though they were true, because in the context of a movie, people would not believe it." However, the opposite, Bailey says, is true for the documentary, where things get more outrageous—and more compelling—as a result. Bailey clarifies, "The film is based in reality, but that reality is hallucinatory." This distinction provides another good reason why the two versions should be seen to get the complete picture.

And while the story itself is shocking, audiences will also be taken aback watching *Home Alone* (1990) star Macaulay Culkin playing Alig. Perfectly cast in the role, Culkin captures Alig's energy and gives a truly brave performance here. Bailey claims, "We had Mac in mind from the outset, but it was a challenge to get him on board. He had retired from the business."

Culkin's performance gets to the heart of what makes Alig tick—a constant need to be the center of attention, however outrageous the behavior.

Bailey speculates on the character of Alig, stating that he was an "attention junkie" who always needed an audience and applause.

As far as the murder was concerned, Bailey's opinion is that it was a combination of factors that lead Alig to kill Melendez. Yet he firmly believes that the murder was "an act of self-destruction. He had reached a dead end."

In filming the events, Bailey and Barbato concentrated on re-creating the club scene with the costumes, memorabilia, and music from the era. "It was tough, but we tried to embrace the original Club Kids aesthetic," Bailey recalls. "We did have some of the original Club Kids in the movie, so they provided some of their authentic costumes."

Like the clothes, the music in the film is pitch-perfect. While *Party Monster* does not include Screaming Rachel's song about Alig, "Freedom/Murder in Clubland" (which is performed in the doc), the feature does showcase "Money Success Fame Glamour," a 1980s tune by Pop Tarts, the band Bailey and Barbato were in before they became filmmakers.

And perhaps this delving into this subculture provides the best understanding of the whole Club Kids scene. "Clothes were sublimation for sex, and drugs took over a lot of the sexual energy. But notoriety was the real turn on," Bailey says. "The Club Kids were satire on celebrity. Alig was parodying the whole thing and he got lost in the process."

Alig is now serving time in jail for Melendez's murder. To date, Bailey says, Alig has not seen *Party Monster*.

KARIM AÏNOUZ: MADAME SATÃ

Karim Aïnouz's *Madame Satã* (2002) is a masterpiece in my mind. Aïnouz gives life to an incredible man—lover, thief, performer, and fighter. And actor Lázaro Ramos gives a dynamic, star-making performance in the title role. Beautifully shot, sexy, and stunning, *Madame Satã* is absolutely remarkable, and Aïnouz establishes himself as a talent to watch.

Aïnouz's Astonishing Satã

Karim Aïnouz, the openly gay writer/director of *Madame Satã*, admits that he is nothing like his film's protagonist, João Francisco dos Santos. A social outcast in 1930s Rio, João eventually becomes a celebrated female cabaret performer.

For one thing, the director says on the phone from New York, "I have no desire to perform in drag. I could never imagine myself in high heels. I am too self-conscious to be that free."

Nevertheless, the single, thirty-seven-year-old filmmaker was attracted to this character he describes as "a burst of life," a man who had equal passions for gay sex, violence, and performing in drag—that is, when he was not serving time in jail for criminal activities.

"I am interested in people who live their lives fully. João was excluded [socially] from everything, but he did not allow himself to be disrespected," Aïnouz continues. "I have respect for people who do not let themselves be oppressed."

Aïnouz spent seven years trying to get *Madame Satã* made. Once the project was finally greenlighted, he shot it quickly in six weeks, with a budget of under $1 million. The director had open auditions and hired two sexy, unknown actors—Lázaro Ramos and Fellipe Marques—for the leads. He has the highest praise for his performers.

"Lázaro is twenty-two and he is so talented. He has such a wide range," Aïnouz says enthusiastically about his film's star. Noting that Ramos is straight, the director says the actor had no trouble with the transgender performance scenes. "I told him, 'I want you to be Marlon Brando and Vivien Leigh in one body.'"

However, filming the love scene between the gorgeous Ramos and the smoldering Marques (who, Aïnouz confides, is gay in real life) was a different story. "Lázaro has a line in his contract that he would not do a sex scene," the director recalls. "But in the end, he was totally fine with it. We shot the scene in the last few days when the actors were very familiar with each other. They were intuitive, and let themselves go. I didn't want to break the spell. It was genuine."

While the sex between the men was hot and spontaneous, Aïnouz claims that he had a much harder time directing the fight scenes. "They were very technical. I watched a lot of action films and took notes, studying the movement. It was very hard to do," he recalls.

In contrast, the cabaret sequences were the easiest scenes to film. "They were rehearsed just before shooting, and freely choreographed. There was no point in blocking them," he says.

Aïnouz also made certain to give his film a distinct visual style. The film's coda, which includes staged Carnival scenes of the performer Madame Satã, was shot in Super-8 to give the images an archival feel. "Every moment in the film has a different grammar or language. The nights in the film are warm, but the days are harsh and acidic, like a hangover," the director explains about his deliberate strategy.

And although *Madame Satã* is his feature directorial debut, Aïnouz had previous film experience working as an assistant editor and assistant director to openly gay filmmakers Todd Haynes on *Poison* (1991) and Tom Kalin on *Swoon* (1992). He also co-wrote the screenplay for the stunning Brazilian film *Behind the Sun* (2001). Yet while he says he likes writing with other people, the filmmaker ultimately prefers directing.

"I like to collaborate. I don't mind writing for hire if I can work with friends. But I don't think I could do a writing assignment," he explains. "But I could direct someone else's script. I like the craft of directing—being with the crew, actors, editing, even promoting a film. It puts me in contact with the world." After the glory of *Madame Satã*, moviegoers should be eagerly anticipating what Aïnouz does next.

JOHN GREYSON: PROTEUS

John Greyson's films are outrageous in all senses of the word—wildly stylish, full of bawdy content, and bursting with outrage. An outspoken filmmaker, Greyson's features are fascinating character studies that mix history, sexuality, and politics. From his AIDS musical *Zero Patience* (1993) to *Lilies* (1996), a play-within-a-film set in a prison, Greyson has always dramatized issues of human rights for homosexuals.

Greyson continues to investigate these themes in *Proteus* (2003), which examines the relationship between Claas Blank (Rouxnet Brown) and Rijkhaart Jacobz (Neil Sandilands) who were executed in a South African prison on sodomy charges in the eighteenth century.*

---

*This interview was originally published at www.indiewire.com.

A Q&A with John Greyson

How did you learn about the story of Claas Blank?

Jack Lewis {co-writer/director} found the court transcript, thought the story of these two guys, their incarceration, their affair, and their execution would make an interesting feature. He asked, "Do you want to make a trilingual, sodomitical, botanical, low-budget feature on location?"

What appealed to you about telling this largely unknown story?

I think for both of us, the interest was reading between the lines. The transcript shows they are caught, guilty, and executed. If you read between the lines, their confessions were coerced. The most interesting thing is that for ten years, the authorities knew about these guys, and looked the other way, then they were brought to trial.

This is your second film set in a prison. Have you ever been arrested?

No. I've tried {kidding} . . . I've been involved in civil disobedience around censorship. Semi-close calls, but nothing particularly dramatic. It's a funny contradiction because I like being part of a demonstration, but the minute someone hands me a microphone, I freeze.

What other influential discoveries did you make in your research?

When we were researching, it was coincidence that the naming of the {Proteus} flower was the same year as their execution. It opened up our story in terms of metaphor of classification and naming. That my father is a botanist—I'm sure that had nothing to do with it.

In *Zero Patience*, your character Richard Burton says, "Sometimes the facts have to be rearranged to get at the real truth." Does that idea apply to *Proteus*?

In Proteus, *we have the Mandela quote—"Some of the things told this court are true and some are not true." It gives an audience a critical sense of what they've just watched. Ironically, much of* Proteus *is true. It's Jack and me telling our version of the story. Interpretation is the central thing to insist on. We can footnote every fact, and the interpretation is always what's at stake. It's very important to understand it is co-written, directed, etc., by both Jack and I. In every way, it was full collaboration. Neither of us could have made this on our own. It was a hybrid, a cross-fertilization of our two brains. We come from different places politically, aesthetically but we share concerns of history.*

You deliberately include anachronisms into the story to get at a larger idea.

Every time you think you're diving into deep history, there is a jeep or radio interrupting your identification. The sixties anachronisms point to Mandela. They are the present coming to haunt the past. The wetbag {a torture device} was used at height of Apartheid struggle. It is recognizable to South African audiences.

Do you think your film has other parallels to the present day?

How many states still have sodomy laws?

What can you discuss about sodomy laws in South Africa, Canada, Holland, and the U.S. both in the eighteenth century and today?

We had to do our research, so I know them all. We started with Claas and Rijkhaart's story, and we tripped over the Amsterdam story of seventy men executed for sodomy in 1730, so that seemed to be something we could move forward on.

All of your films deal, albeit in different ways, with the crime of being gay in society. Why is this issue so important to you?

When I first came out—at nineteen—I was still illegal. There was this irony that living as an adult, I could vote, drive, and drink, but I could not fuck. The work began with that contradiction. It went from being marginalized to being so extremely mainstream in ways I couldn't have imagined twenty-five years ago. Historians traced homosexuality being {condemned} by religion, the state, psychology, etc.—those places we run up against the acceptance of society. It's become the great subject for many of us gay artists who have returned to the names society puts on us and the consequences of those names.

Your films in general deal with issues of classification—from science to sexuality. Do you identify with labels? Do you label yourself a political filmmaker? A queer filmmaker? A Canadian filmmaker?

YES, YES, YES, I am someone who is very interested in words, never so much in claiming them for myself since words are so unstable, their meanings shift and change. I use labels all the time, there is a shorthand, but there is an extreme danger. Being aware of that is more important than taking a pro/con stance.

So which label do you prefer—gay, queer, homosexual…?

Queer fits good.

Do you think Blank is self-defined as queer?

This is what drove us—in the court record, the {sodomy} crimes were mutually perpetrated. The only way he could claim his dignity was in confessing. He says it in two languages and the translators translated it in three. This is how we wanted our narrative to resolve the moment of claiming identity for the first time it condemns him to death.

The word {gay} means something different today than twenty years ago, and in 1735 in a colony that didn't speak English. What we got excited about is to identify the places where self-conscious homosexual identity emerges in the culture. Claas sees himself fucking around. It is not an identity. He says, "I am Claas. I am going to get out of here." His choice in the end, to admit something to the world, is what our film turns on.

Like your other work, *Proteus* addresses issues of sexual shame. Why is this theme important to you?

The shame of yesterday, we are still struggling with today. It turns in to prejudice and homophobia.

What is interesting is the contrast between Rijkhaart, who owns his sexuality, and who claimed it for better or worse, versus someone who hasn't. Claas is an opportunist. He fucks {men} but can't admit it.

The film has probably your most impassioned, erotic sex scenes, especially those between Blank and Jacobz, when the botanist Niven (Shaun Smyth) spies on them. Surprisingly, however, there is perhaps less nudity in *Proteus* than in your other work.

The sex was driven by story issues, establishing the triangle. Just as Niven watches them fuck he also watches them die. The voyeurism is what drove those scenes. If I'm telling a story, a fuck scene has to move the story forward. Every sex scene is development in terms of story and character.

There is more nudity in this one, to the point where distributors said they don't do pornography.

Were the actors concerned about performing the sex scenes, and taking parts in a queer film?

Twenty years ago it was hard to find actors—gay or straight—to play in a gay film or keep their clothes on. Now, they feel playing gay is a smart career move, the roles are richer. The bigger crisis is for gay actors to be out and get work. Somehow there is still a prejudice against it in film. Most are discouraged and give up. Is this homophobia on the part of casting agents, producers, and directors? Sure.

You shot the film on DV? Do you prefer that medium, or would you have rather shot on film?

In some ways, the culture answers that for me. I doubt I'll ever be able to shoot on film ever again. We shot digital and blew it up to 35mm. Next time we won't have to—the theatres will all be digital.

Shooting on Robben Island must have been difficult. Can you describe that experience?

That's the only way we could have made the film, in the actual location where the story happened. It was a priority to get permission to shoot there. Shooting in penguin colony, in the quarry, or on the shores where they fished was very important for visualizing their story. It adds immense production value to the film, and it is so important serving their story and being true to what actually happened.

It made our eighteenth day shoot {difficult}. We spent much of that time in trucks driving madly to the next location to catch the sun.

What was your budget for *Proteus*?

$300,000 US in cash, and $150,000 in deferrals and donations.

You have Strand distributing this film. Do you have trouble getting your films picked up?

I've been pretty lucky considering. This is the fifth film I'll have in theatrical release. Every one has had big festival play and some theatrical distribution. This is the seventh feature. Most of the credit goes to a pretty enlightened arts council in Canada, who doesn't let the market decide what gets {made and played}. Every time I talk to American friends who complain, I realize how lucky I am.

You have always been as much a filmmaker as an activist. Do you think these ideas are what motivated you to make *Proteus*?

When I made Zero Patience, *I got letters from eighteen-year-old, HIV-positive kids, and some of the letters {show} I really made a difference. It reminds you that is the reason I do this stuff.*

Because my films are more artsy, they aren't going to {be widely distributed} . . . but they still can subversively get out there and make ripples. What gay films are mainstream? Real social change happens around gay and lesbian culture—the ways culture has worked—and representation, good, bad, or indifferent, has made a real difference.

Chapter 3
Queering the Lines

The interviews in this chapter are either with queer directors whose films feature mainly straight characters, or with straight filmmakers who tackle queer subject matter.

STEPHEN FRY: BRIGHT YOUNG THINGS

After establishing his career as an actor and novelist, Stephen Fry finally wrote and directed his first film, *Bright Young Things* (2003). This adaptation of Evelyn Waugh's *Vile Bodies* is superb and proves that Fry's talent is boundless. He is also incredibly charming in person, truly a class act.

Stephen Fry Shines Bright

"I'm certainly not idle, and I don't know about young either," says out filmmaker Stephen Fry, about the appeal of depicting the idle, young rich who populate his film *Bright Young Things*.

Fry, does however, have an affinity for the 1930s period when the film is set, having played period before—as Jeeves the butler in the *Jeeves and Wooster* (1990) TV series, and as an inspector in Robert Altman's *Gosford Park* (2001). Best known for his amazing performance as Oscar Wilde in *Wilde* (1997) (another period piece), Fry makes his first foray behind the camera with *Things*.

"I love the idea of doing a period film that was fast and had a pace to it. Because so many times you think period means languor, slowing down" Fry says, clarifying, "That's not a jibe at Merchant Ivory, who I

Independent Queer Cinema: Reviews and Interviews
© 2006 by The Haworth Press, Inc. All rights reserved.
doi:10.1300/5482_04

like very much." (Fry appeared in Merchant Ivory's contemporary *Le Divorce*, 2003.)

Bright Young Things starts out fast, and eventually slows down, mirroring the characters' fates and stories. Fry talks candidly about the pressure of getting the tone and pacing exactly right.

"There are all these rules people propagate about film, about whether you give the wrong impression in the first twenty minutes. If you are too funny, then people get upset if something gets dark. I've never believed that, at least, I've hoped that there is a way of doing it in such a way that doesn't subvert expectation in the wrong way."

His *Bright Young Things* does turn dark, but Fry prefers to talk about the challenges of helming a film, as if to explain why he started directing film at this stage in his career. Fry has been a TV and theater star in Britain, an in-demand character actor on screen, as well as a bestselling author before this opportunity came to him.

"The first time you direct a film, you obviously learn about your ability to control the story, and the mode of narrative—how you move the character, and the pace. I think the essential thing in your first film is to work within a world you understand, so you are assured in what you are doing. I am familiar with the English and the upper class and their odd ways and that period." He adds wickedly, "I have always been absolutely fascinated with the odd eccentricities of my fellow countrymen."

Fry seems to be fascinated by other aspects of the story as well. He talks lovingly about the language the characters use, and the way they express themselves. In adapting Evelyn Waugh's novel *Vile Bodies,* Fry has captured the essence of what is on the page—with one exception. In an effort to make his own imprint on the material, Fry has changed the ending slightly, extending it to the postwar period. Waugh, alas, published his book before World War II, but he was prescient enough to see there was trouble on the horizon.

"It was the First World War that broke down the 'respect for elders' in Europe, because you couldn't trust anymore—the fathers who sent their sons to their slaughter," Fry says, suggesting that there is little change between attitudes then and now.

The filmmaker also recounts the differences between young and old in the way they communicate, which is part of the humor in *Bright Young Things,* particularly in a scene between the story's hero and his lover's father. "The misunderstandings of the older generation . . . I think it is [a] genuine misunderstanding. It's the old generation missing the young generation, people missing each other's meaning all the time, people mistrusting each other. It is worse to mistrust people than to be a sucker."

As such, Fry, who has an ear for dialogue, has placed an added emphasis on language in his film. "The way language hides emotion and reveals emotion, the way it is funny, the language of the young people is very interesting. I like that," he says with a smile. And while the language provides much of the film's humor, Fry is absolutely serious about being funny.

"For me, comedy has always been immensely important in film and literature, because it is one of the absolute staples of human existence. I've always found it extraordinary when there is absolutely no humor whatsoever, because to me, that is like watching a film where everyone has one ear missing without it being commented on. They've gone to all this trouble to make it realistic—they've got proper cars, proper scenes—and there's no banter, no badinage, yet that is the absolute staple of human existence. Wherever you go in the world, there is humor. However grim life is, that is always true."

ROBERT CARY: ANYTHING BUT LOVE

Robert Cary made the affable musical drama *Anything But Love* (2002) as a throwback to the musicals of yesteryear, a straight romance lensed with a queer sensibility. I would love to see Cary make a great gay love story—say, remake a Hollywood classic with two men. He has the talent to do it; he just needs the opportunity.

Robert Cary's Love

"Being gay, my whole worldview is the disparity of way things look and the ways things feel. This is why Billie is the character I connect with. She creates a world that reflects the way she feels inside even though the rest of the world resists that," says Robert Cary, who directed and co-wrote *Anything But Love* with the film's star Isabel Rose.

The idea for the film, which portrays the efforts of singer Billie Golden (Rose) to make it on the cabaret circuit, began when the two friends saw Eartha Kitt at the Café Carlyle back in 1989. "Isabel wanted to tell a story about a woman singing at an airport cocktail dive who longs to be a cabaret singer. I thought it was interesting and added elements of my own to it," Cary explains. He even wrote a role for Kitt, who appears in the film and sings live.

Anything But Love is a throwback to those musical romances of the 1940s, starring actresses such as June Allyson. "It's a woman's picture in the old-fashioned sense," Cary says. "Billie has to make a choice between heart, home, and her career."

Significantly, the director made it a point to shoot the film as if it was a classic movie. He is proud of this achievement, boasting, "We didn't do anything you couldn't do in the 1950s. We even used film that was rich in color and detail and not sensitive to light."

This is not to say Cary's methods did not have their share of challenges. "The split screen scene was hard to do because we didn't have digital equipment." The production crew had to measure everything for a scene featuring Billie and her hunky beau (Cameron Bancroft) talking on the phone to match the shots perfectly.

Given the fact that the film has a budget of under $1 million, Cary's accomplishment is all the more impressive. However, the project's humble origins were initially a drawback. The filmmaker confides that "not being a characteristic indie, *Anything But Love* does not have the hallmark of [being] edgy. It took a long time for festivals to pay attention to us."

The adorable Cary, who lives with playwright Jonathan Tolins *(The Last Sunday in June)*, has always had a creative streak. He grew up in Los Angeles with a family of entertainers, and was a ballet dancer before doing acting, singing, writing, and directing.

Cary developed his interest in cinema watching TV shows and movies being made. What is more, he admits to living in a house that is closer in style to 1955 than 2003, "except that TVs back then were not as big as mine" and that when he listens to soundtracks of MGM film scores—something he does quite frequently—they are on CD. "I find incredible comfort in music," he says. "It is like a beacon for me."

Music, of course, is a crucial element in the film. Cary effuses about being able to use songs by Jimmy McHugh and Arthur Schwartz. "I had not imagined that we could use those composers' songs in such a focused way," he recalls about finding a score for *Anything But Love.* After contacting the appropriate folks, "It was their enthusiasm about the script and the idea that made it possible. Music rights are very expensive. We were thrilled with what we got."

As much of the film contains the performance of musical numbers, it was also important to get these scenes note perfect. "Isabel sang some things live on set when we shot, and she did other things to a playback in the old-fashioned MGM way," Cary described. "Everything had to be right in the shot. If the sync was off, we had to go back and do it again."

Likewise, for a dance number—one of the film's highlights—Cary had the opportunity to shoot the routine he choreographed on a soundstage, just like the musicals of yore. "That was a luxury," he acknowledges, even though he had only eight hours to complete thirty-six set ups.

In keeping with the films of the era, *Anything But Love* is refreshingly unironic and free of cynicism. "That can be corny," Cary realizes, "but I'm fine with that. We did it with our hearts. Life is not a fantasy. I can say that that the idea of not giving up on your dreams and not making compromises for the sake of emotional safety is very close to my heart. In a strange way, my life has imitated the life of the heroine."

With the same determination and hard work, Cary should continue to meet with success. "I am anxious for my next directing opportunity," he says confidently, with one eye in the past and one fixed firmly in the future.

KEITH FULTON AND LOUIS PEPE:
LOST IN LA MANCHA

Keith Fulton and Louis Pepe, the queer documentarians behind *Lost in La Mancha* (2002), are funny and offbeat—not unlike their film. They not only love moviemaking, but understand—and show—why it is so exciting.

Men of La Mancha: *Keith Fulton and Louis Pepe*

"We've been together eleven years," says filmmaker Louis Pepe.

"That's like seventy-seven *gay* years," jokes his partner and co-conspirator Keith Fulton.

Pepe was born in Philadelphia but went to M.I.T as an undergraduate before returning to Temple University for his M.F.A. in film studies. In contrast, Fulton moved to Philadelphia from Boston and attended Haverford College—"a gay man's nightmare," he says about the experience—before entering Temple for his graduate work. The two filmmakers met at film school in 1990, and they now live and work together in the Silverlake district of Los Angeles.

The couple has returned briefly to the City of Brotherly Love on a promotional tour for their new film, *Lost in La Mancha,* a documentary about Terry Gilliam's *The Man Who Killed Don Quixote,* a quirky and cursed adaptation of Cervantes's novel. While Gilliam's film encounters disasters of epic proportions, Fulton and Pepe shrewdly record it for posterity. Not unlike Quixote himself, Gilliam is forever tilting at windmills in the struggle to get his film made against all odds.

"I read the first volume of *Don Quixote,*" Pepe begins, and starts talking how wonderful the book is.

"It was irrelevant," counters Fulton.

The subject is quickly changed, but it is clear that the two documentarians interact well together, playing off each other's strengths and weakness.

For example, they both share the directing duties, but Pepe operates the camera "while I just drink and smoke." Fulton quips. Actually, Fulton is a field producer, a job that involves location work and preparation.

"I'm the aggressive, impatient one," he admits.

"And I'm timid, patient, and compulsive," says Pepe.

They are both very accommodating to the other's "interpersonal skills."

"He's very good about having us get paid," explains Pepe.

And, as if to reveal the secret to their relationship, the couple agrees that they "fight more about personal things than we do about work."

While they have made two documentaries with Gilliam, *The Hamster Factory* (1997) about the director's film *Twelve Monkeys* (1995) and now *La Mancha*, they are thinking about doing a film with a gay character. Although they don't reveal much about this project, Fulton states that his own sexuality "is not an issue" when it comes to their getting work as filmmakers.

In fact, both Fulton and Pepe have strong opinions about how queer films are marketed to gay audiences. They lament about these films luring viewers with the promise of sexy, nude men—it doesn't matter if the film is any good at all. (Incidentally, the closest thing to a sexy nude man in *La Mancha* is one of the trio of shirtless "Giants" that stomp around the Spanish countryside.)

As for working with gays and lesbians, Pepe is always eager to employ them, stating that "it is hard not to make a personal connection [with them] on a set." The composer for *La Mancha*, Miriam Cutler is a lesbian, as were all of the costume designers on the film-within-a-film, Gilliam's *Quixote*.

And while making *Lost in La Mancha* was relatively painless for Fulton and Pepe—they still can not believe their good fortune at Gilliam's expense—it was difficult for the documentarians to watch their friend's project go up in smoke.

"It was very depressing," Pepe says, about the experience. "Everyone wanted to make [*Don Quixote*]. But they had nothing to do but sit around and wait."

Gilliam's production fell victim to extreme weather conditions, the ill health of the film's star, and F16s flying over an airspace during shooting among other things.

"We didn't sabotage it," Pepe says,

"But we'd love it if you start that rumor," Fulton jests.

RICHARD KWIETNIOWSKI:
OWNING MAHOWNY

Queer filmmaker Richard Kwietniowski's *Owning Mahowny* (2003) does not have a single gay character in it, but the ideas he discusses about his protagonist's double life will certainly ring true with queer audiences. The director's first feature, *Love and Death on Long Island* (1997) was a clever rumination on gay love, and *Mahowny* continues the filmmaker's trajectory of exploring the underbelly of men trapped by their own desires.

Kwietniowski's Compulsions and Obsessions

Queer filmmaker Richard Kwietniowski excels at telling stories about ordinary people's secret lives. His first feature, *Love and Death in Long Island,* had John Hurt's character Giles De'Ath chasing after teen actor Jason Priestley to satisfy his long-dormant sexual urges. In his new film, *Owning Mahowny,* the British director studies another driven character, Dan (Philip Seymour Hoffman), a compulsive gambler who downplays his very serious addiction.

"I am very drawn to stories about obsession," Kwietniowski says on the phone from his London home. "I am interested in marginalized, outsider characters—ordinary people who undergo extraordinary things." He acknowledges that the outsider status of his film's protagonist can lend itself to a queer identity. If audiences want to read *Owning Mahowny*—about a man living a double life, deceiving his girlfriend, and dashing off every night—that way it is entirely possible.

As the film shows, Dan get as big a thrill hiding his gambling habit from the bank he works at (where he's stealing money to support his habit) as well as from his long-suffering girlfriend (Minnie Driver) who is unaware of the extent of his addiction.

"Most gays and lesbians in this country don't live openly, and there is a thrill in concealing it," Kwietniowski declares, adding that "there is too much paranoia about this."

He continues to address this topic of secretive sexuality. "The secret is what you fantasize about—not what you would act upon. I don't understand eroticism where heterosexual men only find women attractive or gay men who don't find women attractive. If you look at the homoerotic subtext in straight culture, you should see the same in gay culture. It is a terrible thing to suggest that straight culture is more complex."

This idea of looking deeper at a person or culture offers an insight into why the character of Dan Mahowny appealed to Kwietniowski. "He doesn't have a reason why he is addicted to gambling. He is an enigma to us as much as to himself. [Like gambling], desire/sexuality/love are very arbitrary, chance events. It could happen to anyone." And this is the point of the film—to show how anyone can be susceptible to an addiction.

While Mahowny is certainly an everyman—Kwietniowski wanted to make him a most unlikely addict—the director was fortunate to cast a brilliant actor in the title role. Philip Seymour Hoffman makes the part his own, using both his voice and excellent body language to convey his character's quirky personality.

"Philip plays this character as an exceptionally closed person to show that obsession is actually dull," Kwietniowski says. "Unlike Giles [the hero of *Love and Death*] who undergoes a rebirth in Long Island, Dan is the opposite. He is Canadian, polite and reserved, a bit paranoid, and unworldly. He is not used to exposing himself emotionally, and I wanted him to be a fish out of water as a high roller in a casino."

Recalling the lure of the casino firsthand, Kwietniowski admits that he once had a gambling problem himself. "When I was ten, I asked for six months pocket money to play slots at a resort on holiday. Of course, I lost it and asked for the next six months."

He laughs at the memory, but he continues to talk about casinos. "Anyone who spent a night in a casino can understand Dan reducing his existence to winning or losing. Casinos are desperate places—but you forget that quickly once you are in them. [They] irresistibly invite you to leave reality outside."

And, the director realizes, the same can be said about the power of the movies. "Cinema is especially good at taking you out of yourself, to somewhere you wouldn't go in real life. I try to tell stories in a way that is as compulsive as the subject matter."

And this makes perfect sense. When asked about his own personal obsessions, Kwietniowski simply answers: "Filmmaking."

BRIAN DANNELLY: SAVED!

Brian Dannelly may make a teenpic like *Saved!* (2004) for the mainstream, but it reveals his subversive streak. He shows promise as a filmmaker, and it will be interesting to see what he would do with an independent gay feature.

Dannelly on Sex, Sin, and Saved!

Brian Dannelly, the gay writer-director of the teen comedy *Saved!*, recalls how he felt when he first started questioning his sexuality. "I remember I'd pray every night that I wasn't gay, and please God, please God, anything I could do—just don't make this happen."

He eventually came out at the age of seventeen, and was thrown out of his home by his parents. "Now my parents travel around with my films," he says with some satisfaction about their mended relationship. "It took time."

Yet Dannelly continues to grow comfortable with his sexuality. "I am still in the process of accepting it. It's weird, because I've never been a joiner—I don't like karaoke, line dancing—I've never had a bunch of gay friends specifically, just friends." Nevertheless, his life is certainly happier now than it was in the closet. "I think anyone who is gay—you just know it. It is so denying who you are," the filmmaker offers about wishing for a different life.

Being a gay teen is portrayed in Dannelly's new film *Saved!* as the adorable Dean (Chad Faust) tells his Christian girlfriend Mary (Jena Malone) that he thinks he is queer. After a vision from Jesus, she sleeps with him to "save" him and winds up pregnant.

Dannelly is also familiar with having visions of Christ, having had one of those as a young boy as well. "I think I was like ten or eleven in

Germany, and we were playing with a Ouiji board, and I swear to God I saw Jesus on the wall. Like this glimpse. It was like akin to that oil stain Mary in Florida. I remember thinking, 'that is so weird.'"

Taking these twin themes of religion and sexuality, Dannelly crafted a serious, funny, and seriously funny film. *Saved!* both skewers the Christian teens as much as it tries to explain them.

While *Saved!* does address potentially sensitive issues of gay youth and teen pregnancy, the film is not particularly nasty or mean spirited. In fact, it is rather sweet. While Mary learns to fit in with the misfits—a smart-mouthed Jewish girl named Cassandra (Eva Amurri)—Dean, who is shipped off to a "rehabilitation" center to cure his "deviancy" finds another queer kid (Kett Turton) whom he hopes to take to the prom.

Dannelly describes his sense of humor as not being "cynical or black—more brown or light gray. I think people want me to be more biting, and really let [Christians] have it, but that wasn't interesting to me. The whole idea behind the film was to make a mainstream movie that had subversive undertones. It's for regular people. It had to be accessible. It had to be PG-13."

Still, the writer-director acknowledges, "Regardless of how face friendly the film is, there are certain things that will never ever *ever* be accepted. And those are premarital sex, being gay, being Jewish—can't get much around that—but there are people who are those things."

That said, "The Christian left have been really accepting of the film," Dannelly boasts, before stating, "just not fundamentalists."

The filmmaker claims, "Everything in *Saved!* was born out of the truth, and sometimes it was slightly heightened. We didn't make anything up, we played down stuff—there is stuff you really wouldn't believe. Going to Christian concerts, and having girls in tube tops screaming at these Christian bands, and it's weird because you're not supposed to have idolatry, but . . ." He trails off before adding, "The bands are so much better now. You have Skillet and The Benjamin Gate and you have great music."

And speaking of music, *Saved!* features teen sensation Mandy Moore in as the haughty Hilary Faye, the leader of The Christian Jewels. Moore is terrific in the role—perhaps her best screen performance yet—and she also gets to perform "God Only Knows" during the opening and closing credits. "Mandy ate up the role. She was really into it, committed, fearless," Dannelly says about the squeaky clean Moore's ability to be mean on screen.

With the casting of Moore along with Macaulay Culkin, Patrick Fugit, and Heather Matarazzo, Dannelly expects *Saved!* will appeal to a young audience.

"We used a high school as a microcosm for that society so you could deal with issues in a more simplistic way. We also wanted to speak to kids who are growing up in a time of AIDS, terrorism, and people shooting up their schools, and it's a fearful time. This movement is really comforting and safe, but it is a really fine line and it excludes so many people. My sense is that something's not right," he says, adding, "my religion today is personal responsibility and kindness."

JACOB TIERNEY: TWIST

Jacob Tierney's *Twist* (2003) is an ambitious reworking of Charles Dickens' *Oliver Twist,* and while it does not always work dramatically, it shows Tierney's eye for beautiful images. As an actor turned filmmaker, Tierney certainly understands the process of moviemaking. Hopefully his next project will improve upon the skills he developed in this film.

Twist-*ing with Jacob Tierney*

A new version of *Oliver Twist,* told from the Artful Dodger's point of view, the film *Twist* features a cast of young boys posing as gay male hustlers in Toronto. Writer-director Jacob Tierney's directorial debut is a gorgeous-looking drama, and one that the filmmaker says "subverts the classic expectations of the story." Tierney was inspired as much by his father's obsession for Dickens as by his own interest in themes of child labor, prostitution, and sexual abuse.

"We were trying to create a deliberate fiction—not an accurate depiction of [hustler] life," Tierney says on the phone from his home in Toronto. "I did a lot of research into this world. I was amazed at how dire it was. The strongest thing I took away from it is that it's not fun, sexy, or glamorous."

Neither is his film. *Twist* purposefully plays down the erotic elements of gay prostitution for a darker look at sexuality as a job skill.

"Sex is a way of dealing with love for others. If that's been beaten out of you, then it's something you can sell. It doesn't have an emotional impact," Tierney says, justifying his reasons for making this film. The filmmaker claims he was simply drawn to the material, "I'm not gay, and I've never worked as a prostitute, but I know a ton of guys who have been sexually abused."

The filmmaker shot *Twist* in twenty days with a $200,000 budget. He cast his friend and former roommate Nick Stahl as Dodge and made him the focus of the story because "I felt people would have an easier time relating to a guy who has been around the block a few times versus the innocent being corrupted."

Tierney got the idea for the film after seeing *Oliver Twist* on the stage in London. He hopes that audiences will use their knowledge of the show or the book as touchstones for his film. Though he admits, "structurally, I went more from the musical than the book."

One of the ways *Twist* is distinctive is that the story is much more about mood than action. The film features stunning cinematography and artfully composed shots that provide a stark, despairing atmosphere. The freezing Toronto weather allows the actors' breath to cloud when they speak, lending the film a realism that is palpable.

Tierney says that he "worked really hard on the look of the film," which was influenced by queer filmmaker Terence Davies, who directed Tierney—as an actor—in the film *The Neon Bible* (1995).

He continues, "I did not make *Twist* to look like an urban, underworld film. It's a character study, and my style is observational. You really do just watch these people. I don't tell you how to feel about them. I just present them."

Shrewdly, Tierney places much of the action off screen, in favor of quiet conversations. This stylish technique may, however, distance viewers from the narrative. "I thought it would be easier on the audience," Tierney says, "but it was the opposite! It is so removed that it makes it difficult for people to deal with."

Regardless of one's knowledge of Dickens, or their identification with the characters, the performances are what truly come across in *Twist*. In addition to Stahl's heartfelt turn as Dodge, Gary Farmer has a memorable supporting role as Fagin.

"He was able to play this guy as an abusive softie," Tierney says in praise of Farmer. "He is a phenomenal actor. He takes care of these boys and looks after them, but he is an abusive headmaster. He played both of those things at the same time, effortlessly."

As an actor himself, Tierney is especially pleased with his cast, and although he loves performing, he prefers being behind the camera.

"I have been on movie sets since I was a kid. I love the [process]," he says, before ending on a wistful note. "I had a great time making the film. The role of the director is the storyteller. You have to put yourself out there. But I don't think I realized how much work it would be."

DENYS ARCAND:
THE BARBARIAN INVASIONS

Denys Arcand caught my attention with his film *The Decline of the American Empire* (1986), and I've enjoyed his subsequent films *Jesus of Montreal* (1989) and *Love and Human Remains* (1993) and found his flop *Stardom* (2000) a curious misfire. But I was unprepared for the complexity of *The Barbarian Invasions* (2003), which is his most impressive film to date. This interview concentrates on the queer content in his work, although there is much more to Arcand—and his film—than that.

Denys Arcand Attacks The Barbarians

It should be no surprise that the most well-adjusted couple in queer-friendly writer-director Denys Arcand's latest film *The Barbarian Invasions* is the gay one.

"It is not the traditional view of things, and I like it," the Canadian filmmaker says about his queer characters, before noting that they do "have these little issues between them. They are like this old [married] couple and they quarrel."

This funny and deeply moving film reunites the gay and straight friends from the filmmaker's 1986 production *The Decline of the American Empire*. When Rémy (Rémy Girard) is dying, his estranged son Sébastian (Stéphane Rousseau) arranges for all his old friends to come and pay their last respects. Claude (Yves Jacques), the only homosexual in the group, comes from Rome, where he is living with his partner Alessandro (Toni Cecchinato).

When audiences last saw Claude (in *Decline*) he was pissing blood. Many critics thought this condition suggested he had AIDS. Arcand explains that he was much shrewder with how he portrayed Claude's physical disorder. "What I wanted to show was the state of panic gay people were in at that time [1986]. You coughed, and your body would ache, and you'd say, 'That's it, I got it.' And the actual actor (Jacques) who's gay was living in this state of shock."

Arcand, however, made sure Claude would survive for the sequel seventeen years later. "I gave him a symptom that I had at one point in my life [blood in the urine]. It is a terrifying sight, but it's just a kidney ailment. I thought it would be a visually striking image. You could see his panic. [I knew] he would live a long and happy life. And what I like about it is that he is the most stable of the characters."

The director explains that his love for the character of Claude comes from his strong professional and emotional ties to gay men. Why is Rémy so close to Claude when he is much closer in temperament to the film's other heterosexual characters?

"It has to do with my life," Arcand answers. "I am a filmmaker and always have prominent gay people on the set. I don't have the faintest idea of passing judgment on someone."

In fact, Arcand has had many queer influences in his career, one of which he pays homage to in *The Barbarian Invasions*. The director explains that Michel Tremblay, a gay author, wrote a book called *Bambi and Me* about films that shaped his sexuality. Arcand uses an image from one of the films Tremblay discussed in a clever and poignant way.

Moreover, Arcand tends to gravitate to collaborating with gay writers such as Brad Fraser, whose play became the director's controversial film *Love and Human Remains*. In this 1993 romantic thriller, a group of twentysomething men and women search for their sexuality through various same-sex encounters while a serial killer is on the loose.

Arcand describes Fraser as a "very in-your-face kind of gay person. A lot of his plays came from his anger. He'd say, 'I'm GAY' and I was like, 'Alright, good. What else?'" The filmmaker is attracted to people who are confrontational and openly discuss issues.

"If I have one quality, it is that when I make films I am fearless. You are offended by it—good or too bad!" Arcand is especially emphatic when he says this. The director has no tolerance for narrow-minded people. *The Barbarian Invasions* is in favor of drug use, euthanasia, and adultery; it has contempt for hospital administration, unions, and the church. Arcand is nothing if not political.

"Think of what Philadelphia meant [in 1776], think of Jefferson, think of these people and look at where you are now. It's frightening!" he says, before continuing. "The people who are cultured don't seem to be part of this gigantic phenomena called America. They are the best public—they are vibrant, and totally open to everything. I am discouraged for the others. They never read a fine book; they never see a fine image on their TV. It means that the world totally revolves around their vision of the world. *They* are the barbarians."

ANDREW JARECKI:
CAPTURING THE FRIEDMANS

Andrew Jarecki may be best known for creating Moviephone, but I will always remember him for *Capturing the Friedmans* (2003). An unforgettable documentary, Jarecki's film is seared in my mind.

Capturing *Andrew Jarecki*

Filmmaker Andrew Jarecki was originally going to make a documentary on professional birthday clowns. However, when he met the #1 Birthday Clown in New York, David Friedman, he found an altogether different, darker, and more fascinating story. It was one that had to be told. Jarecki's film, *Capturing the Friedmans* is a chilling saga of a family torn apart by a horrible crime. "The Friedmans are like all of us, only more so," Jarecki said on the phone from Cannes. "Everyone has family secrets—only theirs are more shocking."

In 1988, in Great Neck, New York, the Friedmans became the focus of community attention and outrage when the father Arnold, a celebrated teacher, and the youngest son, Jesse (who was eighteen at the time), were arrested and accused of child pornography, sexual abuse, and pedophilia.

"There was a tremendous amount of material about the case," Jarecki said. "It was important to [tell] the information in digestible bites." *Capturing the Friedmans* tells the family's compelling story using the family's remarkable home movies—of everything from the brothers goofing around to intense family arguments—as well as a series of "talking head" segments.

While David's reaction to his family's skeletons is one of protection, his mother Elaine feels betrayed by her husband, and she is soon alienated from the family. As the home movies present the family coming apart at the seams, Jarecki was thrilled to include them, as he felt they "had great impact. They validated my initial feelings about the case."

Significantly, the middle son, Seth, chose not to be filmed for the documentary. Jarecki states, "I would have loved to have had him," but Seth declined participation because, as he put it, "The last time the family was in public eye it didn't work out so well."

Yet what is interesting about the film is what each subject does reveal. So many people involved in the case—from law enforcement officials to the Friedmans' legal council—wanted to talk to the camera. "Every perspective makes the film better in a way," Jarecki explained. "Parsing the language these people use shows what they are thinking." Citing the example of one of the boys who claims to have been abused telling "a very strange story, [full of] contradictions," Jarecki suggests that the way he films each subject "reflects his feelings about their commentary." For David, it was important to show his clown materials in the background to "see him in his environment. It was part of his personality, and added an understanding of who he is."

While the audience will draw their own assumptions about what did or did not happen, it is to Jarecki's credit that he is able to have viewers think so objectively about the case. "What the film can do is make you think about the difficulty of assessing a situation like this—the risks of relying on highly subjective evidence such as children's testimony and nonphysical evidence," the filmmaker said.

Capturing the Friedmans is certainly provocative not only for the subject matter but also for the way audiences will connect the dots that Jarecki presents. One individual interviewed is a homosexual, whose lifestyle may be the (in)direct result of his experiences with Arnold. For this particular person, Jarecki acknowledges that "some people say [his early sexual activity] 'made' him gay," while others perceive that it helped him "develop an awareness of his homosexuality." Such is the brilliance of the film.

And although the film deals with difficult subject matter, there is a sense of humor on display. The Friedmans were, Jarecki describes, "funny—they loved laughing at themselves." What is more, Arnold was an accomplished pianist, and his music is used throughout the film. "It was the soundtrack of their lives," the director says.

Yet the filmmaker, who has two young sons himself, claims his documentary is ultimately about the "issues of responsibility you have as a father." He continues, "No matter what you believe, Arnold clearly created a situation for Jesse. He made a tragic decision. The son was implicated by every action his father took."

ROBERT J. SIEGEL: SWIMMING

Robert J. Siegel was unknown to me before I was asked to see his feature *Swimming* (2000), which I think is one of those near-perfect films. Of course it received ecstatic reviews and near-zero box office. Graced with a performance by the fabulous Lauren Ambrose (who starred in *Six Feet Under*), this is an indie pic to get excited about. It has pitch-perfect acting, a smart, heartfelt message, and a brief queer scene.

In the Swim *with Siegel*

"If I make a film, I have to be connected to every moment of the picture," says director Robert J. Siegel. "Filmmaking is about the observance of human behavior—the small touches," he continues "I wanted to depict ordinary people in ordinary circumstances." As the enthusiastic reviews attest, *Swimming* is this summer's independent sleeper.

A tender coming-of-age drama, *Swimming* features Lauren Ambrose (of *Six Feet Under*) as Frankie, a tomboy in Myrtle Beach, South Carolina, who is grappling with her budding sexuality. Her character's gradual steps toward independence are played out against the shifting of loyalties between two other young women—her oldest friend Nicola (Jennifer Dundas Lowe), a spitfire, and Josee (Joelle Carter), a new girl in town. And it is Josee, who Frankie develops a crush on, who acts as a catalyst for Frankie's maturation.

The film's relationship-oriented story originated in a SUNY Purchase Film School class taught by Siegel. Lisa Bazadona, a student Siegel describes as "a bad director, but a gifted screenwriter," wrote about her observances working at a tattoo parlor (as Nicola's character does) in Myrtle Beach. When Siegel approached Bazadona to option the film, they ended up writing nine drafts of the story before settling on the finished version.

"Lisa hated me as a teacher," Siegel recalls. "She did not have any experience, but [by the end of *Swimming*] she emerged a real pro. It was a wonderful collaboration."

In fact, the making of the film was a completely collaborative effort with total support from the entire cast and crew. Siegel shot the film on location doing eighteen to twenty-seven set ups a day (a normal film has about nine to ten set ups per day) which translated into shooting six pages a day (compared to the industry average of three). "Everything was preblocked before filming," he explains about why filming went so quickly.

"A director's key job is to know when the actor has 'arrived,'" Siegel says about deciding when to say cut, print, and move on to the next shot. "You have to know where the actors have to go."

In addition to having to find the right physical and emotional cues, however, the director maintains that 90 percent of directing is the casting. "You can't overcome bad acting," he says about finding the right performers. "These people are collaborators. They bring depth to their roles. The more careful you are in picking the collaborators, the better the work."

Obviously, Siegel is blessed with having the rising star Ambrose play the lead in his film, as she has garnered uniformly glowing reviews for her performance. Siegel recognizes that the actress was given a difficult task. He found Ambrose after she made the films *Can't Hardly Wait* (1998) and *In & Out* (1997), and has great admiration for her. "Lauren had to carry the film, and she's playing a passive character with not a lot of dialogue," Siegel says. "That is a tremendous burden for a young actor. But she is smart, and she understood the role. Lauren had grave concerns about [playing] a character who's a 'nobody'—but she moves the audience in a very powerful way."

Siegel also has high praise for the two supporting actresses, Jennifer Dundas Lowe and Joelle Carter. "Jenny was the most experienced, most trained actress we saw. She gave a cold reading and I hired her that day. Joelle is a natural—right in the moment. She improvised her scene in the restaurant and let us film her running at night into the cold water as many times as it took."

Truly an independent filmmaker, Siegel started in the industry at the age of eighteen, making political films such as *Parades* (1972), about the Vietnam War. The fictional *Swimming* is a bit of a departure for the professor. While he produced, directed, and co-wrote this low-budget winner, he also had a significant role in choosing the film's soundtrack which features tunes by Bree Sharp and G. Love & Special Sauce. "We spent months on the music and were extremely selective. We wanted music to be a counterpoint, but not underline the moment."

Siegel has also taken on the monumental task of distributing the film himself. "We began on the festival circuit, to build reviews," he said. "After an overseas deal fell through, we got the film back." When he didn't want a small distributor to handle his baby, he chose to do it himself. "We were given 'slim to none' chances of succeeding" he says, then adds, happily, "and we ran twelve weeks when the film opened in Boston."

STEVE GUTTENBERG:
P.S. YOUR CAT IS DEAD

Steve Guttenberg gave a great performance in *Diner* (1982), and I was pleased to see him springboard from that role to major success. Unfortunately, it was in those *Police Academy* (1984) movies. Still, every once in a while Guttenberg turned up in something good. I think Curtis Hanson's *The Bedroom Window* (1987) is a great little thriller, and the actor gives a terrific performance in the wonderful Jodie Foster film *Home for the Holidays* (1995). Sure, Guttenberg has made crap—he acknowledges this—but I find him immensely likeable. His directorial debut, *P.S. Your Cat Is Dead* (2002) should have received more notice from critics and audiences. It is a fine adaptation of James Kirkwood's novel/play

Steve Guttenberg Is Not Dead

Steve Guttenberg has a sense of humor about himself and his career. The sexy—yes, sexy—everyman who appeared in great films like *Diner* and *The Bedroom Window,* as well as the camp classic *Can't Stop the Music* (1980), also made some of the most profitable franchise films of all time. Guttenberg starred in the *Police Academy* series, the *Three Men and a Baby* (1987) movies, *Cocoon* (1985) and its sequel, as well as *Short Circuit* (1986). He also appeared in 3-D (and in the nude) in what is one of the great bad movies ever made, *The Man Who Wasn't There* (1983).

"I've done a lot of crap and a lot of good stuff," he admits readily in a recent phone interview. But, he says in earnest, "I have more in me than meets the eye."

Guttenberg proves this in the long-awaited film adaptation of the late, great, gay writer James Kirkwood's *P.S. Your Cat Is Dead.* The actor not only stars in this film; he co-wrote the screenplay, served as co-producer, and makes his directorial debut.

While this chamber piece, which was shot in thirty days for under $2 million, may not sound like a typical Steve Guttenberg project, the actor suggests that there is no such thing. A dog owner, he was drawn to this comedy-drama because he liked the story, which involves a down on his luck actor bonding with the gay burglar he has tied up in the kitchen on New Year's Eve.

"It is a really important piece of literature," Guttenberg says. "It is a story of moral conflict. What is the right thing to do? It is to listen. Once you start to do that, the answers come." Such is the "action" in this talkfest, between two characters that slowly learn how to communicate with each other and become better people in the process.

P.S. Your Cat Is Dead is quite faithful to the cult 1972 novel (and subsequent play), though there are some obvious changes. The burglar, named Vito Antenucci in the book, became Eddie Tesoro (Lombardo Boyar) in this version as Guttenberg felt uncomfortable with the novel's Italian stereotypes. The setting moved from NY to LA because it was "more prohibitive" for the director to shoot in the Big Apple. And the ending, which is quite poignant (and anti-Hollywood) in the film, differs from the original in several respects that should not be revealed.

Purists may carp, but the only aspect that really might upset fans of the novel is that the film downplays the book's queer content. Guttenberg's Jimmy Zoole is actually slightly homophobic in the film. He makes a comment about being hit on by his friend Carmine (A.J. Benza, who is terrific) and is threatened (physically) by the film's gay characters. "I can see how it can be seen as anti-gay," Guttenberg says, "but it was never the intent." He adds, in the film's defense, that "the treatment of [the gay character] Eddie was quite realistic."

And speaking of Eddie, the cute Boyar, who is hog-tied to a sink and bare-assed through a good portion of the film, holds his own against Guttenberg. "He was a real sport," the director recalls about his co-star. "It's tough to be in one position and convey a performance with very little movement, but it is also challenging and exciting."

Guttenberg also gave his parents cameo roles in the film, and he dubs his folks "my Stiller and Meara." For the director, casting was one of the perks of making *P.S. Your Cat Is Dead,* and Guttenberg liked being in control. "Acting is the most enjoyable part of the process because it is invigorating once the camera starts to roll. Producing is a twenty-four-hour job, trying to cobble together a deal. Writing is the most civilized part, but directing is great because of the excitement of getting the rhythm, the feeling, and the tone of the story," he says about his multiple jobs.

As for his own personal choice between being serious or funny, Guttenberg says, "There is a skill to both. You have to make people laugh, or you have to make them think. I don't look at either as being harder." He cites *Stalag 17* (1953) as one of his influences in making *P.S. Your Cat Is Dead,* appreciating director Billy Wilder's ability to "use claustrophobia to create conflict." In addition, the balance of comedy and drama, which also appears in both films is "a great cocktail for the audience."

Yet the eternally optimistic Guttenberg explains that making a film—be it a comedy or a drama, a good film or a bad film—requires the same amount of energy and work. "You just need to have heart, diligence, and integrity, and you can [do] anything you want."

As for the character of Jimmy Zoole, who in the film is having *one of those days,* Guttenberg admits to having a few bad days of his own. "They are not always as bad as you think—once you step away from them."

Chapter 4
Fascinating Actors

The actors in this chapter are all straight, but each have played in queer films/roles. Their insights into their work and their careers are interesting, which is why I have included them here.

TILDA SWINTON: THE DEEP END

Actress Tilda Swinton continues to fascinate me. From the gender-bending *Orlando* (1992)—her first starring role—to her magnetic performance in *Young Adam* (2003), Swinton projects intelligence and insouciance. When Swinton was cast in the American film *The Deep End* (2001), I really thought her profile would soar; however, Swinton still remains below the surface. What struck me when I met her was the actress's incredible self-control. I was also dazzled by the large silver spider cufflinks she wore with her blouse. I soon became less concerned with demystifying Swinton as I was with just taking her in.

Swinton Goes Deep

Tilda Swinton is an unusual actress, just check out her performance as Margaret Hall in *The Deep End*—a thriller written and directed by Scott McGehee and David Siegel (*Suture,* 1993)—and watch her expressions change as trouble seems to find her. In this tense and provocative film, the actress plays a mother of three who helps dispose of her son's lover's corpse in an effort to protect her family. However, Margaret gets sucked in deeper when she is blackmailed by a stranger (*ER*'s Goran Visnjic) who is holding an incriminating videotape of her son's sexual activities with the dead man.

Independent Queer Cinema: Reviews and Interviews
© 2006 by The Haworth Press, Inc. All rights reserved.
doi:10.1300/5482_05

It's a meaty role in what Swinton describes as "an action film"—and one that was both very demanding and highly rewarding. *The Deep End* may in fact prove to be Swinton's breakout film, and her role could earn her an Academy Award nomination. Not that she's aspiring to win one. Swinton crosses herself at the mention of an Oscar, more to say "God forbid" than "God willing." [She received a Golden Globe nomination, but the Academy did not recognize her.]

In describing the intense eight-week shoot, Swinton says that "it was like a long-distance run, and I'm a sprinter." Yet her performance is remarkable. Swinton describes her acting process as "concentrating on the dots and connecting them," but it appears completely realistic on-screen. About her character in *The Deep End*, she says, "I am nothing like Margaret Hall. I don't adhere to that style of motherhood. I am lazy."

Nevertheless, Swinton gets the American accent down right and plays this well-written part brilliantly. When asked why she chooses the roles she plays, the actress says simply, "Because of the dialogue."

Swinton is also quick to state that acting is not her main focus. "I do not have a career. I have a life." Her three-year-old twins—a boy and a girl—as well as her husband take up most of her time and energy, although she is working a bit more frequently now. In addition to small roles in Cameron Crowe's *Vanilla Sky* (2001) and Spike Jonze's *Adaptation* (2002), she will next appear in *Teknolust* (2002), Lynn Hershmann's film made entirely on virtual sets. The actress is visibly excited about the project and has tremendous respect for Hershmann, who cast Swinton in her previous movie *Conceiving Ada* (1997).

But perhaps Swinton's greatest collaboration was with iconoclastic filmmaker Derek Jarman, who referred to Swinton as "his muse." The actress responds with a laugh. "If anyone knew Derek [who died in 1994] they knew he was his own muse." Furthermore, in Tony Peake's recent biography of the late filmmaker—a book Swinton decided not to collaborate on—she is referred to as "La Swinton" in a passage about a fight she had with her dear friend. The title "La Swinton" amuses the actress, who says she is "flattered by it."

Asked about her other previous work, Swinton is mute about *The War Zone* (1999), a powerful incest drama directed by Tim Roth.

However, she is happy to talk about *The Beach* (2000), the film that Leonardo DiCaprio starred in after skyrocketing to fame in *Titanic* (1997).

"I call [*The Beach*] my experimental film," Swinton says with a wry grin, as it is her only "Hollywood" film to date. She looks back on the experience as a good one, although she claims that the studio made mistakes in marketing the film. "It was a teenage adventure story, and they made it look like *The Blue Lagoon*" [1980]. Nevertheless, she enjoyed working with Danny Boyle on *The Beach*, and couldn't turn down the opportunity.

And so it seems that Tilda Swinton will continue to do what Tilda Swinton wants to do, making the movies that appeal to her regardless of budget, awards, or box office returns. As if to underscore this fact, Swinton admits—surprisingly—that she once lived for a year on money she won betting on horseracing. Unusual indeed.

JEAN-PIERRE LORIT: A MATTER OF TASTE

My interview with Jean-Pierre Lorit, who played the food taster in the film *A Matter of Taste* (2000), took place in a Paris restaurant/nightclub where we met for lunch. (I insisted on having a meal with an actor who played a food taster.) Lorit, who had featured parts in Krzysztof Kieslowski's *Red* (1994) and André Téchiné's *Alice and Martin* (1998), is ripe for success. Hopefully, it will find him soon.

At Lunch with Lorit

At lunch in a trendy Paris restaurant with Jean-Pierre Lorit, the handsome French actor orders our fixed-course meals—an appetizer and fish for me, the typically Gallic dish of sausage and lentils plus dessert for himself. I don't speak a word of French, so I just sip my Kir and smile sheepishly. Thankfully, Lorit's English is quite good, and we can talk about his César [French Oscar]-nominated performance in the stunning psychological thriller *A Matter of Taste*.

In this unsettling film, Lorit stars as Nicolas Rivère, a poor waiter hired by a powerful executive named Frédéric Delamont (Bernard Giraudeau) to be his food taster. The job pays quite well, but of course, it comes with a catch: Delamont strives to completely remake Nicolas in his image, and he will stop at nothing to achieve his goal. It would spoil the film's thrills to describe exactly how things get out of hand, but needless to say, they do.

Although *A Matter of Taste* was completed in thirty-eight days almost three years ago, Lorit still talks about it as if he had just finished shooting. "What I like about the film," he says, "is that it is about the miseries of human psychology. Nicolas hates what Delamont is, but at the same time, he is—maybe not consciously—fascinated and attracted to the freedom represented by Delamont's power and money."

What begins as a kind of game soon turns into something uncomfortably symbiotic and, ultimately, deadly. "Delamont is the great manipulator. You can see that," Lorit says. "But to me, Nicolas is also manipulating, or trying to manipulate Delamont."

Lorit, himself, however, is not likely to fall into the same trap as his on-screen character. "I don't think what happens to Nicolas can happen to me," he says, but then, considering this some more, he suggests, "I'm not sure—like in the film, you can't be sure of anything."

He continues, "That is another reason why I love this movie—it is full of questions for the audience. No two people see the same movie."

When *A Matter of Taste* screened in Japan, two viewers were convinced that Rivère ate Delamont after killing him, and Lorit is still amused by this idea.

Our meals arrive and Lorit is served a pork loin that looks tasty. As he is about to eat, we realize that this is not what he ordered. Mentioning the error to the apologetic waiter, Lorit insists, "It's no problem. *C'est bon, c'est bon,*" handling the situation more in the style of Nicolas than Delamont. The waiter, however, soon returns to serve Lorit his sausages and lentils, and takes the pork to the proper table.

This break in our conversation is the perfect time to discuss food, which plays a significant role in the film. "We shot in Lyon, a place where food is very important, and in some really good restaurants. Through this film I discovered some wines . . . . it was not boring at all." Lorit smiles almost wickedly at the memory.

Yet I am curious if Lorit—like Nicolas—has a strong aversion to tripe, or if he actually enjoys intestines. "Yes, I love that!" he says, adding that his father made his living selling to butchers, which might explain the actor's taste for organ meats.

Our plates are cleared away, and Lorit is served a gorgeous lemon meringue pie. It takes all of my energy not to ask a man who played a food taster if I can sample his dessert. Instead, I question Lorit about the film's daring skydiving scene.

"They told me that I wouldn't jump because of the insurance, but everybody promised me I would at the end of the shoot. The Sunday we went back, we still had three or four days more of shooting, so everybody jumped except me." We laugh in anguish at this missed opportunity as Lorit sets his spoon down, and I contemplate my own missed chance.

Nevertheless, I am grateful to have had the occasion to eat lunch with Jean-Pierre Lorit and discuss his provocative film. It provided me with plenty of food for thought.

ERNESTO MAHIEUX: THE EMBALMER

Ernesto Mahieux is another actor I'd never seen—or heard of before—but his performance in the sinister film *The Embalmer* (2002) was quite memorable. He brings his character, Peppino, a diminutive taxidermist with a crush on his tall, handsome co-worker, to life. It is an outstanding performance in a creepy film.

Mahieux Brings The Embalmer *to Life*

Ernesto Mahieux, the title character of *The Embalmer*, never expected to play the role of Peppino, a taxidermist smitten with Valerio (Valerio Foglia Manzillo), a handsome young man he meets and employs. A veteran of stage and film in Italy, Mahieux got the starring role through happenstance.

"Some friends of mine (who are also actors) were at a restaurant and they happened to meet the director, Matteo Garrone. They began talking, and Garrone asked if they knew a small actor who could really act. The first name that came to mind was mine," he recalls.

The part was an unusual one to say the least. His character has sex scenes with both men and women, professionally stuffs dead animals, and has ties to the mafia, who ask him to use his skills as a taxidermist to help them out with some delicate situations. Mahieux says that what appealed to him about this role was "how it would challenge me as an actor. I did not really like the story—because it was so violent— but I felt the character was so far from who I am, from my reality."

The actor sees Peppino as a father figure to Valerio, his heartthrob. Yet Mahieux views the relationship between these two opposite characters as one of "respect, not power." He continues to discuss their intense bond. "If anything, [Peppino] had the power that a father would have over his son. Valerio was certainly not stupid. He's somewhere between smart and native."

In making *The Embalmer,* the actor enjoyed the camaraderie he had on the set with his costars. "It was marvelous," he admits, "a pleasure to go to work everyday." However, there were several scenes that were difficult to shoot.

One pivotal moment in the film involves Peppino being confronted by Valerio's girlfriend Deborah (Elisabetta Rocchetti), who figures out why Peppino is so interested in her man. Filmed on a golf course, Mahieux acknowledges that this was one of the more trying moments for him during production, but he does not explain why.

It could be that the actor had to work hard at improvising his speech here. A wonderfully sinister moment, where Peppino lays it out for Deborah—and why she should go away—Mahieux explains that the actors had to come up with their own dialogue. Garrone's methodology involved improvisation in every scene. "He wanted us to read the script and know what was going to happen, but we pretty much created all of the words."

Likewise, the ending, as well as a sequence involving a gun, proved to be some of the more troublesome scenes for the actor to film. Surprisingly, he comments little about the film's taxidermy sequences, which are fascinating to watch. About preserving pets himself, Mahieux says perhaps jokingly, "I have a mutt named Lilly. Maybe when she dies, I'll embalm her."

And speaking of strange occupations, the actor thinks that he has been fortunate not to have too many bad ones. "The worst job I ever had was as a dishwasher," he claims. As an actor, though, Mahieux's career is on the upswing.

"*The Embalmer* has helped incredibly. Now I'm known not only in Italy, but all over the world. This film has made everything that I've worked for in over thirty years in theatre and film worthwhile," he says, before noting that his goal is "to star in my biography."

A longtime performer in cabaret shows and sceneggiata—"a popular type of theatre in Neapolitan dialect," he explains, as well as poetic theatre, the actor says that his life includes "a lot of suffering. I was without a father when I was ten. I learned life's realities at a young age."

Things have certainly improved since then. "My family was very happy during the shooting of *The Embalmer*, but after the success the film has had, they are really proud of me."

JAVIER BARDEM: THE DANCER UPSTAIRS

Javier Bardem is a life force. In a word, this Spanish stud is simply *fearless*. He is also irresistible. Not only is Bardem handsome and then some—he is also extremely polite, achingly funny, and absolutely charming. Bardem is a great storyteller, too. I have the utmost respect for this actor, who defies typecasting. Check out his resume: he played a mullet-headed mystic in *Dance with the Devil* (1997); embodied the spirit of writer Reinaldo Arenas in *Before Night Falls* (2000); and then turned in a quietly powerful performance as a dogged policeman in *The Dancer Upstairs* (2003). Bardem never makes the same film twice, and I will watch him do anything, several times.

Dancing *with Javier Bardem*

Wearing a long, black leather jacket, a black T-shirt, and blue jeans, Javier Bardem ignites a Marlboro Light before settling in to talk about his role in *The Dancer Upstairs*. This superb film, which marks actor John Malkovich's directorial debut, was adapted from Nicholas Shakespeare's novel about the real-life search for Abimael Guzman, the Marxist leader of Peru's Shining Path. In the film, Bardem plays Agustín Rejas, a lawyer turned policeman who is assigned to capture a political terrorist named Ezequiel.

Bardem describes Rejas as "a man in control of his emotions who wants to leave behind what he has been." But as with every character played by this remarkable actor, the role is much deeper. He explains further: "Rejas is a man who tried to construct his life in the way he would like it to be. And he lets himself go through love." As his efforts bring him closer to finding Ezequiel, Rejas becomes enamored with his daughter's ballet teacher, Yolanda (Laura Morante).

A poignant scene in which Rejas and Yolanda sit in a coffee shop and try to guess the identity of people in portraits on the wall is Bardem's favorite. He says it is "specific, small, and very clear," and it reinforces the idea that "we don't know anything about nothing."

Best known for his Oscar-nominated portrait of gay Cuban writer Reinaldo Arenas in *Before Night Falls,* the role of Rejas in *The Dancer Upstairs* appealed to Bardem because it offered him something different. "I did this when I was thirty, so it was quite a challenge to work in a role much older than I was, and so different from what I am emotionally, intellectually, and physically. I'm more . . ." he pauses, looking for the right word or phrase in English, ". . . of a kind of crazy guy."

Bardem is the youngest member of a Madrid acting dynasty. He originally wanted to be a painter and earned money working as an extra in to buy art supplies. He also admits to working—for two weekends—as a stripper. "The first weekend I was drunk, and brave enough to do it. The second weekend I was only drinking water, so I said, 'no, there is no money in it for me.'"

Bardem eventually found what he calls "beefcake" roles, several of which required him to be a sex object. "In the beginning, I was very much into physical roles, with strong sexual content," he says. One of those parts was in a film called *Jamón, Jamón* (1992) that also starred Penélope Cruz. It is perhaps famous for a scene that features Bardem and another actor bullfighting nude.

"That's a great, great scene," Bardem recalls fondly. "It was very cold. The makeup woman rubbed [Bengay] to warm us up—she put it all over our bodies, testicles, everything—and after five minutes we were running, naked, screaming, and 'on fire.' We had to go to the hospital to get an injection to lower our temperatures to go back and shoot!" The actor laughs heartily and then adds, "She was crying . . . she was so sorry."

While Bardem also starred in the comedy *Mouth to Mouth* (1995), in which he played a phone sex operator, the actor believes that his role playing a junkie in the film *Numbered Days* (1994) was the turning point in his career.

That is, until *Before Night Falls.*

"Nobody thought that I could portray a gay man with my face and with the movies I'd done before," Bardem says. Yet he took on what he calls "the huge responsibility" of playing a real person, and brilliantly captures Arenas in the film.

Bardem acknowledges that it was his character in another film, *Second Skin* (1999), in which he played the lover of a married man, that helped him feel comfortable playing queer.

"[Journalists] were asking me if I was ashamed of doing it," he remembers about taking the gay role. "What the fuck are you talking about?" he said in response. "Just that question itself is homophobic!"

In fact, Bardem insists that he has no limits as an actor. "There is nothing I wouldn't play—because when you judge the character you are dead as an artist. I think the artist has to be free to create it. I just want to [play] people who have a struggle inside them. I don't believe in superheroes. It is very easy to judge people, and it very easy to condemn them if they are different from us. And that is something that we should avoid because that brings destruction, and intolerance, and intolerance brings violence."

For Bardem, it is also important for him to have the opportunity to alter his physical appearance—allowing him to find (or lose himself in) a part.

"It is boring to see the same actor with the same look," he says. "I like changing my appearance. It helps me to enjoy [acting]. You can not lose the sense of joy, of play."

In *The Dancer Upstairs,* Bardem has a mustache, which is something he says he would not wear in real life. In *Mondays in the Sun* (2002), scheduled for release this summer, the actor is bearded, and more heavyset.

"*Mondays in the Sun* is more emotional," Bardem says. In that powerful film he plays an unemployed man in northern Spain. "He is someone who is trying to survive those hard circumstances with irony."

In contrast, for *The Dancer Upstairs,* Bardem is effective in a very different part. "I like that it is a thriller in which something is going on but you don't see it." *The Dancer Upstairs* is an intimate film in which much of the "action" is really the characters sitting around waiting to take action.

Perhaps the most difficult scene to film was the one with the least activity—a three-minute-long still shot of Rejas watching his daughter dance ballet. "I kept waiting for John to say 'cut'," Bardem remembers. "I thought I missed it." And yet this scene, Bardem says, speaks to what he enjoys most about acting. "The process of working, I love it. To be there, holding the emotion . . ." Still, he has one complaint. "I can not stand having to wait for the fucking light!"

As for working in English—*The Dancer Upstairs* is the actor's third film following *Dance with the Devil* (aka *Perdita Durango*) and *Before Night Falls* that he has made in a foreign language—Bardem likes it that "cinema allows you to get around [dialogue problems]. When you work in a language that you don't control, it is a matter of working really, really hard to get comfortable with the lines and dialogue. I won't be brave enough to go on the stage in English, but movies you can't get wrong—there is always time to loop. I had two directors [for *Dancer*]—John and the dialogue coach."

That said, Bardem has no trouble expressing himself in English, Spanish, or with his body language. A big, attractive man, Bardem is down to earth, but also full of energy—and extremely gregarious. His current look—long hair and silver loop earrings in both ears—suits him well. He is relaxed, and apparently enjoying talking to the press and telling stories about his life and career.

In contrast, his character in *The Dancer Upstairs* is wound a bit more tightly. This is especially apparent in a tense scene in which a gun-toting Rejas enters a shack where a criminal may be hiding.

"I went to John and said, I think this man starts the movie saying 'I'm a lawyer.' This is his very first police action. If I had to face that situation, I would be very scared. I tried [playing scared] and he liked it," he said.

Bardem understood his character well from reading Shakespeare's book—a lengthy undertaking at the time, because he did not have as sure a grasp on the English language. The actor also admits that he did not know much about the Shining Path when he agreed to make *The Dancer Upstairs*.

Nevertheless, he received some invaluable background information from a reliable source, "I had some meetings with the ambassador to Peru, and he told me a lot of things about the government and what they did wrong." This guidance was particularly notable, as the film could not be made in Peru because of its subject matter. (Malkovich shot the movie in Spain, Portugal, and Ecuador.) Yet he says it was easy to create Rejas because "the real person was more politically involved and more radical in his politics. I did not have to work so hard."

And while *The Dancer Upstairs* features another outstanding Bardem performance, the actor is looking to mix things up a bit in his next acting job. "I think I'm getting too serious. I'd like to make a comedy," he says, before adding slyly, "as long as it is respectful to real life. I try to portray real people."

JENNIFER WESTFELDT AND HEATHER JUERGENSEN: KISSING JESSICA STEIN

I am still giddy from seeing *Kissing Jessica Stein* (2001), the funny, heartbreaking, and intelligent little indie pic about two bi-curious women who find love and friendship. I was so taken by this film that I interviewed the screenwriter-actresses before and after the release. (Both interviews are included here.)

Kissing *Jennifer and Heather*

"We thought it would be funny for two women who decided to give up men to date each other," says actress Heather Juergensen about the inspiration for *Kissing Jessica Stein,* the terrific new romantic comedy she cowrote and coproduced with coconspirator Jennifer Westfeldt.

In the title role, Westfeldt plays a single, Jewish twentysomething who can't seem to find the right guy. When she discovers Helen's (Juergensen) ad in the "women seeking women" section of the personals column, Jessica realizes that she might have found what she's been missing in a partner. (Alas, despite playing gay on screen, both girls are heterosexual).

A sweet, and at times serious, movie in which two ostensibly straight women decide to explore lesbianism—with various and hilarious results—*Kissing Jessica Stein* grew out of a theater workshop in the Catskills where the two women met.

Juergensen describes how the film (which began as the play *Lipschtick*) came to be. "We noticed that we were both writing about men, women, and dating, and we were amused at how books (such as *Men Are from Mars, Women Are from Venus*) told people how to conduct their love lives. We thought it would be fun to skewer that. In taking the friendship of women to the 'next level,' we got the impetus to be more thorough. . . . And suddenly, Hollywood was calling."

However, Westfeldt explains that she was disenchanted with the changes studios wanted to make in their script, and this led to the decision to produce the film themselves. "Hollywood comedies are just *one thing*. Life is more than that. We wanted to make something that could make you laugh and cry." (To its credit, the film succeeds in doing both, well.)

"It's our baby," concurs Juergensen. "With the studio, we were stuck in the middle, and it was our vision, our story."

She continues to say that it was "probably one job too many" to share directing duties, and gay filmmaker Charles Herman-Wurmfeld was brought aboard to helm the project.

Nevertheless, as writers and producers, the actresses had a say in all aspects of the production. "Toughest part of filmmaking," Juergensen says, "was keeping a pace and keeping it tight."

Westfeldt agrees. "Budget cuts forced us to cut locations, and scenes. You have to think on your feet to get the same effect [on screen] as what you wrote."

Westfeldt was particularly involved in the casting. "I had Tovah Feldshuh in mind when I wrote the part [of Jessica's mom]. We have known each other for years, and we were very excited to play mother and daughter."

Westfeldt also had a hand in making an Ella Fitzgerald song on the soundtrack play "gay" in one comic moment, and for those who "get it," this gag generates one of the film's most satisfying laughs.

Since *Kissing Jessica Stein* is a character-driven comedy, the writers were very conscious of how they portrayed the two protagonists, particularly in regard to their sexuality.

"It's complicated," says Westfeldt. "Two straight women meet and fall in love for all the wrong reasons. In our research, we found that there is a sexual continuum for some, and not for others. We wanted to honor both, and judge neither—let people draw their own conclusions. We dared to make Jessica unlikable (at first) because what matters is how she changes. We showed her warts-and-all and how [with Helen's help] she evolves."

About her character's arc Juergensen says: "Helen is part of the downtown hipster scene, and she is tired of that environment. She decides she wants to be with women—and Jessica offers her a real relationship. But she is scared about being gay. Helen's promiscuity [masks] this. She has to reach for Jessica. It's what she needs to discover her truth."

How Jessica and Helen's relationship transforms them will certainly prompt viewers to think about *Kissing Jessica Stein*'s characters for far longer than an ordinary Hollywood love story. And the response from the gay community has been incredibly positive. "Lesbians were laughing at the screenings, thanking us for making a film about gay women that isn't serious, and not about killing themselves," Juergensen says. Still, she has to acknowledge that the piece "comes from a straight person's point of view."

But Juergensen quickly points out that she has reaped personal rewards in addition to the professional satisfaction of bringing *Kissing Jessica Stein* to the screen. "Now, when I hang out with my gay female friends, I feel a different connection. I'm not such an outsider—I've 'been there.'"

Kissing *Jennifer* and *Heather Again*

A breakout hit when it was released theatrically, the DVD of *Kissing Jessica Stein* arrives gives audiences another opportunity to enjoy—and debate—this winning, if controversial romantic comedy about two straight New York women that choose to date each other.

The success of *Kissing Jessica Stein* not only boosted the profile of its three creators, but it also raised issues about the state of queer cinema today.

Whereas queer audiences in urban areas made the film a hit—it earned ten times its budget in box office—director Charles Herman-Wurmfeld says that he "was awed by how many old folks loved the film. It was a big hit in elderly Jewish communities."

Actress/writer Heather Juergensen concurs. "The older audience was surprising. Grandparents, people in their seventies and even eighties, loved the film and some went to see it multiple times."

Yet Jennifer Westfeldt, who also co-wrote and co-starred in the film, expected *Kissing Jessica Stein* to reach a wider audience and had a different perspective. "There was hope we'd become mainstream, but the reality is that most of the county is conservative. It's a sad statistic."

The film, which was praised by critics, occasionally received a mixed reaction from queer viewers. "Certain gay people thanked us for being truthful, while others said 'How dare you—you sold us out.' That was a shocker!" recalls Westfeldt. Still, she maintains her intentions as the film's cowriter, "We made a film with integrity. We were not speaking for the [entire gay] community."

Juergensen, heard a more upbeat responses from viewers. "I've had gay women e-mail me saying things like they experienced huge tension with their parents when they came out, but *Kissing Jessica Stein* was a film they could go to *with* their parents. The whole family enjoyed it and it stimulated healthy discussion. So in that respect I think the film was an advance for the gay community." She continues, "Most gay people I've talked to have said while they would *prefer* that a success like *Kissing Jessica Stein* could happen with a fully fledged gay story—as opposed to a 'gay-themed' story being told through the lens of a straight person—they agree that it is definitely a positive step forward."

Adds Herman-Wurmfeld, "My hope is that I've told a story that illuminates a true human story—as for advancing queer or straight cinema, I'd have to leave those musings to other people."

Whether the film is groundbreaking or not, gay and lesbian viewers will enjoy several scenes on the DVD that were deleted from the theatrical version. A conversation between Martin (Michael Mastro) and Helen (Jeurgensen) following Helen's fight with Jessica (Westfeldt) is a tender moment that unfortunately had to be left on the editing room floor. "It was cut as much as for pace and for remembering who the central character of the story was—Jessica," recalls Juergensen about this marvelous scene that will strike a chord with gay viewers.

Another scene that also happily made it on to the DVD is a monologue Jessica gives in response to a potential suitor. This episode is perhaps the highlight of the film's bonus features.

As for the future careers of the film's three creative talents, they are all pursuing their own projects. Westfeldt, who has finished the draft of a new screenplay, has optioned another film to produce. She says, "There are so few great women's parts, you have to look for projects to spearhead." Not asked to play gay characters, Westfeldt has been propositioned with "extremely neurotic" ones, she says.

Juergensen agreed that her writing/producing skills have helped her gain respect in the cutthroat movie industry, noting, "On the acting side, things can take a bit longer." While she says she has "not been pigeonholed into gay roles, I have had a few women give me their phone numbers" as a result of *Kissing Jessica Stein.* For the record, she is currently engaged.

As for Herman-Wurmfeld, "I get meetings now," he says. "The leap has been quantum. Before it was six years between movies, and now I have consistent opportunity to work." His plans are "to make the films I want to make. *Kissing Jessica Stein* is a small movie, but it always inspires discussion. I love this—and it's something I will look for in every movie I do—makes smart movies with social and political purpose."

[For the record, Herman-Wurmfeld directed *Legally Blonde 2* (2003). I think he sold out.]

DALLAS ROBERTS:
A HOME AT THE END OF THE WORLD

When I saw Dallas Roberts in *A Home at the End of the World*, he was so convincingly queer, I was taken aback to learn otherwise in our interview. In person, Roberts was charming and extremely likable. He even answered questions that most actors avoid. As the unknown actor in a film that few people saw, Roberts might be forgotten; however, this would be a crime. His performance was fantastic, and with any justice, he will be more visible soon.

At the End of the World *with Dallas Roberts*

Dallas Roberts makes an auspicious big screen debut as Jonathan in *A Home at the End of the World*. A thin, boyishly handsome young man—currently sporting a beard—Roberts's first film role has him playing gay and getting sexual with Colin Farrell.

"It was a really, really good time," the actor says about working with his notorious costar. "That's the great thing about being an actor, is that you get to experience all of these things. There's no way in heck that I would ever lay with Colin Farrell naked in my bed, if it weren't for getting the chance to make this movie."

That said, Roberts admits sheepishly, "I could not get him to let me lead [dancing]. He's certainly a good kisser, my joke has been that it's all fireworks and confetti when it happens, but the notion of kissing anyone with fifteen people standing around pointing lights is inherently not an intimate thing."

Yet *A Home at the End of the World* is a very intimate story about three friends trying to make a life and a home for themselves. Based on the book by Michael Cunningham—which Roberts has read and re-read—what appealed to him about the part of Jonathan was "his humanity, his sense of humor. I'm near him in the way that most people are, in that we're all sort of looking for a place to belong, an identity, a definition of what love is going to be and what were going to call all that."

As for his own identity, Roberts is straight, and expecting a baby boy in October. His girlfriend, whom he describes as "the love of my life," is a scenic designer who works in the New York theater. They have decided not to get married because "what she and I [have] is between us, and we didn't need to involve the state, or blood tests, or ask anyone's permission." The actor acknowledges the irony that in the era of states trying to legalize gay marriage, he chooses not to exercise his power to wed.

Perhaps this is Roberts's own way of creating a home for himself. In the film, Jonathan, Bobby (Farrell), and Clare (Robin Wright-Penn) set up an unconventional household in Vermont, where the two men play daddy to Clare's child. Another link to home is revealed when Roberts talks about his screen mom Sissy Spacek, who, like the actor, also hails from Texas.

"It was amazing to work with Sissy. I grew up with her in many ways, so sitting across from her on my first movie pushed it from the ninth dream mode to the eleventh!" Roberts describes his own childhood as "happy" even though his parents divorced when he was eleven, and he was shuttled back and forth between them.

Roberts is thrilled to appear with his famous costars in a high-profile film, but in person, he is also incredibly down to earth. His soft-spoken demeanor suggests that the acting bug is his true passion, and nothing less. In real life, he is quiet and a little shy. It is as if he is saving his energy for a performance. When Roberts admits how he spends his time when he is not on stage or screen, the reason for his being bashful becomes clearer.

"I am a computer nerd. I fix them, for both hobby and cash," he demurs. "With any luck, I'll be able to give that up sometime in the next ten years. But until I can pay all my bills pretending to be other people, I'll continue to pretend being the computer guy."

Lest anyone think Roberts is a complete geek—and his character Jonathan does walk a fine line—the actor loves to rock out in his living room at any opportunity. "I pretend that I am a rock star and I crank up the amp and play guitar," he admits, adding that his interest in music extends to being "in silly bands that never went anywhere."

And if his music career goes nowhere, his plans to keep performing seem to be solidifying. Although he will not discuss any acting projects—for fear of jinxing them—he is drawn to meaty roles such as Jonathan.

"My actor self is interested in [playing] human beings, stuff that is not green screen and laser beams," he says. "But the kid in me wants to ride horses, shoot guns, and fly a starship, and be a lawyer, a farmer, a pirate, and a baseball player. If I have my way, I'll have a varied career." Hopefully, Roberts will.

Chapter 5
Promising Starts

The films in this section went "straight to video." And while that is usually deemed to be a curse, the titles in this chapter all have their merits. New queer filmmakers are given very little theatrical exhibition outside of film festivals, and like the ones interviewed here, they deserve to be discovered.

RICHARD BELL: TWO BROTHERS

Richard Bell's drama *Two Brothers* (2000) is notable not just for its microscopic budget ($545 Cn), but also for its heartfelt treatment of the relationships between the story's four characters. Given more money, there's no telling what Bell can—or will—do. This calling card, however, proves him to be a talent to watch.

A Q&A with Two Brothers *Creator Richard Bell*

Two Brothers is the remarkably self-assured directorial debut from Vancouver filmmaker Richard Bell. Made for $545 Canadian, this labor of love was shot with a video camera and four friends over the period of one year.

A story of two brothers—natch—this feature concerns the gay Riley (Norbert Orlewicz) who reunites with his straight brother Chad (Cody Campbell) after the death of their mother. As Riley falls in love with Gavin (Kevin Macdonald) and Chad deals with tensions with his girlfriend (Karen Rae) the brothers each revisit painful secrets they have long held dormant.

Independent Queer Cinema: Reviews and Interviews
© 2006 by The Haworth Press, Inc. All rights reserved.
doi:10.1300/5482_06

The film, which gained favor with audiences at various film festivals around the world, was recently released on video/DVD. I recently spoke with the twenty-four year-old Bell about his production, his cast, and his own family.

How/why did you decide to make this film?

Two Brothers was originally written as a one-act play in my scriptwriting class at theatre school. I entered it into a student play festival and hoped it would be produced after I graduated, but it was declined. I got the idea of making it into a film, or video—I wanted the project to have a little longevity. In hindsight I'm very pleased that it was never accepted for that play festival, because if it had, I would be on an entirely different course now.

Where did you come up with the story?

I wanted to make a movie about how people (particularly twentysomethings) have to face the demons of their teenage years and accept or deal with their pain before they can find happy, adjusted adulthood.

How did you come up with the budget?

The $545 came from the day job I had at the time: bussing and food-running at a fine dining restaurant. The real expense for Two Brothers *was the promotion aspect of it: travel expenses, photocopying, Fed Ex, etc.—that probably cost up to $10,000!*

What would you do differently if you could make the film again and had more money?

I would show Riley and Chad's history: them growing up as boys, living on the farm, dealing with their parents, etc.

Would you ever want to remake it with a bigger budget?

Definitely! I remember in the spring of 1999, when the cast and I first assembled to discuss the project, I told them that what we were about to do was create "the rough draft" of a larger, better film we would eventually do. So I must make good on that promise one day—I don't think I will revisit it until I am in my thirties though.

Is the film autobiographical?

I have always maintained that Two Brothers *was not about my family or me (for one thing, my mom is alive and well and living in the suburbs of Vancouver). But there were "seeds" of truth, from which more dramatic and cinematic ideas grew.*

Do you have any siblings?

Yes. I have two brothers(!). One is older, thirty, and the other is younger, sixteen.

What is your relationship with them, and what did they think of the film?

My older brother has been very difficult regarding this film. He confronted me before the film came out on DVD, and accused me of stealing things from his past. For him, the similarities between Two Brothers *and his life were too close, but frankly, I think he was searching for them. What my brother fails to realize is that this is my past, too, and I have every right to explore it, be it personally or artistically.*

My younger brother has been very supportive, and kind of looks up to me. He's still waiting for me to release a "real film" in a "real theatre" though—I think he's hoping for something bigger budget and more mainstream. He first saw the film when he was fourteen years old at the Queer Film Festival in Vancouver. He dealt with it pretty well. I came out to my brother when he was eleven, and although I think he would rather I was straight, he's very proud of me and respectful.

Which character was hardest to write?

I think Gavin was the hardest to write because although he does a terrible thing to Riley, I didn't want to judge him or paint him as an irresponsible or evil character. I kind of feel like I shortchanged him as a character. Thankfully though, actor Kevin Macdonald filled in the holes with the life he brought to his part.

How did you find the actors to play the four roles?

I went to theatre school (at Studio 58, Langara College) with all of the actors who were in the movie. I chose people who I knew would be loyal to the project and would see it through. This is obviously because they were all working for free.

Which—if any—of the actors is gay?

I was the only gay person to work on this project!

Did the straight actors have any concerns about the kissing/love scenes?

Not at all. Norbert had done it in plays before, and I think Kevin might have as well. They were both in touch with their "feminine sides" and were very easy to work with. And their girlfriends were so excited about it and loved it! If anyone was nervous during the love scene it was me!

Did you choose not to do a cameo?

No. I was the camera operator and the director, even the lighting guy sometimes—I had way too much to do!

What has been the strangest reaction(s) you've had from audiences?

A woman at a screening in Utah challenged me for using straight actors for the gay roles. I thought that was ludicrous. I choose people based on their acting merits, not on their sexuality.

Where do you ultimately see yourself going as a filmmaker?

I am a very ambitious person and I plan on having a very successful career. I want to keep making uniquely human stories, where the sexuality of the characters is incidental to the storyline.

Have you had any offers for your next project?

Two Brothers *allowed me to meet a variety of different people (producers, actors, a D.O.P., etc.) who are now working with me on my new film,* Eighteen *(2004). It also introduced me to patrons who modestly support me financially.* Eighteen *is a much larger film about two eighteen-year-olds—one is a street*

kid living in modern times, and the other is his same-aged grandfather fight-
ing in the Second World War. We just got development funding from City TV
and we are awaiting word from other government agencies. So far, so good.
There's more information on the project in the Eighteen *window of*
www.bellmovies.com.

MICHAEL AKERS (WITH MATTHEW MONTGOMERY): GONE, BUT NOT FORGOTTEN

Michael Akers's film *Gone, But Not Forgotten* (2003) proves that he has the talent to accomplish great things. Akers is not looking to reinvent gay cinema, rather, he wants to make a good, sexy queer romance. His cinematic influences are more mainstream than avant-garde, and this goal to be gay and mainstream is admirable. I wish him both luck and success.

Remember His Name

The debut film by writer/director Michael Akers, *Gone, But Not Forgotten*, is a low-budget drama starring Matthew Montgomery as Mark Reeves, an amnesiac rescued by a forest ranger Drew Parker (Aaron Orr). As the two men slowly get to know each other, they find themselves falling in love. Of course, as Mark's memory is triggered and returns, he learns the truth about his life and whom he loves.

While the story may be oft used, Akers really wrote *Gone, But Not Forgotten* to examine his own sexuality. "I had just come out myself," the director explains, stating that he had also just left home in Pennsylvania for life and work in Los Angeles. "I was looking for a plot contrivance—leaving one's old life behind—but still feeling the pressure of family and friends. I wanted the character to have 'social anchors,' but be free to live how he wanted to."

Akers, who produced the film with his partner Sandon Berg (who has a funny cameo in the film), wrote the screenplay in 1995. He was working in LA in a TV movie/feature film production company, and read many script treatments before quitting the business to strike out on his own as a filmmaker.

"I vastly underestimated what making a film is all about," he admits now. Akers used his credit cards to make *Gone, But Not Forgotten*, shooting in seven weeks in Pine Crest, California, outside Yosemite National Park.

Although he never went to film school, the filmmaker took his job as director very professionally. "I storyboarded each section of the film, and posted the script on a Web site [for actors]. We auditioned 200 people for the six principal roles, and 'matched' the talent so the actors playing brothers looked like brothers."

Both leads, newcomers Montgomery and Orr, are nonunion actors and were, according to the director, "excited about the roles and the movie."

"I loved the script, the premise, and the role being a challenge of two different people," says Montgomery. "I met with Michael and Sandon, and I was fascinated by their dedication and vision." The actor said he never had concerns about working for a novice director, because he was starting out himself, as well. "Michael took a chance on me, and I'm honored that he did," he said.

Akers was equally happy with his performers as well. "I am very concerned with the actors, their safe space, their process, and achieving the best performance they can. I [was] inexperienced as a director, but I know that even if a scene is as well lit as possible, if the person on the screen isn't entertaining you, there's a problem."

While a boat scene had to be reshot in February—"it was fucking freezing," recalls Montgomery—"that was my most difficult, least favorite scene" Akers claims to have had more trouble filming the steamy love scene between the two men.

"I closed the set, except the camera girl, me, and the two actors," the director remembers. "We started it and it was awkward. I had to guide the performances along. We were all terribly nervous—about putting ourselves out there, about what we find sexy—and that was weird. It became a big deal."

Montgomery himself had some issues as well. "Michael was really open and communicative with me. We talked about what the sex scene would entail—how much I wanted to expose myself in the film, and how it would be edited. By the time we shot it, I was much more comfortable with doing the nudity."

Yet Akers worries that viewers will be overly concerned with the film's sex, and not care about the central theme of *romance*.

"When we were making it, a lot of people had asked if there would be nudity. It's an important part of gay cinema, I think, that a lot of people go right to the penis. I wanted to show what is sexy about a man and two men together. I don't see that in films. The guys are kissing and then their pants come off. What about all the stuff in between? In normal life, in gay culture, it's right to the sex. There is no drama, no introspection. We struggled with that, and wanted to show the searching."

Montgomery concurs. "I think that it was important to see these two characters connect on an intimate level. We focused on the caressing."

Now that *Gone, But Not Forgotten* has been a hit on the gay film circuit, playing to sell out shows in over twenty cities, Akers hopes his romance will be embraced by audiences on DVD. Still, he says, "I'm blessed we've gotten this far."

GEORGIA RAGSDALE: WAVE BABES

Georgia Ragsdale's *Wave Babes* (2003) was so funny and charming that I hope she makes good on her promise to make the sequel *Babes Go West*. Ragsdale is one of those comediennes who should have her own TV show, but does not for reasons unexplained. (She's assured me that she's tried.) Ragsdale is so funny and engaging, I hope that people will sit up and take notice of her. I was an instant fan, and I want to see more from her soon.

Riding a Wave *with Georgia Ragsdale*

"Aging, body image, and not being alone is what we laugh about all the time," says out comedienne Georgia Ragsdale, about her motivation to make *Wave Babes,* a hilarious new comedy now out on video and DVD.

"My job to make fun of everything. I get my material from painful, uncomfortable, and vulnerable situations, and turn them into some kind of win." The comedienne continues, "I like to create a high relateability factor and point out the silliness in every kind of behavior."

To wit, *Wave Babes* is a parody of those "You go, girl" movies, as well as the surf-girl film *Blue Crush* (2002)—but with forty-year-olds. *Babes* features Christina Carlisi as Val, a newly divorced woman who reunites with her gal pals Sam (Ragsdale), a frisky lesbian, and Maureen (Carolyn Hennesy), a tough-talking lawyer, to share a reckless weekend at the beach.

The film, which was shot in four days and for $15,000, has been well received on the gay and lesbian festival circuit—it won Best Comedy Feature at the New York International Film and Video Festival—and inaugurates what Ragsdale hopes will be a series of *Babes* films.

"We are trying to contribute to and create more comedies that have women in them. Gay men are known for their sense of humor. Lesbians are stuck with social causes and saving the world. We wanted to be silly and have fun," the screenwriter/actress says, getting serious for a moment.

Wave Babes is filled with terrific humor of many varieties. "We really wanted to keep the campy, cheesy factor going through the whole thing," Ragsdale recalls. From song spoofs of Melissa Etheridge's "Come to My Window," to a gag involving a character slipping in a hot tub, and cheesy sound and special effects, the film will keep audiences highly amused. Ragsdale herself even tries hard to suppress a laugh when she has to say the line "I could eat her for lunch" in one scene.

Then there is "The Shoulder Master," Sam's exercise device that was inspired, Ragsdale says, by "Suzanne Somers squeezing a paper clip between her legs."

She confesses, "One of my private fantasies is infomercials. I'm always trying to create an invention that is a complete parody to me, but people in the Midwest will buy."

Adding to the film's fun are Sam's numerous kissing scenes, which defy the Hollywood stereotype of the gay best friend not getting any.

The comedienne jokes that viewers could have a great drinking game if they imbibed whenever Sam is in a lip lock with another woman in *Babes*.

In contrast, the love scene between Sam and another character "had to be shot three times to get it right." Ragsdale explains. "There were lighting issues, wardrobe issues, and hitting the right tone was hard. The scene needed to be tender, and in the cute, appealing genre. It was not meant to be hot, sexy love scene. We had to drink a lot of beer to get the scene to work properly."

Another problem that hindered filmmaking was beach noise. "We shared the beach permit with *Charlie's Angels 2* (2003), and even in that film there was overly loud ocean noise [to mask the beach noise]. Our sound editor called and said, 'See, even they couldn't get it right!'"

At least the weather was consistently reliable for *Wave Babes*. "By luck, we had gorgeous sunsets. There was no fog on the beach the four days we were shooting. It was a miracle," Ragsdale says.

Ironically, actress Carolyn Hennesy—who steals the film and channels Eve Arden in the role—hates the beach and the water. "She not been in the sun more than two minutes in the last twenty years," the comedienne confides. "She had full body makeup on, but still looks very pale."

Although Hennesy acts as if she and her costars have been friends for years, the performer was not a known entity. Director Lisa Knox-Nervig and Ragsdale invited their friends (and family) to participate in making *Wave Babes*, and found Hennesy through a friend of a friend. Her character has received such an enthusiastic response that Maureen is likely to be prominently featured in *Babes Go West*.

And Ragsdale is excited at the prospect of another project. She gushes, "We've got lots of great western locations and props. It's a natural fit for us. And besides, there is so much to make fun of in the west."

Hopefully that film will be complete in time for next year's festival circuit. After audiences get a look at *Wave Babes*, they will no doubt be eager for more.

BRAD FRASER: LEAVING METROPOLIS

Brad Fraser, the playwright, does have his own TV show of sorts—he is a writer for *Queer As Folk*. While I do not watch his program, nor have I ever seen his plays on stage, I am familiar with Fraser from the films he has worked on. Denys Arcand's *Love and Human Remains* (1993) was an adaptation of one of his plays and Fraser's directorial debut, *Leaving Metropolis* (2002), was a film version of his play *Poor Super Man*, which charted another stage of life for his character David. As Fraser continues to be involved with film projects, I will keep watching him, even if I miss his work for TV and theatre. Fraser's investigation of various queer identities is political and compelling. He may raise questions, and he may raise people's ire, but this is what makes his work so riveting.

Queer As Fraser

Brad Fraser, the outspoken, gay, Canadian playwright, has always been very "in your face." Not one to shy away from controversy, Fraser pens characters that he says, "do not know who they are sexually." He also addresses topical issues such as the AIDS crisis and the treatment—both positive and negative—of gays and lesbians in our society.

"I had a role to play coming out in Canada when I did. If you were gay and did not speak loud and hard, you did not get people's attention. That was how I was accustomed to being heard," Fraser admits. "I am still as angry now at forty-four as I was at thirty-three, but I use anger as fuel, not weaponry. It goes further. I choose my battles, and have become more diplomatic over the years. It's a natural part of the aging process."

The writer is back in the spotlight—and once again in people's faces—with three concurrent projects. First, *Leaving Metropolis,* a film version he directed of his play *Poor Super Man,* is now available on video/DVD. Second, his play *Unidentified Human Remains and the True Nature of Love* is now being staged in New York. And third, Fraser continues his job as a writer for the hit television series *Queer As Folk*.

Fraser's strength as a writer is to feature damaged men and women who grapple with their sexuality, and find their place on the sexual spectrum between gay and straight. "We live in a world where people—especially Americans—like to put people in categories. You are gay, you do this. . . . I write about people who are a lot more complex than this. Most people are elastic—they fall 'in between' because of their situation, time of life, etc." He says adamantly, "I can't write about people who don't have issues. The most interesting people blur lines and step outside of boundaries."

In both *Remains* and the film *Leaving Metropolis*, Fraser features straight characters who, he says, "are completely out of touch with who they are, and end up hurting a great many people." Likewise, his gay men "have to overcome their self-loathing, get beyond it."

Shrewdly, the playwright uses elements from pop culture to imbue his work with meaning. From comic books and video games to music, films, and television, his characters live in the moment and talk realistically.

"I have always tried to write dialogue that truly reflects how people speak to one another," Fraser says about developing the "rhythm" of his work. "I spend time listening to the words and sounds people make."

With *Leaving Metropolis*, the playwright also got the opportunity to develop his story visually. In this erotic drama, the gay David (Troy Ruptash) takes a job as a waiter in a diner, owned by a married couple Matt (Vincent Corazza) and Violet (Cherilee Taylor). Before long, David and Matt begin a hot and heavy affair that has lasting consequences for everyone involved.

"*Leaving Metropolis* was not meant to be naturalistic or contemporary," Fraser explained about his highly stylized movie. "When I knew I wouldn't be able to use [*Superman*] comic book imagery, I {gave} everyone a color key to provide a clear signal to the audience. David had bright, vibrant, daring colors to show that he was an artist and this is how he saw things."

While the color scheme of the film is terrific, Fraser also coaxes great performances out of his cast of unknown actors. He describes some of the challenges he had as a director in casting the film. "It was hard to find actors to read for these roles in a predominantly gay film with sex scenes. A lot of people wouldn't consider it. It takes exceptional actors."

While he announces, "I grabbed Troy Ruptash when he came along," Fraser was perhaps happiest with the discovery of Corazza. "Vince needs to be a guy who reads as straight and is ruled by his emotions, not as a closeted gay guy who is cheating on his wife. When I saw [Corazza] at the gym one day, I thought 'if that guy is an actor, he'd be perfect.'" Fraser went home and happened to see Corazza in a commercial and decided to ask him the next time he saw him. "He was naked in the locker room. It was not the right moment to ask," Fraser recalls. "I eventually had to track him down through his agent."

Even though he got the right performers, the director found that filming the love scenes was pretty difficult. "I was never comfortable with it. The actors were concerned, rightly, about the nudity. On film, being naked involves leaving an image behind. I wouldn't say the actors were comfortable with it, but they were professional. For me, I concentrated on the kissing. I wanted to see the real intimacy that went on—mouth to mouth contact—everything else followed naturally."

One particular sequence involves Matt fucking David and Violet separately, but, as Fraser cuts it, the scene fluidly shifts back and forth between the two couplings. "There was no time to rehearse it," Fraser remembers. "The actors choreographed it on my hotel room bed with their clothes on. A lot of shots are staged with one actor sneaked in and out of the frame." The result, however, is seamless and beautiful, and one of the film's highlights.

As for his other projects, Fraser is excited about their development. He meets the theatrical revival of his hit play *Remains* with both anxiety and excitement, "I don't know how NYC is going to react to it, but I'm hoping it holds up," he says optimistically.

Fraser is also looking forward to working on the fourth season of *Queer As Folk*, his second season with the hit show. He is one of four writers, not including the two head writers, and works on shaping the storylines, and, as he explains, "keeping the continuity and the characters connected."

While the playwright enjoys being a part of the show's team, he also appreciates being flexible enough to work in theatre and film.

"I could never work in just one medium," he exclaims. "I have too much to say."

GIL D. REYES: FAKE ID

Gil D. Reyes's *Fake ID* (2004) is a first effort geared to a young audience. The film is the DVD equivalent to a home movie—a bit amateurish, and a bit embarrassing. And while the low-budget parody is fitfully entertaining, writer Reyes came across quite sure of himself in this interview.

Fake-*ing It*

The new DVD *Fake ID* is a satiric comedy about two best friends and theater queens who discover their true sexual identities. Eric (Brian Gligor) and David (Stuart Perelmuter) are performing with a local theater group when Eric finds himself attracted to another guy at a party one night. As a result of his buddy coming out, the straight David begins questioning his sexuality, wondering if he might be gay too. Before long, it's "Queer Eye for the Straight Guy" as two gay guys try to help David learn how to swing his hips and gesture like a gay man.

Directed and cowritten by the queer Gil D. Reyes, this sweet parody is based not so loosely on his friendship with the film's co-writer and star, Perelmuter. "The film shows the way we really interact," Reyes said on the phone from his home in Louisville, the city that serves as the film's setting. "We would try the scenes out and get other friends involved, get the timing down."

Reyes explains that the purpose of the movie was "to explore the way people communicate with each other. It is sometimes a completely different language—gay/straight, male/female. We tried to be true to these characters who were young and still trying to figure out how to read other people."

Fake ID is an ultra-low-budget production, shot in three weeks and costing less than $500,000. Reyes was anxious to shoot his first feature, even if he was somewhat unprepared for all of the responsibility.

"I love directing because of the adrenaline." Reyes says, having helmed theatre productions since high school. "It's a lot of power, and easy to make huge mistakes. My gaffer said if I known all the things that could go wrong in shooting a film, I wouldn't have done it," the twenty-five-year-old director admits. "But I like fostering the creative juices of all of the talent. There's quite a bit of performance being a director, especially in something small like this. I had to keep my cool all the time. Even if things looked bleak—that required acting [on my part!]. I'm quite the little performer—trust me," he says with a flourish.

Reyes chose to make a comedy, because he and Perelmuter "wanted to tell the story in a big campy way. I didn't want to be an angsty director being all dark and brooding. People respond well to the stereotypes and the camp."

One of the more flamboyant bits in *Fake ID* involves Eric and David posing as superheroes named "The Glorious Outsiders" that look like the ambiguously gay duo and have costumes that say "GO GO" on them.

"We spent a lot of time designing them," Reyes recalls. "We wanted them to look as shiny and gay as possible, so when the characters said 'We're straight' it was just outlandish."

And while the film has its share of outrageous moments—a few fantasy sequences come to mind—*Fake ID* is really geared toward younger viewers coming to terms with their sexuality.

The film deliberately features only chaste kissing between the male performers, and despite the cute Perelmuter appearing shirtless quite frequently, there is no nudity. "The actors weren't shy—I probably could have gotten them to do a lot of things," Reyes says almost mischievously, "but we wanted a 'PG-13' [equivalent] rating. So there is no romantic male kiss in the film. I never really give my [mostly gay] audience that payoff. I am trying to cater to a larger audience. We hope to get a straight audience to see this film and empathize with Eric's character."

However, Reyes believes that gay viewers will laugh at *Fake ID* because it plays up the stereotypes it tries to debunk about sexuality. He states, "I think there's a lot of power in acknowledging [queer] stereotypes. At the same time, I hope we get to the point that everyone knows that they are stereotypes. It is not how everybody really is."

He continues this line of thought. "The film has a good message for adolescents. They will be more responsive—more likely to take that in—if it doesn't deal with the level of sex that most of us deal with. It's cute and romantic, the [gay] guys are 'going with' each other. It is a dangerous stereotype to promote that people just jump into sex. It's not the only option."

Perhaps the writer-director is motivated by his own experiences, having struggled with his homosexuality as a teenager. Reyes regrets being closeted in high school. "I really wish I had been [out]. I tried to put on too many different faces, and everyone wanted me to be more honest. I came out as soon as I got to college, and became a bit of a campus activist. The sort of thing where I learned to put up a front about being comfortable with my sexuality—I put myself in a leadership role. I couldn't show any weaknesses."

Now, he realizes the strength of living honestly and openly. "As a gay activist, the most important thing you can do is to be clear about who you are. The most effective way to change people is on a one-on-one basis."

And for discovering that, Reyes should be proud of himself, but he finds pride elsewhere. "I am very proud of making this film. The odds are against a young indie filmmaker out for the first time," he says. "I am proud that I am still plugging away at it—that I am still following my passion."

Chapter 6
Not Their True Calling

The performers interviewed in this section are not actors, though they have been known to appear in front of the camera and make a strong impression.

PAUL LEKAKIS: CIRCUIT

Paul Lekakis turned my head as the best (and sexiest) thing in Dirk Shafer's ambitious film *Circuit* (2001), and I hope he is able to parlay his singing and acting talents into greater success. I recently noticed him as a dancer in the so-bad-it's-good Chippendale's murder movie *Just Can't Get Enough* (2001), and I hope he gets even more exposure for himself in the future.

Circuit *Boy*

"I was a circuit boy before it was called 'The Circuit,'" said singer-turned-actor Paul Lekakis with characteristic flair during a recent phone interview. Describing his experiences making director Dirk Shafer's controversial new film *Circuit*, Lekakis says that the part of Bobby, an HIV-positive dancer/performer "was a very sexy role" and one that he identified with to a large extent.

In the film, Bobby describes circuit parties as "tribal—they're the gay man's Super Bowl,"—but Lekakis himself has mixed feelings about the intense events he used to frequent with some regularity as a club singer. "I had the opportunity to go to the 2002 White Party in Palm Springs, and I had a good time for a couple of hours. J. Lo performed, and the party aspect of it was fun, but I think I got enough of it when I was performing, so I don't miss it that much. I miss the music, but I was burnt out on it. I couldn't even dance anymore."

Fortunately, Lekakis was able to bring his musical talents to Shafer's film. The performer scored a big international hit a few years back with the dance tune "Boom Boom Boom (Come Back to My Room)," and wanted to do a song for the *Circuit* soundtrack. "I threw it out there, and Bruce Roberts and Allan Rich had written a song—'Assume the Position'—and wanted to work with me." Lekakis performs the dance number while Bobby strips out of a cowboy costume, and down to a G-string.

"I personally wouldn't wear one," Lekakis said about the G-string, "but it was fun 'going there' because I *never* get to go there." Part of what attracted him to the role of Bobby was the chance to do something daring. In addition to wearing the G-string, appearing in *Circuit* also meant that the buff Lekakis would also be in the buff during multiple nude scenes.

"I didn't have a problem with the nudity," he says. "When Dirk offered me the part, that was the last factor. But I wanted to know how he was going to shoot it!" Because the filmmakers wanted *Circuit* to get the all-important R rating, Shafer used smoke and diffused lighting to hide some of the skin. Nevertheless, Lekakis almost bares all.

One particularly difficult sequence involved Bobby sticking a needle into his groin. "The needle scene was really tough. You are supposed to wear a pouch [over your genitals], but it was getting in the way—so I pulled it off," Lekakis recalls. "Then I'd be totally naked, standing there, and they'd have to change some lighting. I'd stand there for thirty minutes, with everyone looking at me, and I just had to be comfortable with my body and let it go. I had to trust the director was not going to get a bad angle."

While most of the G-string moments were part of choreographed dance routines, there were various sex scenes involving Bobby and the film's other characters. Lekakis said that he had no problem getting intimate with his costars, John (Jonathan Wade-Drahos), the naive hero, and Hector (Andre Khabbazi), John's looks-obsessed boyfriend, or Tad (Daniel Kucan), a young videographer with whom he had to share several passionate kisses. But he remembers "they had to lighten up a bit" during the love scenes. "When they did, it was all good," he recalls devilishly. As for a favorite on-screen partner, Lekakis admits, "Hector was more my type" but unfortunately, Lekakis's favorite scene with this hot Latin costar wound up on the cutting room floor. "Hector and I had a shower together that was pretty racy, but it got cut. They got so much footage!" He wonders aloud if it will be made available on the DVD. [It's not.]

In addition to sex and rock and roll, playing Bobby also meant that Lekakis had many scenes involving drugs. "That was the biggest challenge for me," the actor said, "because I've been sober for four and a half years." When Lekakis snorted the "drugs" in the film—they were some sort of ground vegetable powder—he said, "it was very triggering. I never thought I'd be in that position again." Yet Lekakis also advised director Shafer on certain aspect of the drug culture. "I explained that you [have to] cook Special K in a glass bowl. I had been around these [kinds of] people, and I had seen them do it." True to his research, Bobby is filmed "baking" the drug in *Circuit.*

Lekakis also relished the opportunity to select some of Bobby's outrageous costumes, and he was especially pleased with the fabulous feather outfit in the film's extravagant White Party scene. "Bobby would wear skintight clothes almost everywhere. In fact, some of his clothes were mine," he said.

Yet for all of the fun the actor had playing a role—and Lekakis, who has charisma to burn, steals every scene he is in—what makes Bobby perhaps the film's most sympathetic character is his HIV status. "It gives him a method to his madness," Lekakis stated about the role. "It explains why he does what he is doing and how it alters people's lives." Lekakis, who himself is HIV positive (and undetectable), said it was a very important facet to his character. Describing his own experience with being positive, he says, "It was a turning point in my life and career," and something that has fueled his desires to want to work even more.

And hopefully, with the success of *Circuit,* Lekakis will continue to perform on stage and in movies. "I want to do everything I can," he says. "It is what I'm focusing on in all aspects of the business. I want to be noticed for the work."

GREG WALLOCH (WITH ELI KABILLIO): F**K THE DISABLED

Born with cerebral palsy, Greg Walloch has made a splash as a stand-up comic/storyteller in New York City. He has won the attention of many fans with his performance pieces, some of which were documented/presented in the film *F**k the Disabled* (aka *Keeping it Real*) (2001). The film, directed by Eli Kabillio (also interviewed) shows not only Walloch's routines, but also features interviews and dramatic re-enactments of some of his material. A second interview I conducted with Walloch a few years after we first spoke is included here as well.

Enabling Greg Walloch

Greg Walloch, the gay, disabled stand-up comic who lives in Harlem wants to be the most beloved disabled performer in America— no, in the world. If director Eli Kabillio's remarkable documentary/concert film *F**k the Disabled* reaches the wide audience it deserves, Walloch should have little trouble achieving his goal.

Originally released theatrically under the more printable title *Keeping it Real,* this amusing and poignant film—based on Walloch's act titled *White Disabled Talent* —is now available on home video and DVD. Hopefully, audiences will see this winning documentary and become familiar with Walloch's wicked sense of humor.

"I wasn't looking to get a film made from that source material," says Walloch in a recent phone interview, "but Eli met me through a mutual friend and enjoyed the show and approached me to make the film." The result eschews the normal "talking head" documentary approach by incorporating both footage of Walloch in concert at clubs such as Dixon Place and Joe's Pub, as well as vignettes that "dramatize" some of the material in Walloch's act.

"Greg's comedy is based on real events—such as the woman who asked him if he was gay because he was crippled," says Kabillio. "The best way to hammer that point was to create a comedy skit from it." To wit, several of Walloch's stories are presented throughout *F**k the Disabled*. One involves the hunky Stephen Baldwin as an illiterate gym bunny, while another features Anne Meara as a frustrated restaurant customer. (To explain more would give away the joke.)

Whereas these episodes showcase Walloch's creative mind and "anchor the ideas," as he says, Kabillio's film is significant for also featuring the stand-up comic's body. Born with cerebral palsy, Walloch relies on walking sticks, and *F**k the Disabled* is notable for showing not only the ease with which Walloch gets around in the streets, on the subway, up stairs, and through doors, but also the painstaking completion of everyday tasks.

"That was done purposely," says Kabillio, who deliberately and frequently uses close-ups of Walloch throughout the film—so that viewers might "forget" his handicap.

Although Walloch was comfortable shooting the concert scenes—primarily because he was used to performing his material—filming the interview footage, which required some spontaneity, was a bit more difficult for the comedian. "I didn't necessarily enjoy having a camera in my personal life. It reinforced my appreciation for my solo work—and my privacy! It was strange to experience the reality component of it," he said. Nevertheless, Walloch was very pleased with the end result.

"Through this process I really learned how the documentary becomes—through choices made by the director and the editor—its own creative form of storytelling." Walloch, ever the storyteller, acknowledged, "I have my whole life to choose from for source material. Eli chooses portions."

At its best, *F**k the Disabled* focuses on the comedian's mesmerizing stories. A marvelous tale he tells about visiting a Baptist church with a friend, or informing a male member of the audience that he would like to "fall in love with him, for just a moment" are powerful, captivating sequences.

However, filming the concert scenes did not always go smoothly. Kabillio explains that when they shot Walloch's first show at Dixon Place the audience purposely didn't laugh because they thought they had to be silent for the filming. "It was deadly without an audience," the director recalls. Thankfully, Walloch's performance at Joe's Pub, which comprises a good portion of the final cut was, in Kabillio's eyes, probably the best connection the comedian has had with a live audience.

Walloch's dry wit also comes across especially in the film's title piece, or in an extra scene on the DVD, which features him auditioning for *Sesame Street* and being referred to as "the white disabled talent." (Hence the show's title.)

One of the stories from Walloch's routine that is described in his routine but not filmed as a sequence involves his anticipation of eating a piece of cake. "It would not have been difficult to catch me doing that," Walloch said, his mouth probably watering at the thought of his favorite bakery. Then he deadpans, "But I'd have to do extra sit ups."

Ultimately, Walloch explains the recipe behind his humor. "I use disability and sexuality to make people see that we are 'all disabled in our very own special way.' We all have things that make us different. What I show in my work is that we all have things to embrace."

It's an important, inspiring message, and one that comes across both clearly and cleverly in this enormously heartfelt and enjoyable film.

Walloch Redux

"A lot of my work is about being a gay disabled guy, talking about these things, but the show is for everyone, not a specific crowd," Walloch said in a recent phone interview. "Whether it is the gay community or the disabled community, we're working so hard to define ourselves to our own community and to the community outside, that self-definition is important to articulate, but [one must] also be malleable. I think my work is helping redefine the image of disability. We are funny, and smart, and have sex, and say dirty words. There is humanity there. It is an interesting journey."

His semi-autobiographical act has been recorded in the film *F**k the Disabled,* but Walloch should be seen live to get the full impact of his performance. He asserts, "People always say, 'The book is better than the film.' I feel like my show is the original, that it's better than the film. Seeing my work live gives people a direct hit, a live and unfettered experience."

And the thrill of performing live motivates Walloch, who enjoys the interaction he has with different audiences. "It's a very warm and personal show. I talk directly to the audience, and so naturally it changes night to night and audience to audience."

Walloch explains that although his show is very conversational, it allows him to form an intimate bond with theatregoers. And he is always open to the excitement of the curtain being raised. On one occasion, Walloch did however, have an unpleasant experience. "I stepped off the wrong part of a raised stage in the dark and fell six feet, but hey, I already had the crutches, so there's a bright side to everything," he jokes.

Walloch's sense of humor is indeed unerring. "You have to laugh in this world to keep from crying. Pleasure, pain, funny, and sad are all so close. I can always find the funny thing in the saddest situation and the saddest thing in the happiest events, either way it makes me a fun guy to invite to your wedding," he says.

Perhaps it is the suspense of what will happen in any given night that will make seeing Walloch such a rewarding experience. The writer/performer improvises certain segments of his act, because, he says, "what is most important is working on the honesty in a performance, then you don't really have to worry about jokes, because the truth in a story is what is actually funny."

As his stories—about going to a church in the South, or auditioning for a role on *Sesame Street*—from his show *White Disabled Talent* prove, Walloch finds humor almost without trying. While his "art" is steeped in reality, the writer does not go in for angsty navel gazing. He admits, "I walk down streets I probably shouldn't, talk to strangers on the bus, and have engaged in various sexual situations just so I could write about them. Writers watch and listen, but they also like to play in traffic."

He is also not afraid to get political. "It's not the time to be timid about who we are," he said passionately. "This is not a time to hold back because there are already other forces that are doing that."

A contributor to the Lammie-winning anthology *Queer Crips*, Walloch recently completed principal photography for the film *Steam Cloud Rising* (2004) set in Three Mile Island in the 1970s. Walloch was pleased with the opportunity to appear in the film because it offered a change of pace for him. He said, "I play the best friend who's super smart about nuclear power. It was interesting to make, because I wasn't being Greg Walloch, I was actually *acting*."

Yet the film experience was eye-opening for Walloch for reasons other than simply performing. "It is interesting travelling around to see that the world is not NY or LA," he says. Describing a disconnect he had with a woman he met in central Pennsylvania, he recalls, "She was grappling with her own son's sexuality—she rejected him for being gay—but she said she loves Rosie O'Donnell. It goes back to breaking thought the barrier of being defined by these elements."

In addition to acting, the writer/performer, who is currently single, has other ambitions. "I would love to be knocked off my feet by a man," he says dreamily and with determination, and, he adds, "I want to learn to play the saw."

MARGARET CHO: NOTORIOUS C.H.O.

The Korean-American comedian who scored with her hit one-woman show *I'm the One That I Want* (2000), Margaret Cho has gone on to a devoted following of gay (and straight) fans. When I spoke with her about her second concert film, *Notorious C.H.O.* (2002). I found her to be somewhat humorless—her comedy is very serious business. In fact, when I asked her to recite one of her signature catchphrases from her first film—"My name is Gwen, and I'm here to wash your vagina"—Cho agreed, but delivered the line perfunctorily, as if to emphasize that she was not performing for me. I have to respect that, and her, as Cho makes me laugh with her insight on relationships, her hilarious expressions, and her deadpan comic timing.

"It's about being a woman of color and stepping into power—wearing my greatness on my shoulders and being ostentatious and outrageous," says Margaret Cho, explaining the hip-hop title of her latest concert film, *Notorious C.H.O.*

"To step into our political power is essential," she continues. "We may be liberal in our politics, but we're very conservative in dealing with ourselves. This internal struggle is something that affects everyone—not only minorities, but it holds minorities back." Pretty heady stuff coming from a comedienne.

After developing a loyal following with her last stand-up tour turned documentary, *I'm the One That I Want,* two years ago, Margaret Cho has returned with another film—one that is actually funnier than her first—even if the language and humor is particularly raw for some audiences.

"That's what I'm like. That's what I think about. It's what I find funny," she says, defending her crudeness. And when she cites Richard Pryor and Sandra Bernhard as her influences, it comes as no surprise.

"My storytelling is a kind of mythmaking and myth-breaking," Cho answered in a phone interview about her work. "It's mostly fables, but it is very political and motivational in its own way. To me, [stand-up] is the *best* thing I can do. With the energy of the audience and the physicality of the show, it {becomes} a very magical experience. I feel like this is what I was born to do."

The thirty-three year-old Korean-American performer bases her shows entirely on her own life, relationships, and experiences. Her stories, which range from poignant to vulgar, explore her evolving relationship with her mother—whom she is famous for imitating—to sexual experimentation, and her struggles with anorexia and bulimia. She also disses and discusses gay men, straight men, drag queens, and one of her boyfriends, whose failure to return an adult movie got her into hilarious trouble at the video store.

"I've done all the things in my life because I've wanted to at that moment—not for the benefit of telling others. It was a kind of discovery," she explains about her more unusual experiences such as participating in a sex club, getting a colonic, and having an occasional lesbian partner.

"I feel very strongly about being very honest in my work, since I exaggerate very little," she says. However, Cho is careful not to talk about what she calls "the true intimacies in my relationships—that is private," adding that this behavior is also not as interesting as what is in her show, the main reason why she does not include it.

As for the creation of her one-woman act, Cho acknowledges that "very little of my show is improvised. It is all well rehearsed in front of an audience and planned out beforehand. Everything is [performed] in the order it's written." During her act, Cho often pauses dramatically, especially when she is mimicking voices of various "characters." Her expressions—of disgust, or despair—are often pricelessly funny.

"My timing comes from doing college tours when I was inexperienced and I had to fill an hour-long show with fifteen minutes of material. I learned to make every moment count," she said. However, Cho claims that she does not practice her work in the mirror or study her expressions. "I don't know what I look like until I see the film." Even Cho's decision about what to wear is pretty haphazard. "I choose what is clean, available, and not wrinkled," she says—and she does not seem to be joking.

Ultimately, the comedienne sees her work as being a way to define herself and allow the audience to identify with her. "I realized that I had the ability to combine my need to be funny with my desire to help people. And by that, also help myself. I think it was just discovering the ability to combine the two that made me the artist I am now."

DANNY ROBERTS: BOYS BRIEFS 2

Danny Roberts, the host for a short film collection titled *Boys Briefs 2* (2002) was one of the housemates on MTV's reality series *The Real World* (New Orleans). He used his fame from that show to create a popular Web site for gay youth, and he has talked openly to teens about homosexuality at various public speaking engagements. Roberts is incredibly down to earth, a quality that seems to bode well for a young role model. And although he may not aspire to being a performer, he is a natural, and the camera loves him.

A Brief *Chat with Danny Roberts*

"In gay culture, there is a lack of role models," says Danny Roberts, host of *Boys Briefs 2*, a video/DVD of short films about gay teen lust. Roberts, the hottie who is best known for his stint on the New Orleans edition of MTV's *The Real World,* however, has worked hard to fill this void.

As a spokesman for gay youth, Roberts is awed by "the power of television and media in our culture." Now a frequent guest speaker at colleges and universities he conducts "candid conversation about sexuality and coming out in America." In addition, Roberts continues to work on his Web site, www.countrytoconcrete.org, which provides a forum for gay teens.

"It's an honor to be in this position," he says about being a role model. "I never would have imagined this. Somebody should have been doing it already."

Contacted by Picture This! Entertainment about hosting *Boys Briefs 2,* Roberts accepted the opportunity as it provided him "a test run for future projects." The episodic introductions, which were filmed at Laguna Beach, California, feature the occasionally shirtless Roberts sunning it up on the beach, despite having the flu on the day of filming.

The short films in the video all send "gay is good" messages. Yet some, such as the Spanish entries *Doors Cut Down* and *Backroom,* announce this more explicitly than others. Both feature young boys having frank sexual encounters with strangers in public venues as a means of developing their pride.

"People are so repressed when it comes to showing their affection," Roberts says. "Gay or straight—there should be more [affection] in our culture. It's not so taboo." However, he also acknowledges that all teens, hetero or homo "have sex too early. [They] get the message that it's not only all right, but also expected." Roberts blames the media for this, citing that "MTV is very guilty."

Roberts's own experiences with queer lust began in high school, "I first started experimenting with my best friend. It was pretty whack. After a year, we realized what we were doing was gay as hell," Roberts remembers, probably with a smile. He stills stays in touch with the guy, who, by the way, is straight.

Roberts also admits that he first fell in love in college. "My boyfriend scared me so bad," he recalls. "I was so in love with him, I quit talking to him."

Similar issues are examined in the *Boys Briefs 2* collection. In the German film *Breakfast?*, one boy loves his best friend who is, instead, interested in sleeping with other people. The tension between these characters is quite palpable as they work out their love. Likewise, *Chicken*, from Ireland, examines the silent bond between two teens, neither of whom is able to verbally express their fears or desires.

Roberts also feels that it is important for teens to develop "an identity outside of a gay identity," citing that his life with Paul—his boyfriend of three years—is very healthy. (*Real World* viewers will recall Paul was in the military and while they were dating the show could not film his face because of the "don't ask/don't tell" policy.) "He's happy-go-lucky, and it's nice to be [stable] and with someone who has their shit together and is not bothered by the odd situations and people in my life."

Furthermore, Roberts is happy to stay out of what he describes as the "gay clone" scenario: "If you are gay, you have to mold into the 'gay identity.' That's lame as hell," he says adamantly. He is into breaking gay stereotypes.

"I hate the gay club music. Gay clubs are all about hooking up. They are nothing but trouble."

Instead, Roberts prefers the outdoors, and he loves travelling—he has been all over America and Africa, as well as to Mexico, Canada, and France. Comfortable in foreign countries, the *Boys Briefs 2* host hopes that audiences will respond to the international shorts, and not be put off by the few entries with subtitles.

As for his future, "I have no concrete plans," Roberts says. "I want to travel more. I started working on a book of inspiration and advice, but it didn't work out—it was dropped. I'd like to do TV, or movies, it depends on the project. I want to be involved in positive projects." Spoken like a true mentor.

PART II:
FILM REVIEWS

Chapter 7
Hot and Sexy

Come Undone (2000), *O Fantasma* (2000), *Burnt Money* (2000), *Bad Education* (2004), and *Madame Satã* (2002) are hot and sexy films that stayed with me for days. I think the reviews explain why I enjoy them so much.

COME UNDONE

Come Undone may traverse familiar coming out territory, but this poignant French film is a bittersweet coming-of-age drama about a teenager's first gay romance.

Mathieu (Jérémie Elkaïm) is an eighteen-year-old vacationing at his family's beach house near Nantes. His mother is ailing and his father is absent, leaving Mathieu to spend most of his days sunning on the beach with his annoying younger sister (Laetitia Legrix). One afternoon, hunky local teen Cédric (Stéphane Rideau, the hottie from *Wild Reeds*, 1994) becomes smitten with Mathieu and pursues him. The next evening the two boys meet outside Mathieu's house and go for a walk. The night ends with a passionate kiss and the beginning of a hot and heavy affair.

However, the sullen Mathieu is not fully prepared for his sexual awakening with the lusty and enthusiastic Cedric, and the differences in their personalities create tension in their relationship. Although Mathieu finds Cedric irresistible—and enjoys horsing around with him on the beach or in the water—he occasionally rebukes his boyfriend who constantly demands physical attention. Furthermore, Mathieu is reluctant to come out to his family, and he tells lies about his friendship with Cedric to deceive his sister and Annick (Marie Matheron), a family friend, who harbor suspicions about the boys' closeness.

Come Undone focuses largely on the intimacy between Cedric and Mathieu, and these moments of the young lovers dancing at a night-club or stealing a kiss in a public place are highly erotic and beauti-fully realized. Director Sébastian Lifshitz (who also cowrote the screen-play) uses a hand-held camera to craft a realistic and very sensuous film. Many scenes of the boys lying naked in bed together or caressing each other in the sand contribute to the film's seductiveness. Moreover, scenes of Cédric dancing on the beach at night or having sex with Mathieu in the dunes feature ample nudity.

Yet the film's compelling love story is more than just a series of sexy encounters between two beautiful boys. As the title indicates, Mathieu has "come undone," and when the film opens, he is recovering from a suicide attempt (which is explained later). These "flash forward" scenes take place in winter, and include one in which a psychiatrist tells the concerned Cédric that Mathieu has returned to the summer house to "find himself."

Significantly, Lifshitz deliberately fails to explain the events that prompted Mathieu to try to take his life, and the director is equally shrewd to omit scenes of Mathieu and Cédric's breakup. But despite the arty narrative structure—it is very easy for viewers to follow the juxtaposed "summer" and "winter" scenes—sometimes Lifshitz cuts away from a romantic moment too quickly or ends conversations too soon. Likewise, the film's abrupt and open ending may frustrate view-ers who want more. The director is, of course, being cagey on purpose, but his oblique storytelling slightly mars an otherwise satisfying film. At least audiences will appreciate the deft handling of the complex plotting and the sensitive characterizations.

To his credit, Lifshitz has cast two wonderful actors in the lead roles. Both Elkaïm and Rideau are incredibly sexy, and they give re-markable performances as the affectionate teens. Elkaïm conveys Mathieu's happiness about being with Cédric through excellent facial expressions and body language—he completely transforms when he is in love. Elkaïm is terrific, and he gives a sympathetic portrayal of a distraught gay teen.

Stéphane Rideau is also fantastic as Cédric. Although certainly not as meaty a part, Rideau makes his character someone who is deeply in love with Mathieu—mind, body, and soul. Rideau invests all his emotions in the role, and he is as moving frolicking on the beach with Mathieu as he is trying to understand what caused his lover's breakdown. Although the part is slightly underwritten, Rideau is extraordinary.

So, too, is the film.

O FANTASMA

O Fantasma is a fiercely erotic film that oozes sensuality and strangeness in equal measure. From the intense opening scene—in which a man nude, handcuffed, and gagged is fucked from behind by the sexy Sergio (Ricardo Meneses) in a skintight black latex bodysuit—it is clear this film is one for the raincoat brigade.

Director João Pedro Rodrigues includes plenty of steamy sex, but there is actually a point to all the pornography. Specifically, unrequited love can be a bitch—albeit, a sexy bitch in heat.

Sergio is an incredibly hunky garbage collector in the north of Lisbon who spies a studly motorcyclist on his rounds one night and becomes obsessed with him. His would-be lover is a "phantom" in Sergio's fragile mind—and someone he must possess at all costs.

Pursuing his conquest through fetish objects, Sergio first masturbates with the biker's dirty gloves, and later breaks open the guy's garbage bags—with his teeth, no less—to find a torn swimsuit. To satisfy his urges, Sergio heads to a shower in the swimsuit to pleasure himself.

Yep, this is that kind of film.

Much of *O Fantasma* consists of Sergio spying on or stalking the object of his affection. However, the young man also embarks on a series of extremely graphic sexual encounters to relieve his pent-up frustrations. Sergio gives a hand job to gagged and handcuffed cop in a parked car; gets fucked against a metal gate by a stranger; and experiments with autoerotic asphyxiation in the shower.

Although these moments are certainly titillating, the film's most explicit tryst involves Sergio, bare assed against a urinal, receiving a blow job from some guy in a bathroom. For many viewers, this scene will be *O Fantasma*'s highlight.

Should anyone care, in between these escapades, garbage gets collected. There is also a digression involving Sergio's female co-worker Fatima, who has a crush on him.

Despite all the "shut up and fuck" content, *O Fantasma* does actually have something to say about the nature of its protagonist's animalistic desires. Sergio lives solely by his passions and instincts, not unlike his best friend Lorde, a dog. Sniffing, licking, and growling at both men and women, Sergio also breaks into his phantom lover's house—and marks his territory by pissing on the guy's bed.

Significantly, Rodrigues portrays these bestial actions as a descent into madness that culminates—it does not climax—in the film's most unusual sequence, a bizarre twenty-minute finale during which a feral Sergio prowls around in his skintight black latex body suit. It simply has to be seen to be believed.

Needless to say, the gorgeous Meneses, who was discovered in a bar by the director, gives one hell of a performance. He may not provide much insight into his character, but he appears equally comfortable in the extended nude/sex scenes and rolling around in the trash.

An indelible portrait of unbridled sexuality, *O Fantasma* is startling smut.

BURNT MONEY

Burnt Money is a stylish and sexy crime melodrama. This great, gay, period gangster romance—which features a trio of thieves on the lam in Argentina and Uruguay in 1965—is also based on a true story.

Nicknamed "The Twins," Nene (Leonardo Sbaraglia) and Ángel (Eduardo Noriega) are lovers and bank robbers who share a special bond. However, although they were once extremely romantic—just watch how seductively Ángel removes a cigarette from Nene's mouth and crushes it in his fingers—at present, there is something "broken" in their relationship.

Hired for a holdup, The Twins are partnered with the cold-blooded Cuervo (Pablo Echarri), a sedative addict who drives getaway. Cuervo has contempt for Nene and Ángel, and his presence adds further stress to their already tense relationship. Things get worse when the heist turns out to be a rainy, bloody mess. Although the crooks walk away with the $7 million loot, Ángel is injured, and they must flee to Uruguay to obtain passports for escape.

Director Marcelo Piñeyro deliberately paces this elegant, absorbing film to establish the rhythm of the lives of these criminals, allowing viewers to understand and even sympathize with them. Scenes of the men "buried" (waiting to pull off the heist) or "in hiding" give the characters a chance to develop, and they are shown to be troubled, anxious, and bored. Moreover, *Burnt Money* spends considerable time observing the characters tormenting themselves and/or one another. Ángel, who hears voices, is self-destructive, while the frustrated Nene embarks on clandestine sexual encounters. Similarly, Cuervo displays a recklessness that may lead to the trio getting caught. What emerges is less an action film than a fascinating character study occasionally interrupted by intense bursts of violence.

Although the film is certainly grisly, Piñeyro finds a kind of intimacy amid all of the bloodletting. A sequence in which Nene tends to Ángel's chest wound may be uncomfortable to watch, but there is such tenderness it becomes an incredibly touching love scene. This episode rivals an incident in which Nene spies Cuervo having sex with his girlfriend—who catches Nene looking, and teases him by exposing Cuervo's ass—for the film's most passionate moment.

Burnt Money also boasts gorgeous cinematography, a lush tango soundtrack, and outstanding period detail in the vintage clothes and cars. The film only sags a bit in the middle, when the characters (and the audience) wait for something to happen. The drama eventually picks up in the third act with the introduction of Giselle (Leticia Brédice), a femme fatale who brings the story to its forgone conclusion. (The title gives it away.)

Nene succumbs to the charms of Giselle and begins a secret, erotic relationship with her. The catch is that while Giselle offers him a chance to escape, Nene's freedom comes at the price of leaving Ángel behind. Piñeyro emphasizes this point by cross-cutting Nene and Giselle's coupling with the despondent Ángel taking drugs.

As Nene makes his fateful decision, the tragic consequences are played out in a breathtaking finale that drips literally and figuratively with atmosphere. Set inside Giselle's fiery apartment, the heat in this scene is absolutely palpable. As the criminals, stripped and sweaty, attempt to survive a maelstrom of violence, a thrilling shootout takes place.

The performances by the three sexy leads are uniformly excellent. As Nene, Leonardo Sbraglia projects both intelligence and sensuality that is utterly captivating. Likewise, Pablo Echarri is quite impressive as the impudent Cuervo. Yet it is Eduardo Noriega (he starred in the Spanish thriller *Open Your Eyes*, 1997, which begat the wretched *Vanilla Sky*, 2001) who steals the film with his moody performance. Noriega communicates his character's despair with little dialogue, and his response upon learning of Nene's affair with Giselle is remarkably affecting. In support, Leticia Brédice performs her moll role with noticeable élan.

Violent, and sexy as hell, *Burnt Money* smolders.

BAD EDUCATION

In gay filmmaker Pedro Almodóvar's excellent and complex *Bad Education*, the irresistible Gael García Bernal plays multiple roles—including one in drag—and he is absolutely captivating. So too is the film, an absorbing noir drama about topics as diverse as love, sex, and obsession, identity, blackmail, and revenge, as well as murder.

With flashbacks within flashbacks, and both real and imagined plotlines, *Bad Education* has a complicated narrative that unfolds slowly. Considerable attention is required to keep all of the characters and stories straight, but the work is worthwhile. This film is as satisfying emotionally and visually as anything Almodóvar has ever made, and the director's distinctive style is in evidence in every frame. From the bold background colors and costumes to the deft interweaving of the multiple characters and narratives, the filmmaker is in control, and audiences who go along for the ride will enjoy it immensely.

The story begins with Ignacio (Bernal), an actor who is now called Ángel, reuniting Enrique (Fele Martínez), a childhood friend who works as a filmmaker. Ángel has brought a story along called *The Visit*, which describes Ignacio's and Enrique's youth realistically, but also imagines what might have happened between these characters when they grew up. Wary of this at first, Enrique becomes very interested in this story upon reading it. However, the truth of the tale, Enrique learns, proves to be stranger than fiction. The filmmaker agrees to take on the project as much for its content as an excuse to get to know the fascinating Ángel further.

It would spoil Almodóvar's clever plotting to reveal how the stories evolve. Suffice it to say, Enrique and Ángel get caught up in a twisted, tricky relationship that involves the production of *The Visit*. A scene in which the two men go for a swim one afternoon features tremendous tension between them both sexually and otherwise. (Almodóvar teasingly tantalizingly films the hot and sexy Bernal in and out of his underwear, causing viewers' hearts to race as fast as Enrique's.) Following a debate about the film's casting and ending, Enrique and Ángel decide to enter into an intense physical relationship—one that blurs exactly who is taking advantage of whom.

What can be revealed is that the drama in *The Visit* concerns Ángel's attempt to blackmail a childhood English teacher, Father Manolo (Daniel Giménez-Cacho), who developed an obsessive love for his star pupil Ignacio. In the film's second half, the truth about Father Manolo's behavior becomes clear, and viewers will be intrigued learning how the stories both onscreen and off, real and imagined, are connected and resolved.

Almodóvar sensitively addresses Ángel's desire and despair as he enters into a new gay relationship to resolve one from the past. Yet *Bad Education* goes beyond the simple revenge fantasy to present many significant issues, including a loss of faith. Most interesting are the parallels between the real and fictionalized stories in the film within a film that offer viewers a prism through which to consider the (not always appropriate) behavior of the characters. As the layers are slowly peeled away, and more is revealed, many ambiguities remain.

One of the reasons the film is so effective (and affecting) is because of the strong central performances. The swoon-inducing Gael García Bernal is absolutely fearless in his role(s), and he looks quite fetching in drag as the female performer Zahara. Bernal's expressions and emotions are remarkable, and he makes the conniving Ángel and Zahara sympathetic, even if these characters are not always likable. Furthermore, Bernal's riveting performance of "Perhaps, Perhaps, Perhaps" (in Spanish) as Zahara is a showstopper. Likewise, Fele Martínez is perfectly cast as Enrique, who is inspired both professionally and emotionally by Ángel's arrival. Martínez may not have the showy role that Bernal does, but he gives a very accomplished performance.

In support, Daniel Giménez-Cacho is suitably sinister playing Father Manolo in the flashbacks, while Lluís Homar fares well essaying the same character in the more contemporary episodes. Rounding out the all-male ensemble are three actors who deserve credit for their excellent work. Javier Cámara as Paquito, Ángel's amusing gay best friend, provides the film with its comic relief; Francisco Boira makes a terrific impression as a transgendered character who appears in the story's second half; and Alberto Ferreiro, whose sex scene with Zahara is *muy caliente*.

Bad Education is certainly a demanding film, but for those who accept the challenge, it is a story that truly resonates.

MADAME SATÃ

Madame Satã is an extraordinary film about João Francisco dos Santos (Lázaro Ramos), an Afro-Brazilian man who ultimately finds a measure of happiness performing as the title character. Director Karim Aïnouz's exotic, erotic, and ecstatic film traces João's life through his daily struggles, which include battling against racism and sexism in a society that cares little for gay men of color.

A remarkable man who lives in the *favelas* (slums) of the city and works as a dresser for a chanteuse at an upscale bar, João knows all the routines but is never given the chance to perform them. This is actually a very good metaphor for his life as a whole, for João, a poor, black homosexual, is a powerless second-class citizen in 1932 Rio.

However, João is worshipped and feared by members of the underworld. Although he is close to his makeshift family—João lives and cares for Laurita (Marcélia Cartaxo), a prostitute with a baby, and Tabu (Flávio Bauraqui), a gay drug addict who owes him money—he has a vicious temper, and commands respect from the locals. In fact, João's penchant for violence gets him into trouble often. As *Madame Satã* shows, much of his life was spent in and out of jail cells.

Although the film depicts only a ten-year period, which culminates in the creation of Madame Satã in 1942, it is a vibrant time nonetheless. João begins an intense and steamy relationship with a ruggedly handsome Brazilian man, Renatinho (Fellipe Marques), which illustrates his capacity for love even though Renatinho's intentions may not be entirely honorable.

Another defining moment for João is his need to reinvent himself after his first stint in prison. Finding his voice as a cabaret performer (and as an icon for the disenfranchised and marginalized) in the guise of Madame Satã, João experiences true happiness for the first time in his life. This rapture is communicated not only in his dazzling performance, complete with lavish costumes and period music, but also by João's expressive face, which lights up during the show.

Madame Satã may be episodic, but the various pieces create an impressive mosaic. As João flits from the glamour of backstage to the shadowy *favela* alleyways looking for love or money, the many facets of his character are revealed: seductive when João removes a man's wedding ring with his tongue before going to bed with him, and tense as he initiates a brawl in the streets after Laurita is threatened by an unwanted john. And then there is the joy he radiates watching his idol, Josephine Baker, in *Princess Tam Tam* (1935). Aïnouz beautifully captures these moments, and the film eloquently displays its affection for its hero.

Audiences, too, will respond positively to this larger-than-life character. João's self-empowerment is inspiring, especially when he declares, "I'm a queen by choice—it doesn't make me any less of a man!" in one of the film's most dynamic moments.

Madame Satã boasts a miraculous performance by Lázaro Ramos in the title role, and his ability to convey both sensitivity and candor is tremendous. Even when João does something as simple as straighten his hair—to look more sophisticated, less wild—he is moving. Likewise, his physical behavior, which shifts seamlessly from passionate sex to punishing kicks and drag performances, is mesmerizing. Ramos commands the screen every minute he is on it, and he brings João vividly to life.

The film is also deeply indebted to cinematographer Walter Carvalho, who shoots each scene as if it were a still photograph, and the result is indelible. There is a crispness and clarity to every image Carvalho makes—even the slums look beautiful.

Bravo to Karim Aïnouz for telling this unusual story, and for telling it so well. *Madame Satã* is a memorable film about a truly exceptional individual.

Chapter 8
Intimacy

Among the films reviewed in this chapter, gay male sexuality is only a part of the intimacy on display. What appealed to me about these movies—*Kinsey* (2004), *His Brother* (2003), *Smokers Only* (2001), *1,000 Clouds of Peace* (2003), *Lan Yu* (2001), and *Yossi & Jagger* (2002)—was the absolute, undeniable realism of the characters and their emotions.

KINSEY

Queer filmmaker Bill Condon's biopic of the bisexual *Kinsey* is an eye-opening and engaging look at the man who changed America's attitudes toward sexuality. Condon presents Alfred C. Kinsey's (Liam Neeson) life as if he was one of the noted doctor's own research subjects—asking questions about (while depicting) the man's childhood, his relationships with his parents, his early sexual activity, as well as his marriage and current bedroom practices. Much like he did with filmmaker James Whale in *Gods and Monsters,* Condon shows the human side of a man whose methods and ideas may have been unusual, especially for their time, but in fact, marked genius.

The film, like Kinsey himself, takes a nonjudgmental approach toward the sometimes embarrassing to discuss subject of sex. Condon is deliberately clinical in his depiction of some of the racier material (verbally and visually), yet there is much to arouse the viewer's interest. What is more, *Kinsey* addresses the issue of homosexuality quite frankly, both in the doctor's research and his life itself.

Independent Queer Cinema: Reviews and Interviews
© 2006 by The Haworth Press, Inc. All rights reserved.
doi:10.1300/5482_09

After a lengthy exposition establishing Kinsey's difficult relationship with this stern father (John Lithgow), and his courtship of Clara "Mac" McMillen (Laura Linney), he eventually decides to study what becomes his book *Sexual Behavior in the Human Male*. His research is initially of questionable merit, but he heads to a gay bar in Chicago to start talking about sex, even if he acknowledges that "homosexuality is out of fashion in society." While one gay patron (John Epperson, out of his Lypsinka drag) rejects his request to discuss his bedroom behavior outright, a few men begin to open up to the doctor and his assistant Clyde Martin (Peter Sarsgaard), leading them to a fulfilling path of discovery. And perhaps buoyed by the success of these interviews, if not his own not-so-latent tendencies toward homosexuality, Kinsey begins a short-term sexual relationship with Clyde.

Condon uses this queer affair as just one example of Kinsey differentiating "sex" from "love." His work is celebrated for breaking down the bedroom activities of ordinary individual, and classifying them scientifically. Of course, this leaves little room for emotion, a point made clear by Mac's impassioned response to her husband's behavior, as well as her own pleasurable sexual activity with Clyde, who tires of his mentor.

Kinsey gets a bit tedious when it shifts away from its subject's personal story and concentrates on his success and its impact on Kinsey's life, but the film is fascinating nonetheless. An unexpected best seller, his book's triumph leads to a sequel that foments conflict not only among Kinsey's staff—where the men are encouraged to sleep with one another's wives—but also his university board and the Rockefeller Foundation that funds him.

The dramatic downturn of his career certainly garners sympathy for Kinsey, but Condon draws out these episodes, bringing up a customs case (involving pornography) without sufficient resolution. And while an interview in a hotel room with a man (William Sadler) who tells of numerous unsettling sexual conquests is curiously unsatisfying, Kinsey's interview with a woman (Lynn Redgrave) who describes her sudden attraction to another female is fantastic. This scene is especially heartbreaking not only because of Redgrave's moving performance, but also because her words serve to validate the doctor's life's work.

Kinsey is intelligently written, even if it never goes too deep below the surface of its subject. Condon has a firm control over the material, and he elicits pitch-perfect performances from his cast. Liam Neeson is exceptional as the relentless sexologist, and he is ably supported by the radiant Laura Linney, who is flawless as his wife Mac. Linney imbues her character with such warmth and humanity that she threatens to steal the film in every scene. In addition, Peter Sarsgaard is both sexy and impressive as Clyde Martin.

Condon certainly rose to the challenge of making *Kinsey* a respectful film—one that does not insult its subject or its audience. On a scale of 0 to 6, it rates a 5.

HIS BROTHER

There is a stunning, six-minute sequence in *His Brother (Son frère)* that most viewers will find hypnotizing. The main character, Thomas (Bruno Todeschini) is lying in a hospital bed, and two nurses slowly remove all of his body hair. This sequence is dramatized not only to convey the medical necessity of the operation—Thomas is about to undergo a splenectomy—but also the more symbolic act of transformation and change.

His Brother, directed by gay French filmmaker Patrice Chéreau is about the estranged relationship between Thomas and his younger sibling Luc (Eric Caravaca). Thomas is straight and Luc is gay, and they have not had much contact during their adult years. Now, Thomas contacts his brother to say he is dying from an exotic blood disease—not leukemia, not HIV—in which his platelets are dwindling, and he could hemorrhage at any moment and die. This may be the last chance for the brothers to make amends.

Although the film's story sounds like something out of the bad disease movie of the week genre, *His Brother* is far superior to anything on television. Chéreau gets up close and intimate with his characters. Many scenes are shot in silence, with a handheld camera, and the effect lends an urgency to the action that is vibrant. The film pulses with an immediacy that is hard to shake—if viewers can bring themselves to watch. This is a difficult, at times painful film, but also one that has its rewards.

Significantly, Chéreau does not flinch from showing uncomfortable things. From medical procedures and surgical scars to a tense argument between the brothers, there are many raw, absorbing moments. When one brother says to the other, "You deserted me when I needed you most," the effect is gutwrenching.

Despite the power of much of the film, Chéreau presents the events out of sequence, starting in the summer and flashing back and forth to the winter. This nonlinear structure provides an interesting prism for the action, but it robs the story of some of its impact.

Instead, *His Brother* excels in depicting the way the characters react to Thomas's condition. Whereas some of his loved ones cannot deal with his deterioration, Luc becomes emboldened by it. Viewers are also likely to have the same response.

The performances, however, are nothing short of miraculous. Bruno Todeschini, who was nominated for a César (French Oscar) for this role, is simply astonishing. Gaunt and fragile throughout, he conveys the anguish and suffering of a patient who cannot understand why his body is failing. Todeschini is superb, and he is well matched by his costar. As Luc, Caravaca is wonderfully expressive. His response to Thomas's weakening condition is remarkable, but he also has great moments interacting with other characters. When he meets a nineteen-year-old patient in the hospital (Robinson Stévenin) or argues with his boyfriend Vincent (Sylvain Jacques), his reactions to these men and their conditions are perfect.

His Brother is an unusual film because there are doses of sentiment amid all of the harsh realism. Yet Chéreau avoids making the film overly emotional, and this may actually be a drawback. After viewers become so engaged in the lives of these characters, the drama of watching Thomas dying is more of a chore than a relief. Even though a sad, somber Marianne Faithfull song plays on the soundtrack—perhaps to help jerk the tears—viewers may find themselves curiously unmoved. It is a strange if not entirely inappropriate response to a curious but compelling film.

SMOKERS ONLY

A hypnotic and complex character study, *Smokers Only* is an exquisitely filmed drama about two aimless youths drawn to each other in the Argentine night. This haunting film—leisurely paced and episodically structured—boasts a seductive yet seedy atmosphere that pulls the viewer into its dreamscape.

Reni (Cecilia Bengolea) is a suicidal singer in a band who feels her life lacks meaning and purpose. One night, she spies Andrés (Leonardo Brzezicki), a bisexual hustler, turning tricks with various men in the city's ATM vestibules. Reni finds Andrés intriguing, and after watching him participate in several of these highly erotic encounters, she befriends him.

Although Reni is attracted to the sexy Andrés, she "does not pay for love," and while she wants to sleep with him, she also wants to work the streets. Andrés, however, is mostly concerned with getting paid. Sex, he says, is the thing he does best. He also likes to be watched—his anonymous encounters in the city's banks are captured in grainy black and white on closed-circuit video cameras.

Smokers Only deftly chronicles the unusual relationship that develops between Reni and Andrés with appropriate detachment. Director Verónica Chen casually observes her protagonists—alone or together—as they wander the empty streets of Buenos Aires searching for their self-respect. Holed up in a cheap hotel room, or eating pizza on the street, the quasi-lovers slowly reveal themselves to each other as Reni hopes for some kind of intimate emotional connection. Perhaps the most moving image in the film is Reni clinging to Andrés as if for support as they embrace. The scene grows more powerful as the camera circles around them, capturing Reni's expressions of despair.

Chen wisely does not provide her characters with any backgrounds or history, nor does she try to explain or even understand their behavior. The director simply presents Reni and Andrés as they are, filming them in close up, reflected in glass, or against urban backdrops. The images have a documentary feel to them with all the vivid urgency and visual textures.

Although not much actually happens in *Smokers Only,* the film has gritty atmosphere galore. There are several astonishing, impressionistic—and often wordless—sequences that show the city and its inhabitants eking out an existence late at night. Unknown faces populate the bars, streets, and cafes, and the dark sky filled with ominous skyscrapers threatens the wandering Reni. These visuals are suitably poetic, and they speak volumes about the film's protagonist, lost among them. Chen is not so much making judgments as she is commenting on the character's isolation and loneliness.

Yet not all of the pieces fit together perfectly in this mosaic. A dreamy sequence late in the film, set in a field outside the city is out of place (though this very well may be its point). The film has such a thin narrative that viewers may object to the drama being little more than a series of beautiful images that sometimes fail to connect.

Nevertheless, the characters come to life because of the bold performances by the two leads. Cecilia Bengolea gives a stunning portrait of a young woman looking to be transformed by *some* experience. She makes her character's journey absorbing at all times. Likewise, Leonardo Brzezicki has a cool moodiness that is wholly appropriate for Andrés. Brzezicki keeps an air of mystery about his character, and his naturalistic performance is highly sensual and effective.

Decidedly not for all tastes, adventurous moviegoers will be transfixed by the stylish imagery of *Smokers Only.*

1,000 CLOUDS OF PEACE

Luminous black and white cinematography—and a gorgeous lovesick young man—are two of the highlights of *1,000 Clouds of Peace Encircle the Sky,* a fabulous if somewhat arty romantic drama from Mexico. Every frame in this beautiful mood piece about memory and desire is exquisitely filmed and looks like a still photograph. In fact, the cinematography, by Diego Arizmendi, is so crisp and real that the film is able to convey its subtlest emotions by just the images alone. And this is a good thing. *1,000 Clouds of Peace* contains minimal dialogue and long silences that invite viewers to soak up its strong visuals.

Directed by Julián Hernández, this simple but eloquent film is a low-key drama about a very handsome young man named Gerardo (Juan Carlos Ortuño) who experiences heartbreak. Although Gerardo may appear to be a hustler, he is not fucking men for the money. He gives a blow job to a guy in the film's (discreet) opening scene but discards the cash he is offered. Throughout the film, Gerardo has trouble accepting money from anyone, making it clear that he is really searching for companionship to ease his loneliness, not sex.

One afternoon, Gerardo meets Bruno (Juan Carlos Torres) at a pool hall and the couple pairs off to spend the rest of the night together. Yet what begins as a sexy affair, filled with tender hugs and passionate kisses, is soon cut short. After the two guys arrange to meet the next day, Bruno fails to show up, and Gerardo spirals into a funk. He later receives a letter from his beloved.

To cope with this rejection, Gerardo tries to re-create his magical night with Bruno—he buys a recording of a song they heard at a cafe, he masturbates and touches himself as if he was (with) Bruno, and he revisits the places where they spent time together. Gerardo is in love, and yet he is told, "Nothing hurts more than love."

1,000 Clouds of Peace chronicles the various characters Gerardo meets after his brief encounter with Bruno. One man offers him advice, and a hug from this stranger triggers Gerardo's memory. Other people who make an impact on his life include a pregnant waitress he befriends and a lonely lady he finds on the bridge where he was supposed to meet Bruno. Each woman tries to jar Gerardo out of his melancholy state. And although he is coddled by these women who want to take care of him, Gerardo is also abused by various men who want to fuck him, or worse. Perhaps the most poignant meeting is a brief reunion Gerardo has with his mother, a woman who sees that her son is troubled, but scolds him for being so. Her expression as he leaves is quietly devastating.

Hernández certainly sympathizes with all of the lost souls depicted here, not just Gerardo. His film is a poetic meditation on loneliness and romantic suffering, because the emotions are so clearly portrayed. Much of this is courtesy of Juan Carlos Ortuño, who gives an amazing performance as Gerardo. The filmmaker uses the actor's boyish face to full advantage—his blank expressions speak volumes about his interior feelings. Hernández also shoots the actor's head and body to full advantage—a close-up of the back of his neck to a beautiful shot of his naked torso are imbued with lust and eroticism. The director even coaxes his star to do some sensual full-frontal nude scenes that are also quite sexy.

However, it should be noted that some audience members may find this slow-moving film to be sleep-inducing. There are many silent passages, and parts of the dialogue are done in voiceovers—as they are meant to express the characters' interior thoughts. This gives the story another layer of context and meaning, but for some, it will simply seem pretentious.

1,000 Clouds of Peace may be a sparse drama containing very little action, but the emotion it does show is profound.

LAN YU

Director Stanley Kwan's mesmerizing new film *Lan Yu* has a real *noir*-ish quality to it—dark, atmospheric lighting, an edgy, cynical tone, and a palpable sense of fatalism—that perfectly suits this moody gay romance. Filmed illegally in China, this hypnotic drama about love, trust, and truth is both intimate and intense.

Chen Handong (Hu Jun) is a wealthy Beijing businessman who pays an architecture student named Lan Yu (Liu Ye) 1000 yuan to spend the night with him. Although it is the first time Lan Yu has ever provided such a service, the two men become extremely fond of each other. When they next meet four months later, however, Handong is quite clear about communicating the status of their relationship. He insists that they will be together for "as long as it feels right." In addition to giving him this warning, Handong lavishes Lan Yu with expensive gifts and ravishes him with kisses.

Kwan's film traces these characters as their lives intersect, diverge, and reconnect over time. Handong, who is determined to always be in control, wants to sow his oats with a male lover before settling down with a wife and child (to keep up appearances). In contrast, Lan Yu is a simpler, country boy who dreams of going to America. He may be a bit naive, but Lan Yu is fiercely loyal and extremely proud.

The relationship may be doomed, but the power struggle between these two lovers is fascinating. Scenes of Handong and Lan Yu together, which start out tenderly, with seductive embraces, soon become painful as the two men try to hurt each other emotionally.

When things start to sour—and Handong throws Lan Yu over to take a wife who is good for business—there is a startling confrontation. In this scene, Lan Yu drops his pants to offer Handong the only exchange he can in protest of his lover's bad behavior. In doing so, Lan Yu forces the closeted Handong to confront the exact nature of their relationship, as well as his own homosexuality. Kwan finely underscores this chilling moment by filming the characters at a slight distance—their expressions do not need to be seen for their feelings to be fully understood.

All of *Lan Yu* is as artfully composed. The film uses shadows and smoke effectively, and there are many elegant shots of the handsome actors framed in windows or mirrors. Adding an erotic component to this dark romance is the sensuous display of lithe, naked bodies bathed in dim light.

Furthermore, the director employs several interesting cinematic techniques to tell the melodramatic story. Jump cuts used in a sequence where Lan Yu is given a scarf by Handong emphasize the bond developing between the characters. Likewise, a tracking shot in the film's final moments is thrilling for its tremendous emotional impact. *Lan Yu* also features a wonderous (though staged) episode concerning the Tiananmen Square massacre.

Kwan coaxes brave performances from his leads. As Handong, Hu Jun is remarkably cool, even as his character experiences reversals of fortune both personally and professionally. Jun shrewdly plays the part of a businessman who sees affection as a transaction or a contract—he is unable to give or receive love properly.

In the title role, Liu Ye is a revelation. Given the more challenging character, Ye handles the film's love scenes and the dramatic moments with great aplomb, and he earns the audience's sympathy through his restrained but forceful portrayal.

Sexy, political, and even controversial, *Lan Yu* is a minor masterpiece.

YOSSI & JAGGER

A love story between two male soldiers in the Israeli army, *Yossi &
Jagger* is a poignant gay romance. Based on a true story, director Eytan
Fox presents a riveting portrait of queer lovers who keep their rela-
tionship secret from the rest of their unit.

The film opens with Yossi (Ohad Knoller) the troop commander
asking Lior (Yahuda Levi)—nicknamed Jagger, because he looks like
a rock star—to accompany him on a trek to check drill zone positions.
Once away from the other soldiers, the two men have a snowball fight
and cuddle. They talk about their feelings for each other and the pos-
sibility of having a future together. It has all the innocence and excitement of first love.

Jagger is especially interested in taking their relationship to the
next level. He dreams of being together with Yossi, but will even settle for a long weekend vacation in a double bed. Yossi, however, is less
inclined to be so open about things; he has yet to say the words "I love
you" to his boyfriend. His comment to Jagger is "live with it or leave."

Despite this attitude, the tenderness of the couple's relationship is
evident, and their contrasting personalities actually mesh well. Yossi's
concerns about the impact their affair might have are valid because of
his rank over the other men. Although he is more reserved and serious, Yossi makes small romantic gestures that indicate the extent of
his love. Meanwhile, Jagger sings, dances, and acts like a goofy teenager in love, which in fact, he is.

One of the points of *Yossi & Jagger* is that these soldiers are very
young adults, still learning about love and life. The fact that these
teenagers must complete mandatory army service, particularly on the
tense and deadly Israeli-Lebenese border (where the film is set), is not
lost on filmmaker Fox.

When the boys return to base camp, their romantic bliss evapo-
rates. The colonel (Sharon Raginiano) has arrived with news that they
are to prepare for a hot ambush. Even though Yossi says the men are
too tired, he must ready them for battle. It is very telling when the
colonel admonishes Yossi, "Don't be a faggot," for trying to protect
his men.

This idea of machismo is artfully explored by Fox, particularly when Jagger suggests "what if I am a faggot?" to his fellow soldiers during the same meal. The silence this comment brings is broken with hearty laughter, but the unspoken idea of him "coming out" hangs in the air.

Tensions also escalate as two female soldiers who arrive with the colonel cause romantic trouble among the troop. One young woman, Yaeli (Aya Steinovitz), has a crush on the adorable Jagger, and she hopes to ask him out. Her intentions, however, foment jealous feelings with another soldier, Ofir (Assi Cohen), who fancies Yaeli himself. When Yaeli asks Yossi about Jagger—because the two men are so "close"—she tells the commander that she is drawn to him because he is "different." Again, the unspoken acknowledgement of Jagger's true nature is raised but not remarked upon.

Yossi & Jagger sensitively conveys the depths of this whole hidden relationship, which builds inexorably in the film's melancholic finale. Running just over an hour in length, the film eloquently explores the reality of what life is like in the Israeli army for these soldiers.

Another reason the film is so moving is that the lead actors are both excellent. Yehuda Levi has the showier role as the good-looking Jagger, and while he is charming making up lyrics to his favorite pop song, Ohad Knoller steals the film as Yossi. Knoller conveys so much of what his character is thinking and feeling with just the tiniest facial expressions, it is a masterfully understated performance.

Yossi & Jagger is a lovely, perceptive romance, but one that packs an enormous emotional wallop.

Chapter 9
Seductive

The films in this section are all undeniably sensual and erotic. The characters in *Secret Things* (2002), *Confusion of Genders* (2000), *His Secret Life* (2001), *Swimming Pool* (2003), and *Strayed* (2003) are all seductive—inviting the protagonists as well as the audience into their intimate lives.

SECRET THINGS

Secret Things is a titillating drama about two women who use their "guts and asses" in an attempt to gain power and privilege over men. Loaded with steamy sex scenes as well as talky characters, writer-director Jean-Claude Brisseau's film is like a fascinating cross between the sleazy Zalman King (*Red Shoe Diaries*, 1992) and the smart Eric Rohmer.

The film opens with the unforgettable image of Nathalie (Coralie Revel) writhing nude and masturbating in front of a crowd of people in a strip club. In her "act" there is also a bird and a ghostlike vision, and for a moment *Secret Things* borders on pretentiousness. However, it quickly recovers when Sandrine (Sabrina Seyvecou), a bartender at the club, takes an interest in the performance artist. Sandrine, a shy young woman, wants to learn more about "crossing the forbidden line" of being comfortable sexually in public, and enlists Nathalie's aid to do so. Soon the women are sitting nude under their raincoats in outdoor cafes and, after removing their bras in a metro station, are canoodling in the recesses of a subway tunnel.

Yet the film has much more on its mind than chronicling the sexploits of these two beautiful women. *Secret Things* is really about subverting the desires of men, and how women "at the bottom of the social scale" such as Nathalie and Sandrine can beat men at the games of money, sex, and power.

The pair hatch a plan. They will work their way into a company and use their (sexual) skills to humiliate men and get what they want. And sure enough, in no time at all, Sandrine is working for—and sleeping with—Mr. Delacroix (Roger Mirmont), an important executive at a major bank.

Despite this initial success, however, Sandrine and Nathalie really have their sights set on Christophe (Fabrice Deville), the firm's gorgeous, high-powered boss. But Christophe has a reputation as a ladykiller—he is rumored to have caused more than one woman he loved and left to immolate herself. The game of pretending begins, and as it does, *Secret Things* becomes quite intense and wholly absorbing. Even if Nathalie and Sandrine swear not to get attached to their victims, viewers will be totally sucked in by this melodrama.

Although *Secret Things* includes some very explicit sex scenes, most of them are provocative for being either between two women, or because they involve Sandrine, Christophe, and Christophe's sister, Charlotte (Blandine Bury). What is more, the film includes an orgy sequence that makes *Eyes Wide Shut* (1999) look like a Disney picture. Significantly, the eroticism is not exploitative. Nathalie and Sandrine are making the point that as "poor women," they are "forced" to use their sex as a weapon against men. Emotions are another thing altogether. "Love is risk," one character says. They are willing to suffer the consequences if things backfire. The fact is that they are in charge of their sexuality—however they choose to use it.

This point will certainly engage audiences in argument, and that is precisely the filmmaker's purpose. This is not mere porn for the raincoat brigade; it is a thoughtful, intelligent film about manipulating class and gender. It just happens to feature plenty of hot sex, much of it featuring lesbians.

As shrewd and as savvy as it is, *Secret Things* would not be successful were it not for the daring, accomplished, and courageous performances by its two attractive leads. Both Coralie Revel and Sabrina Seyvecou are exceptional in their roles, playing the sex scenes and the dramatic moments with the same diligence. These actresses are also to be commended for taking chances and appearing so naked and passionate on screen. In support, Fabrice Deville and Roger Mirmont are terrific as the men who fall under the spell of these two alluring young women.

Ultimately, Brisseau's film is as beguiling as its seductive heroines.

CONFUSION OF GENDERS

Confusion of Genders is a frisky French romance about a man who desires almost everyone he meets (but not all at once). While the various relationships all involve high drama and unrequited love, the sordid affairs presented here play out like a dark-humored farce.

Alain (Pascal Greggory) is involved with Laurence (Nathalie Richard), who is his boss at a law firm. They reluctantly agree to settle down as partners—especially after she discovers she is pregnant. However, the couple constantly snaps at each other, and their love is more like war.

One obvious barrier to the union is Christophe (Cyrille Thouvenin), the yummy, much younger brother of an ex-girlfriend Alain seriously fancies. Although he acknowledges that their relationship has no future, Alain is frequently intimate with Christophe, who kisses him ardently whenever they are together.

Adding to this confusion is a subplot involving a criminal Alain is defending named Marc (Vincent Martinez). Depressed at the thought of possibly never seeing his girlfriend Babette (Julie Gayet) again, Marc asks Alain to bring her to him in jail. As compensation for this, Marc says he will fuck Alain, who is undeniably attracted to the sexy prisoner. Of course, Alain falls for Babette in the process, causing further complications.

As each of the four couples in the film are in different stages of their relationships, the film depicts the power struggles that consume their characters. Although this makes for compelling viewing as Alain and Laurence fight, or Alain and Christophe fuck, *Confusion of Genders* is weakest when it depicts Alain's courtship with Babette. The dynamic between these two characters is the most unbelievable—perhaps because it lacks real passion.

Wisely, writer-director Ilan Duran Cohen uses Babette to show how men fall under a woman's spell, and a scene in which she visits the lovesick Marc in prison is particularly intense. As Marc's desire for Babette is too fervid, Alain literally comes between them as the couple embrace, forming a bisexual trio. It is one of the more erotic moments in a film full of sexy scenes.

Nevertheless, *Confusion of Genders* is less about sex than it is about love. Alain's inability to choose whom he should be with is more frustrating for the characters than it is for the viewer. Audiences will enjoy watching Alain jump into bed with everyone he meets. In fact, this concept of a revolving bed is best illustrated in the film's opening segment, a back-and-forth conversation between Alain and his various male and female lovers.

Whereas Cohen may be satirizing a sexually compulsive man by presenting all of his foibles—"You're married, you're not. You're gay, you're not," one character says to Alain—at the same time, the film's shrewd ending leaves the subject open to debate. In essence, Alain may be a man who can't decide what he wants, but he is also one who refuses to let other people tell him.

In the lead role, the good-looking Pascal Greggory gives a fantastic performance, full of feeling, and he expresses his character's emotions, ranging from pleasure to indecision, beautifully. Greggory's performance energizes this fast-paced film—things sag a bit during the few moments he is not on screen—and he has an excellent rapport with his various costars.

Confusion of Genders may be risqué and cynical, but it is also dead on about relationships.

HIS SECRET LIFE

His Secret Life is a rich, rewarding Italian melodrama about a woman who discovers the hidden truth about her husband's seven-year-long affair with another man. Although this sounds like a story for the Lifetime channel—and the film kind of plays like an R-rated movie of the week, complete with pauses for commercial breaks—director Ferzan Ozpetek (*Steam: The Turkish Bath*, 1997) has crafted something quite beautiful and moving out of this sentimental tale.

Antonia (Margherita Buy) is a doctor who treats patients with HIV. When her husband Massimo is killed in a car accident, Antonia finds a note from Massimo's lover, and she becomes determined to track down his mistress. However, the recent widow soon discovers that the lover is in fact a man named Michele (Stefano Accorsi). Unable to handle this betrayal, Antonia retreats, but she soon returns to Michele in an effort to understand her husband's secret life. Suddenly, a mutual friendship blossoms between the two grieving people.

Most of Ozpetek's heartfelt film chronicles Antonia's interactions with both Michele and the extended "family" of Michele's friends. There is a genuine warmth to these scenes that invite not only Antonia, but also the audience, to get to know where and with whom Massimo spent his spare time. Although viewers may need a scorecard to keep track of all the characters, they include a butch Turkish woman, a transsexual, an AIDS patient, and a half dozen gay men—all of whom take a special interest in Antonia as a way of keeping Massimo alive.

Through these strangers, Antonia herself learns a few things about her late husband she never knew, and she also uncovers the secrets and desires of Michele and his friends. As she learns to relax and enjoy her new companions, Antonia soon starts keeping secrets of her own. Things get tense, however, when she finds herself falling in love with Michele.

Ozpetek deftly explores the power struggle between Antonia and Michele now that they are no longer fighting for Massimo's affection. When she spies Michele checking out another guy in the supermarket or kissing two men on a dance floor, Antonia becomes jealous and even acts petty. Similarly, Michele, who has often wondered about Massimo's wife and his "other" life, feels guilty because of Antonia's presence. Their conversations, which range from intimate and understanding to cruel and contemptuous are the film's highlights because they feature such honesty and intensity.

These raw emotions are expressed by the two leads, both of whom give excellent performances. Margherita Buy (who looks a bit like Meg Ryan) is wonderful as Antonia, and she provides tremendous depth to her role of a woman who is energized by her experiences and slowly rejects her ordinary life. Buy superbly handles her character's transformation, making it truly memorable. She can outact any of those Lifetime TV actresses.

Equally good is the sexy Stefano Accorsi. This outstanding actor, who recently appeared in *The Son's Room* (2001) and *The Last Kiss* (2001), is incredibly affecting in his portrayal of a bereft gay man, and Accorsi imbues Michele with the appropriate measure of sadness and hope.

Despite these strengths, the film does have a major flaw. Ozpetek bites off more than he can chew—and he deliberately avoids bringing closure to some of the subplots. This is extremely frustrating for viewers who become engaged with the colorful supporting characters and wants to know what happens to them.

Nevertheless, *His Secret Life* is a lovely, bittersweet film, and certainly one worth discovering.

SWIMMING POOL

François Ozon, the gay French writer-director, has excelled in crafting films that feature two (or more) characters in taut, erotically charged power struggles. While not overtly queer like most of his previous films, Ozon's latest drama, *Swimming Pool*, is a deliciously sinister character study, and one that is a fine companion piece to his other nongay film, *Under the Sand* (2000).

Like that drama, *Swimming Pool* stars the incredibly impressive and extremely expressive Charlotte Rampling. Delivering a mesmerizing performance here, Rampling is able to convey much of her uptight character's emotions simply with her mouth. As she eats, types, or even grocery shops, Rampling's expressions speak volumes. And when Rampling smiles—as she does when she first arrives in France, or later when she cuts loose dancing—the emotions are a particularly vivid. Her performance is superb.

The story concerns Sarah Morton (Rampling), a British crime novelist who is in a bit of a creative funk. When her publisher John (Charles Dance) offers her his house in France for rest and rejuvenation, Sarah agrees, and she soon begins to work on her next book. But when John's oversexed daughter Julie (Ludivine Sagnier) arrives, Sarah's peace and quiet is destroyed. Before long, however, there is a corpse, and suddenly Sarah is inspired to write.

The tension between Sarah and Julie, which forms the crux of this very fine film, slowly develops into something pretty extraordinary. Ozon suggests some rather interesting connections between these very different women, and his camera also makes some clever visual parallels. A slow pan across Julie's sunbathing body and up that of her lover is mirrored later in an important shot featuring Sarah. Likewise, the habits of these two characters, how they smoke, eat, drink, and sleep are captured with Ozon's unerring eye. These compositions go a long way in subtly providing information about these characters as well as their sexuality.

Of course, once Sarah is bewitched by the irritating Julie, *Swimming Pool* goes off into some rather deep but invigorating waters. As both women are transformed by their sudden association, their loyalty to each other is tested. When things get complicated, viewers will delight in deciding which one (if either) to trust—as both are not to be crossed—and plans may be afoot for revenge.

Part of what makes this thriller such fun is Sagnier's lusty performance as Julie. This French actress has a terrific command of English and she spits out her bitchy dialogue with tremendous relish. Furthermore, her naked or near-naked body is on almost constant display, teasing not only Sarah with her sexuality, but also the audience.

Furthermore, Ozon continues to prove himself a master filmmaker with his distinctive cinematic flair. Shrewdly using silence and sounds, the director seductively moves his camera around the actors to create an air of real menace. Ozon manages to create some great tension when things turn nasty, and yet he also tosses out a red herring (or two) to keep the audience's nerves jangled. Yet the film is so pleasurable, viewers will not feel manipulated, alas, until the very end.

Despite Ozon's extreme care in revealing—or concealing—information, it is a damn shame that *Swimming Pool* muddles its dénouement. Audiences no doubt will be expecting a twist—and there is one—but it is largely unsatisfying. It is as if he empties the pool while audiences are still enjoying the water.

But this is a minor flaw in what is largely an intriguing and captivating film. There are enough enticing elements to keep viewers actively engaged, and there is atmosphere to choke on. And of course, there is the remarkable Rampling.

Swimming Pool may not be Ozon's best film, but it is certainly another enjoyable one.

STRAYED

Gay filmmaker André Téchiné has a talent for finding emotional truth in relationships. He also excels at placing his seemingly ordinary characters in tough situations that force them to confront their fears. From his candid portrait of a queer teen coming to terms with his sexuality in *Wild Reeds* (1994) to siblings at odds with one another in *My Favorite Season* (1993), Téchiné's films bristle with psychological tension.

The French writer-director's latest film, *Strayed,* a beautifully realized historical drama about a widow and her two children during the war, is no exception. Using the German bombing of France as the backdrop for what is essentially a chamber drama played out at an abandoned country house, this outstanding film is deeply affecting right up to its tense conclusion.

Odile (Emmanuelle Béart) is on the run with her thirteen-year old son Philippe (Grégoire Leprince-Ringuet) and her younger, thumb-sucking daughter Cathy (Clémence Meyer). When German bombs destroy their car and they have nothing left—and nothing to lose—the family follows a mysterious and sexy seventeen-year-old, Yvan (Gaspard Ulliel), into the countryside. After spending a night under the stars, Philippe sees Yvan as their hope for survival, while Odile is wary of the stranger. The next day, Yvan finds a mansion nearby and the family agrees to establish a temporary household.

Once ensconced in the country home, Odile, Yvan, and the children start to reveal their true selves. The love and hate, trust and shame that were initially expressed all reverse and transform—culminating in a betrayal (of sorts), and it is this drama that unfolds that makes *Strayed* so compelling.

The central narrative revolves around the enigmatic Yvan, who is prone to fainting spells and often behaves strangely. Deliberately (and secretly) cutting the phone lines after entering the mansion, and heading out day and night to rob the dead of their guns and grenades, Yvan may have an unexplained agenda for hiding out. Yet Odile and her children who are seduced by his talents, not to mention his good looks, see him as their protector, and perhaps lover.

In fact, the burgeoning Philippe—who aspires to be an opera singer—follows Yvan around like a puppy dog, treating the young man like an older brother. Philippe obviously desires a more intimate relationship with Yvan, but Yvan, it appears, is obsessed with Odile.

Odile, however, tries to mask her desires, and she copes with her situation by cleaning the house and learning about the owners. Eventually, Odile must confront her pent-up frustrations.

As this love triangle unfolds, Téchiné milks every glance, every word, and every touch for maximum impact. Philippe's longing for Yvan comes to a head one afternoon, and this encounter perfectly encapsulates the safe/scared dichotomy each character is feeling.

Strayed builds inexorably to its final twist, never hitting a false note in the process. The film benefits tremendously from the masterful performance by the beautiful Emmanuelle Béart, who displays a full range of emotions in a single moment—as when her crying jag is interrupted by her curious daughter. In addition, scenes of Odile lying in a bathtub, contemplating her next move with Yvan and her children, are incredibly revealing.

Ulliel is equally impressive as Yvan. The actor has a magnetic screen presence, and like Béart, he is able to convey what is really going on in his complex character's mind simply through his expressive eyes.

Strayed contains all of the hallmarks of Téchiné's finest work, passion, sensitivity, and truth. It is another instant classic from the skillful queer filmmaker.

Chapter 10
Heartache

The films in this chapter depict various gay men in the throes of romantic despair. The heroes of *Luster* (2002), *The Rules of Attraction* (2002), *Lawless Heart* (2001), *Testosterone* (2003), *Love Forbidden* (2002), and *The Embalmer* (2002) all handle their heartache and unrequited love in different—and sometimes disturbing—ways. And of course, it is always fascinating to watch.

LUSTER

Low-key and ultra-low-budget, *Luster* is a sexy queer romance that features an ensemble cast of good-looking actors talking about life, love, and sex for ninety minutes.

This unassuming film, which takes place over the course of three days—and looks as if it was shot in as many—depicts the trials and tribulations of a blue-haired L.A. skaterboy poet named Jackson (Justin Herwick). Like the story's protagonist, writer-director Everett Lewis's film is appealing, but it is also somewhat rough around the edges.

As *Luster* opens, Jackson is having "one of those days." He suffers from writer's block with his poetry and has issues with customers asking for Madonna at the indie music store where he works. His love life is not much better. Jackson lusts after an unattainable stud named Billy (Jonah Blechman) and finds himself being pursued by Derek (Sean Thibodeau), a shy, good-looking young guy who appears entirely too wholesome for him.

Totally uninspired, Jackson's mood improves when he comes home to find Jed (b. Wyatt), his attractive cousin from Iowa, taking a

Independent Queer Cinema: Reviews and Interviews
© 2006 by The Haworth Press, Inc. All rights reserved.
doi:10.1300/5482_11   *147*

shower. Not only is Jackson thrilled by the unexpected appearance of this hunky visitor—his cousin likes to parade around the house in the nude—but the magnetic Jed also proves to be a valuable muse. Soon Jackson is writing tunes for his idol, musician Sonny Spike (Willie Garson) and struggling with the question, "Is it incest to fuck your cousin?"

Luster treats Jackson's romantic entanglements as seriocomic farce. While he mulls over his awkward feelings for Jed, Jackson gets involved in two other sticky situations. He helps Billy escape from a bad S&M scene, and learns that Derek fell in love with him at first sight. Although neither of these guys provide what Jackson thinks is a suitable alternative to his feelings for Jed, he gains some insight into the nature of gay relationships in the process of sorting things out.

Alas, the film is both amusing and disheartening as the self-absorbed Jackson make a series of bad emotional choices in the name of slacker angst. At least Herwick imbues Jackson with just enough goofy charm to be endearing. The film could have been unbearable had the lead actor not been so engaging.

Yet while *Luster* establishes Jackson as the protagonist, the film really provides a showcase for the talents of actor b. Wyatt. Even though Wyatt has the supporting role, he is easily the film's main attraction. His relaxed screen presence is captivating, and his enthusiasm is genuinely infectious.

He is also a very good sport. In one scene, Wyatt's hairy chest serves as a tablet for a writer to pen a review, and in another, his whole body provides a canvas for a photographer to make some pretty pictures. And in case those activities were not kinky enough, Jed also gets handcuffed—naked, of course—to a showerhead by Billy who calls him "the best fuck he's ever had."

Wisely, Wyatt takes all of this in stride. In fact, Wyatt appears to be Lewis's own inspiration as well. As this film is the actor's third collaboration with the director following *The Natural History of Parking Lots* (1990) and *Skin and Bone* (1996), perhaps *Luster* is truly art imitating life.

Whatever the case, this is an enjoyable film that is easy on the eyes, and not so rough on the brain, either.

THE RULES OF ATTRACTION

Writer-director Roger Avary's adaptation of Bret Easton Ellis's *The Rules of Attraction* has moments that are so good it is a shame the overall film is not better.

As in the book, the film opens (and ends) in midsentence. Avary introduces the three main characters, Lauren (Shannyn Sossamon), Sean (James Van Der Beek), and Paul (Ian Somerhalder), in a brilliant twenty-minute sequence that unfortunately can't be sustained.

In graphic detail, the film shows their joyless lives at Camden College (a fictional Bennington, Ellis's alma mater). Lauren has just lost her virginity to a vomiting townie while a visiting NYU film student videotapes it. The bisexual Paul gets kicked in the crotch when he makes a pass at a flirtatious straight boy. Sean, a self-described "emotional vampire," has to decide between going back to his room to play the guitar and surf for porn on the Internet or sleeping with a blonde girl he hardly knows.

As the plot unfolds, Avary assembles a series of vignettes that substitute for a proper narrative structure. Sean is a sleazy drug dealer who breaks other people's hearts unknowingly, while Lauren—the girl he thinks he loves—is unattainable. Lauren, for her part, is pining for Victor (Kip Pardue), although he never once thinks of her. Meanwhile, Paul pursues Sean—they even share a kiss—without ever realizing that not only is Sean straight, but he barely knows who Paul is.

Had the film concentrated just on these three main characters, *The Rules of Attraction* might have had some emotional heft. The unrequited love triangle is comprised of a trio of interesting people. But Avary (following Ellis's lead) hopscotches around a variety of supporting characters that distract from the central storyline and end up diluting the impact of the action.

Sometimes the gamble pays off, such as a fantastic monologue by Victor as he recounts his European adventures. There is also a fabulous, show-stopping sequence in which Paul and his friend Richard Jared (Russell Sams) lip-synch George Michael's "Faith" while dancing on a hotel room bed in their underwear.

Less successful is a darkly comic sequence in which Paul helps an overdosing friend to the hospital, which never quite amuses. There is also a suicide that stops the film cold—it simply takes too long to dramatize. These scenes are poorly paced and could have been done much more subtly.

And this is part of Avary's problem as a filmmaker. He has some wonderful stylistic touches, such as playing the film backward, or employing a split screen when two characters are approaching each other. But all too often he sabotages the film because he either goes too far or not far enough. The whole tone of the film is uneven.

The central performances, though, are right on the money. James Van Der Beek seems to enjoy behaving badly. He spits, farts, picks his nose, and masturbates throughout the film, single-handedly erasing any of his earnest Dawson Leery characteristics. Although his kiss with the gorgeous Ian Somerhalder is not quite as stunning as some viewers might hope, Van Der Beek deserves credit for taking the role and making it his own.

Even better is Shannyn Sossamon, who proves in this film that she really can act. Her Lauren is truly convincing and captivating throughout the drama. Lauren is perhaps the one character viewers will care about most, and it is because of Sossamon's strong portrayal that Lauren comes to life.

Rounding out the leads, Ian Somerhalder does not have nearly enough screen time, but he makes the most of it appearing mainly in his underwear—doing yoga, deciding what to wear on a date, or dancing on the bed with Richard. Somerhalder certainly plays the role of a gay young man on the prowl with the right charm and sorrow. Too bad he didn't have a larger part to sink his teeth into.

The supporting cast, however, is a mixed bunch. Jessica Biel is quite good as Lara, Lauren's coke-snorting roommate, Eric Stoltz amiably plays a college professor, and Kip Pardue is terrific as the scene-stealing Victor. But Clifton Collins Jr. overplays his role as a drug dealer Sean owes money, and Fred Savage has a bizarre bit as a stoned student. Even Faye Dunaway and Swoosie Kurtz have an uncomfortable scene at a hotel restaurant, and they look uncomfortable in it.

Ultimately, *The Rules of Attraction* is an interesting misfire. It is certainly provocative, but it never quite lives up to its potential.

LAWLESS HEART

The impact a gay man's death has on three very different men he knew forms the basis of *Lawless Heart,* a profound and deeply touching drama about misplaced feelings. Written and directed by Neil Hunter and Tom Hunsinger (*Boyfriends,* 1996), this melancholic British film unfolds as a triptych in which each of the three stories—told consecutively, but happening concurrently—ultimately link up and form a complete portrait at the film's end.

The first chapter concerns Dan (Bill Nighy), a married man who meets a French woman (Clémentine Célarié) at his brother-in-law Stuart's funeral. Their deep conversation—so achingly realistic, audiences will feel like they are evesdropping—stirs something in Dan, and he finds himself in an emotional quandry. His feeling are further complicated by the fact that his wife has the responsibility of handling Stuart's estate, and the idea of giving Stuart's lover his money agitates Dan's homophobia.

Stuart's boyfriend Nick (Tom Hollander) is the protagonist of the second, and perhaps most interesting, segment. Unable to find solace for his grief, Nick unexpectedly finds himself taking care of a motor-mouthed young woman named Charlie (Sukie Smith), who crashes in his flat during a party. Their unlikely friendship soon turns into a more complicated relationship—one that raises questions about Nick's love for Stuart.

The final episode involves Tim (Douglas Henshall), who was once Stuart's best friend, but has been away for nearly a decade. Stuart's passing has little impact on Tim's life, and he spends most of his time back home pursuing a young woman he fancies named Leah (Josephine Butler).

To be sure, the unusual narrative structure of *Lawless Heart* is a gimmick, but thankfully it is not overly distracting. While some members of the audience will content themselves looking for clues in the dovetailing storylines, savvier viewers will pay closer attention to the rich dialogue.

Hunter and Hunsinger wisely gave their characters private moments that are sometimes more revealing than any of the overlapping incidents that pepper the film. The most significant of these scenes takes place in a bar one night, when Nick's sudden arrival stifles Dan's impulse to act on his emotions. As the two men talk, Dan's impolite questions about faithfulness turn into a telling discussion about the courage to cheat or the consideration not to. The ideas expressed in this simple chat have repercussions in all three storylines.

Despite the talkiness of this bar scene or the fascinating discussion Dan has with the French woman at the funeral, these intimacies provide much of the film with its dramatic momentum. The utter realism of these scenes, or the casual ones shared by Nick and Charlie, are what makes the drama so penetrating.

Lawless Heart also succeeds because the directors deliberately had their gifted cinematographer, Sean Bobbitt, film each of the three segments with a different camera style. The decision pays off handsomely as the elegiac mood varies in each sequence and creates the appropriate atmosphere for each story.

In addition, the film features magnificent performances of the ensemble cast. Bill Nighy is absolutely mesmerizing as Dan, a man who thinks he might regret the life he has made for himself. Likewise, Tom Hollander is fantastic as the grieving Nick. The security Nick finds in caring for Charlie when he cannot care for himself is palpable, and Sukie Smith's winning performance helps cement their bond. But perhaps the best actor in the film is Douglas Henshall, who plays Tim. Henshall masterfully conveys his character's every emotion—and he goes through a wide range of them—with the simplest of facial expressions and body language. His performance is a tour de force.

And although some viewers might take umbrage with the storytelling, *Lawless Heart* is still a very shrewdly made and highly affecting drama.

TESTOSTERONE

Testosterone will probably be most notable—and seen—for the fleeting glimpse of Antonio Sabato Jr.'s naked penis, but there is much more to this nasty, twisted film than meets the eye. With the help of writer Dennis Hensley, writer-director David Moreton (of *Edge of Seventeen*, 1998, fame) has created a seductive, darkly comic thriller from James Robert Baker's book.

The opening credits depict the relationship between Dean (David Sutcliffe of TV's *Gilmore Girls*) and Pablo (Sabato Jr.) using panels from Dean's graphic novels. "It was love at first sight," the caption on the image reads, describing the "one-night stand that never left." Yet when the story opens, Dean is searching frantically for Pablo, who "went out for cigarettes and never came back." At an art gallery with his agent Louise (Jennifer Coolidge), Dean has an altercation with Pablo's mother (Sonia Braga), who says her son has returned home, to Buenos Aires.

Armed with this information, and considerable determination, Dean hops a plane to Argentina with a plan to get Pablo back—or at the very least, get some closure. What the heartbroken Dean encounters, however, is the stuff of *noir* nightmares. He is threatened by the police whenever he rings Pablo's doorbell; he befriends Sofia (Celina Font), a coffee shop waitress who may be more *femme fatale* than friend; and he also meets Marcos (the delectable Leonardo Brzezicki) an ex-lover of Pablo's who wants to seduce Dean himself.

As Dean navigates these obstacles in the path of his reunion with Pablo, he becomes angrier, more obsessed, and more persistent. Yet while most of the characters see Dean as a patsy—and fuck with him accordingly—when he finally has had enough and becomes seriously hellbent on revenge, the already complex story spins a bit out of control.

There are some delicious plot twists that should not be revealed, but once Dean gets a gun in his hand, he unleashes a series of unfortunate consequences that strain credibility. What should be a series of gleefully nasty episodes, however, are not particularly beguiling. Dean's character arc is supposed to be intriguing—he is pushed to the edge and starts to fight back—but the way things unfold defies logic. For example, Dean accidentally shoots someone, and the characters act as if almost nothing happened. What is more, the wicked ending of the story fails to provide a satisfying payoff. Viewers may yawn rather than cheer at the film's finale.

This is a shame, because *Testosterone* builds the sexual tension between the male characters extremely well. Dean's dalliances with Marcos are particularly erotic, even though the two men shed little of their clothes. In fact, Moreton's film, as sexy as it is, surprisingly contains only brief nudity. Significantly, the film's sex scenes do move the story along—telling much about the characters in the process—and making the heat between the various men so palpable.

And while Dean may be a stubborn, sarcastic bastard, David Sutcliffe makes the most of his meaty role. He does manage to make Dean sympathetic even while he is going off the deep end. If his co-star Antonio Sabato Jr. does not have much to do in the film, at least he looks good doing it.

Better yet are the supporting players. Celina Font and Leonardo Brzezicki are sure to be unfamiliar to American viewers, but they make great impressions in their enigmatic roles here. Likewise, Sonia Braga is fantastic as Pablo's mother, and of course, the always reliable Jennifer Coolidge is hilariously deadpan in her brief role as Louise. Coolidge's phone call with Dean contains what is easily one of the funniest film lines this year.

Testosterone is a wild ride. It may be a bit uneven, but it is not easily forgotten.

LOVE FORBIDDEN

Love Forbidden, written, directed by, and starring Rodolphe Marconi, is a gripping film about love, death, and romantic obsession. This provocative drama builds slowly toward its inexorable and excruciating climax—one that will no doubt leave audiences talking (if not gasping).

Bruce (Marconi) is a French filmmaking student who leaves Paris for the Villa Medici in Rome to study his craft and find inspiration. He spends his days making notes in his diary as well as smoking, eating, sleeping, and drinking in a nearby bar. Bruce is haunted by his past, which, as he slowly reveals, includes an ex-girlfriend and a brother who recently died. He is trying to forge a new life in Italy, and when Bruce meets Matteo (Andrea Necci), his spirits unexpectedly begin to rise.

A hunky intern at the Villa, Matteo studies philosophy and wants to be a writer. Matteo bonds instantly with Bruce over cigarettes and small talk, and the Italian soon finds comfort in the French man's apartment.

In fact, Matteo is so relaxed in Bruce's presence, and in his home, that he invites himself to spend the night. Although the two young men share the same bed, nothing untoward happens. Matteo sleeps soundly, but Bruce watches over his new friend and quickly becomes enamored with him.

What begins as a platonic friendship, however, becomes something much more intense. After their first few encounters, Bruce starts having fantasies about talking to Matteo and kissing him—even though he is not around. Furthermore, Bruce takes to spying on his (boy)friend, even stalking him at night. He is simply waiting to seduce his beloved.

Although Matteo does succumb to Bruce's desires, he admits beforehand that he does not share Bruce's feelings. And despite an artfully filmed sex scene—in which the characters' passions are beautifully conveyed through images of skin against skin—their relationship is headed for trouble. It arises in a way that should not be revealed.

That said, the film's third act introduces the character of Aston (Echo Danon), a New York writer who becomes romantically involved with Matteo—and unbeknownst to her lover, befriends Bruce as well. This romantic triangle quickly turns into a sinister psychodrama, and one that yields the film's shocking finale. The ending will certainly trouble some viewers, but Marconi does make his point clearly and effectively.

Yet despite the film's deliberate pace and somewhat uneven tone, *Love Forbidden* excels at keeping the sexual tension between Bruce and Matteo palpable throughout its ninety-plus minutes. The body language between the two men—from the touch of a shoulder to the lighting of a cigarette—is filled with hidden depths. So too are the silences and glances between them. Marconi directs the film with such precision that viewers will be scanning every frame for additional layers of meaning.

One of the visual clues the filmmaker provides are the various statues, sculptures, and artwork whose expressions quietly comment on the character's emotions. The film's crisp images suggest several possible identifications, and the performances by the two leads are suitably ambiguous. Marconi—who took the role when his original actor dropped out—is well matched to Necci, and their rapport is wholly credible. Each actor has a speech or two that reveals much about their characters, but they are much more haunting as actors when they gaze off silently into the distance.

Unfortunately, as talented as the men in the cast are, Echo Danon is awkward and awful in her pivotal role as Aston.

Love Forbidden may be a disturbing, unsettling romance, but it is certainly a worthwhile one. This engaging film is challenging and also highly rewarding.

THE EMBALMER

The Italian film *The Embalmer* is both a hypnotic character study and a sly psychological thriller. It is also a complex and highly unusual love story.

The title character, Peppino (Ernesto Mahieux), is a fifty-year-old dwarf who befriends the gorgeous Valerio (Valerio Foglia Manzillo) at the zoo one afternoon. Secretly in love with this tall young man, Peppino begins his slow, steady seduction of Valerio by offering him a better-paying job doing taxidermy work. Valerio graciously accepts, and he soon asks to move in with Peppino to escape tensions at home.

Before long, this odd couple are spending every day and night together, and Peppino starts initiating some casual physical contact with Valerio. With the touch of an arm here and a brief caress there, Peppino thinly masks his much stronger desire for his companion. This point is driven home when the two men end up in bed together (along with a pair of ladies) and Peppino is resting on Valerio's smooth, bare chest.

Valerio, however, becomes sexually involved with Deborah (Elisabetta Rocchetti), a lost young woman he meets one afternoon. Deborah's presence drives a wedge between the two male friends, and a fierce power struggle for Valerio's affection begins. Needless to say, the story does not end happily.

The Embalmer uses its mismatched romantic triangle to comment on the pain of jealousy and unrequited love. Peppino is a misfit—he wears loud clothes and has ties to the mafia—but the fact that his dream of being with someone like Valerio is realized even briefly makes him fight harder to prolong it. Although Deborah catches on quickly to Peppino's game, she finds it difficult to maintain complete control over her man. In perhaps the film's creepiest scene, Peppino lures Valerio away from Deborah and gets him drunk so that he can undress him under false pretenses.

Either Valerio is either incredibly naive or he is happy to be a pawn for those who love him. It is to the credit of director and cowriter Matteo Garrone that the film remains largely ambiguous (and even slightly frustrating) on this critical issue. Why Peppino has such command over Valerio is one of the film's more engaging mysteries.

The Embalmer, which is beautifully shot in a realist style, is a haunting film. The idea of preserving something that is loved—be it an animal or a relationship—is the overriding theme, and Garrone keeps the tension mounting right up to the film's shocking finale. As the lovelorn characters get more and more manipulative—each trying to outdo the other for Valerio's love—the sense of doom becomes stronger.

Unfortunately, the ending, which makes perfect sense, is a little unsatisfying. It should be noted, however, that it does not involve any taxidermy.

The performances in the film are top-notch. In the central role, Ernesto Mahieux creates a man who is so unhappy with his life that he will risk anything to improve it. Mahieux imbues Peppino with a sweaty desperation that is devastating. As the object of his desire, the incredibly good-looking Valerio Foglia Manzillo proves himself to be an accomplished performer as well. Manzillo uses clever body language to give his character depth, and scenes of the two men walking together provide an amusing visual. In support, Elisabetta Rocchetti projects intelligence and craftiness that serve her unlikable character well.

Although *The Embalmer* falls just shy of being unforgettable, it is a stylish and strange film nonetheless.

Chapter 11
Such a Drag

The films in this chapter all showcase transgender characters, in different genres and, alas, with mixed results. *Transfixed* (2001) is a tense thriller, while *Gaudi Afternoon* (2001) is a lesser comic one. *Girls Will Be Girls* (2003) stars gay men playing women, but the documentary *Venus Boyz* (2002) features lesbians posing as men. Then there is *All the Queen's Men* (2001), which features transvestite performer Eddie Izzard teaching straight men how to dress and pass as women.

TRANSFIXED

The hypnotic Belgian film *Transfixed* is notable not just for featuring a transgendered heroine named Bo (Robinson Stévenin) but also for being an above-average thriller. Director Francis Girod takes all of the standard crime conventions—a serial killer, red herrings, and obsessive love—and turns them on their head to create an absorbing story.

"People have their secrets," says one character, and this line is particularly apt, as no one is quite sure who or what they seem to be. In fact, the filmmaker's dark humor suggests that Bo is the most well-adjusted character.

Transfixed opens with Bo's father being carried off by the police after being charged with molesting young boys and a detective, Paul Huysmans (Richard Bohringer), pressing Bo to testify in the case. Bo is uncomfortable drudging up painful childhood memories, but since Bo is also a suspect in the murders of her transsexual prostitute friends, she cooperates with the cops.

Bo also encounters trouble in the form of her sexy neighbor Johnny (Stéphane Metzger), who is attracted to Bo—note his erection when he waits on her at a restaurant—but he hates her for turning him on. Bo, however, is smitten, and will go to great lengths for her man, even if this means accepting abuse from him. Their unique "romance"—if that's what it can be called—is charged with erotic tension, and just one of the provocative elements in this audacious story.

The mystery element of *Transfixed* does not disappoint either. The film contains a few sequences—such as one in which Bo breaks into a friend's apartment—that generate real suspense. And even though astute viewers may identify the killer early on, knowing "whodunnit" does not detract from the suspense.

What is more, the victims are all endearing characters, making the impact of their deaths on Bo more affecting. It should be noted that the body count in *Transfixed* is quite high, and there is considerable bloodshed.

If the film has a flaw, it is that the story does get a bit far-fetched toward the end. There is more than enough plot in the film—probably too much—and perhaps in an effort to wrap things up neatly, are a few coincidences simply strain credibility.

What is noteworthy, though, is the struggle of Bo's character to be seen as a woman, not as a transsexual. The film wisely portrays Bo's efforts to live a normal life, and though she continually shows up at the wrong place at the wrong time to discover a dead (or nearly dead) body, she almost always maintains her dignity. This makes her scaling walls and rooftops in the name of justice not only ironic but also exciting. Bo is a terrific detective, and the film crackles as she pieces together the clues.

Of course, the film's success belongs to actor Robinson Stévenin, who gives a miraculous performance as the haunted Bo. Stévenin had a brief but memorable part in *Son frère (His Brother)* (2003), and *Transfixed* shows that he has the talent to carry a feature-length film. Bo is attractive, determined, vulnerable, and confused—often in the same scene—and Stévenin is riveting in the role. He is well matched by Stéphane Metzgar, whose brooding good looks and attitude are completely captivating. Like Stévenin, Metzgar displays a star quality here.

In support, the great French character actor Richard Bohringer (*Diva*, 1981) nicely underplays his role as a seen-it-all cop who may have met his match in Bo. Bohringer's performance may look effortless, but it is masterfully subtle. The transgender actors also deserve special credit for bringing dimension to what are usually stereotypical characters.

And this is precisely what makes *Transfixed* so, well, transfixing. The film cares about its characters and treats them—and the audience—intelligently. It makes this extraordinary film even more exceptional.

GAUDI AFTERNOON

Judy Davis, Marcia Gay Harden, Juliette Lewis, and Lili Taylor—you can't find a more mannered cast of actresses. To put them all in the same film is extremely volatile. Making them all lesbians is like mixing highly combustible chemicals. However, Susan Seidelman's film *Gaudi Afternoon* is not only a playful adaptation of Barbara Wilson's lesbian-themed novel, but it also gives each of these fine actresses a choice role to play.

Davis stars as Cassandra Reilly, an American translator of Latin American fiction currently living in Barcelona. Cassandra just quit smoking—there is a running gag about everyone offering her a cigarette—and she is struggling with both her work and her rent. Enter Frankie Stevens (Harden), a mysterious stranger claiming to be "a friend of a friend" who offers her a large sum of money to locate her ex. Of course, there is more to this arrangement than meets the eye, and to say any more would spoil some of *Gaudi Afternoon*'s delicious surprises.

Suffice it to say, Cassandra soon becomes involved with a bisexual magician (Christopher Bowen), a tough butch dyke (Taylor), and a hippie named April Schauer (Lewis), all of whom rock her world.

Gaudi Afternoon has considerable fun chronicling the comings and goings of all of these wacky people and the weird events that befall them. As a custody battle erupts between two of the characters, Cassandra finds herself not only befuddled by the domestic arrangements but also questioning her own sexuality. Moreover, Cassandra also reconsiders her own maternal instincts, something she has repressed for years.

Seidelman, who scored a hit with *Desperately Seeking Susan* (1985) two decades ago, whips up a frothy film here, and once again is dealing with issues of mistaken identity and magical realism. And while it is good to see this gifted filmmaker at work, *Gaudi Afternoon* is not quite as fresh or as funky as her previous triumph.

Although the film gets off to a fine start, things get sluggish in the final act, when the mystery overtakes the characters and plot holes overtake the plot. Seidelman just does not seem to be able to keep the momentum going. There is an excellent set piece early on in the magician's lair—where Bowen does a show-stopping lip-synch routine—but then there are numerous chases sequences and reversals that are more tiring than thrilling.

Wisely, Seidelman makes excellent use of the city of Barcelona and the architecture of Antoni Gaudi, which is suitable backdrop for the zany story.

And *Gaudi Afternoon* does manage to mine some considerable humor from its wacky characters. Judy Davis is as good as always as Cassandra. Her expressions of despair and disbelief (sometimes both at once) are priceless, and Davis also makes effective use of her body language in this very active role.

But the film is stolen by Marcia Gay Harden's gaudy performance as Frankie, an absolutely hilarious creation. Quick with a witty retort, and stunning in her vivid outfits—she wears red especially well—Frankie is the film's highlight, and the Oscar-winning Harden proves that she is no flash in the pan.

Fortunately, the film is not lacking for colorful characters. When Frankie is off screen, Lewis's April Schauer injects some life into the proceedings. Even if April is a caricature of New Agey types—didn't they go out of style years ago?—and the humor is a bit forced, Lewis manages to be very amusing.

Rounding out the cast is Lili Taylor, who does her best with the weakest written role. Taylor has some very good scenes, just too few of them.

Ultimately, it is the performances that make *Gaudi Afternoon* more than just a passable time filler. As Cassandra discovers that nothing is what it seems, audiences, too, will enjoy unraveling the mysteries of this strange quartet of females.

GIRLS WILL BE GIRLS

Guys play the girls in the drag-queen comedy *Girls Will Be Girls*. Written and directed by Richard Day, this very funny low-budget film about a trio of female roommates contains laughs aplenty. From the hilarious bloodcurdling shriek of profanity that opens the film, to the madcap "special-mercial" that concludes it, there is plenty of campy humor to amuse almost everyone.

Evie (Jack Plotnick) is an aging, alcoholic B-movie starlet—her career high was a 1970s disaster film called *Asteroid*—who shares an apartment with the long-suffering Coco Peru (Clinton Leupp). When Varla Simonds (Jeffery Roberson) arrives one afternoon to live in the spare room, each woman tries to regain her self-respect.

For Coco, who longs to reunite with the handsome abortion doctor she once silently loved, she must first overcome such barriers as her chronic flatulence. For Varla, who follows in her dead mother's footsteps to becoming an actress/singing sensation, it is her constant binging. And for Evie, a selfish, martini-fueled legend in her own mind, it is just about everything. Hell, Evie's "falsies" include not only her breasts, but also her hair, teeth, and an eyeball.

Girls Will Be Girls unfolds episodically in little vignettes. The main plot has Evie—described by one character as "a walking ball of ambition"—crushing everyone and everything in her path on her way (back) to the top.

When Varla the newcomer goes off in search of a glamorous movie career and finds herself attracted to Stevie (Ron Mathews), Evie's incredibly handsome son, Evie tries to put an end to the affair. Mom actually takes pleasure in pointing out the fact that her son Stevie has a very, very, very tiny penis. (It makes a great sight gag during the film's sex scene.) And, seriously, with the bitchy Evie as a mother-in-law, does love have a chance?

Meanwhile, Coco has troubles of her own. Recovering from a car accident (Evie, of course, was driving drunk), Coco is drugged and raped by her doctor. However, the couple eventually discover they share a common bond. Yet with sexpot Evie as a roommate, can their relationship last?

Day infuses each of these storylines with achingly funny zingers as well as fabulous hair, costumes, and sets.

However, *Girls Will Be Girls* eventually aims more for crass than class. There is a droll comic bit with a character who has "visible" body odor, and a running joke about a series of dead dogs, but some viewers may find themselves unamused by the onslaught of gross gags.

What is more, the film's big finale, a routine titled *All About Evie,* is not nearly as enjoyable a train wreck as the brief clips from her role in *Asteroid.* Like the character, the film seems to be struggling quite a bit by this late stage. Perhaps this is because Day had to tie up all the loose plot strands quickly. Alas, even with a trio of men playing women for eighty minutes, *Girls Will Be Girls* starts to drag just before the big finish.

Nevertheless, the male actors give *Girls* their all. Jack Plotnick, who executive produced, certainly gets the best lines, and his perfectly timed delivery makes them all priceless. Clinton Leupp, who is probably the most recognizable member of the cast, steals the show as Coco. Leupp is so good, he can get a laugh just by rolling his eyes. And the sublime Jeffery Roberson displays considerable talent, as Varla especially when she sings and sucks down a large quantity of "shaving cheese" at the same time.

Sure, *Girls Will Be Girls* is silly, even stupid at times, but for the most part, it is great fun.

VENUS BOYZ

The inspiring documentary *Venus Boyz* explores the realm of drag kings—women who dress up and perform as men. As director Gabriel

Baur's film vividly illustrates, there is a certain amount of camp and parody to this form of gender-bending which originated at the Club Casanova in New York in 1996. However, the half dozen women profiled here claim that they don male apparel simply because there is just something (more) empowering about being a man.

This rationale suggests that many of these women are self-hating, and one woman admits that she was unhappy growing up because she was unpopular as a girl. This idea may actually be one of the keys to the drag king culture. Each of the interview subjects talk about how much more "credibility" they have in society posing as men—for they claim that they are not judged by their age or appearance when they walk into a room as a man, but they are when they are women. What is more, these drag kings are adamant about not only never wanting to put on a dress, but they describe the erotic pleasures of wearing a pin-striped suit.

In contrast, although one drag king says that she is "happy with the genitals she has," and another claims that she does not want to change being a woman, there is an amusing scene of a female using a prosthestic penis to pee standing up. Other sequences involve women constructing a fake penis, taping down their breasts, or adding facial hair to create the illusion of masculinity. These scenes are insightful to watch because they help viewers understand the amount of time and energy involved in the process of female-to-male transformation.

Yet the performances by the various drag kings really showcase the women's talents. From Mo B. Dick to Storme Webber, the acts are the film's highlight. Watching these women's alter egos truly reveals what it means for them to negotiate their sexuality in this particular fashion. Perhaps the most amazing scene involves Dréd Gerestant and her drag queen friend heading out into Times Square and asking strangers about their thoughts about male and female sexuality. This episode really captures people's ideas about gender and the stereotypes surrounding masculinity and femininity.

Venus Boyz features a handful of interesting females, but the most fascinating subject among them is Diane Torr, the self-described "Daddy Drag King." Torr is a leader in the movement, and she runs workshops to help women find their masculine selves. She talks with an Argentine woman about how masculinity is perceived in her culture, as a way of getting to the root of being a man. Torr works very hard at constructing her characters, such as Jack Sprat, who are composites of the men she knows and meets, and she is quite good at it. Baur also shows how Torr develops her confidence through Akido, or by simply living as a man. A brief discussion of her personal life explains the complexity of Torr's sexuality. While she had a daughter with a guy she met in Amsterdam, Torr also began a relationship with a woman named Jane. Unfortunately, as she explains, being a mother, lover, and man strained her affair with Jane and they split up.

Such confusion seems to be commonplace. As Mo B. Dick (aka Mo Fischer) says at one point, "My inner man overtook my inner woman." To correct this, Mo poses as a half-man/half-woman, and the result is a stunning photograph.

Venus Boyz clearly addresses "female masculinity," and the discussions of the butch/femme dichotomy are useful for understanding these women. Although there is considerable overlap in the message, it still is a provocative topic. Baur's film is most notable for the way it explores these women's self-image and their expression of sexuality.

ALL THE QUEEN'S MEN

All The Queen's Men is a goofy little movie about the "poof platoons"— men who dressed as women to infiltrate enemy lines during World War II. Although this ramshackle action-comedy is about as subtle as a tank, it offers a few smiles amid all the buffoonery.

Matt LeBlanc stars as the dashing Steven O'Rourke, a Yank in the OSS who never finishes a mission. While in prison for assaulting an officer, O'Rourke is asked by Colonel Aitken (Edward Fox) to lead a crew of men into Berlin to capture an enigma machine. The team, however, consists of misfits—Archie (James Cosmo), an aging pencil pusher, Johnno (David Birkin), a sensitive code breaker, and Tony (Eddie Izzard), a transvestite chanteuse—and the catch is that they *all* have to go undercover in drag.

Whereas Tony instructs the guys to be feminine and act delicate, O'Rourke must teach the "poof platoon" how to use weapons and protect themselves. Needless to say, these inexperienced men are not very convincing women, and they are even less successful as soldiers.

All The Queen's Men has fun mixing genres, but the results do not always mesh together well. Whereas the group's mission quickly goes awry, so too does the film. Director Stefan Ruzowitzky seems unable to decide if it wants to concentrate on comedy or action, and he does both, sloppily. There is never enough dramatic tension during the action sequences or sufficient laughs in the comic moments to make the film memorable.

That said, LeBlanc looks quite fetching in a dress, and he carries the flimsy material well. It is diverting to see him prancing around with an enigma machine under his skirt, or slap a German officer who grabs his ass. However, his requisite flirting with Romy (Nicolette Krebitz), the team's resistance contact, is a bit contrived.

What is more, the film is so broadly played (pun intended) that when Romy and O'Rourke are invited to a party given by General Landssdorf (Udo Kier), a high-ranking German official who may have critical information pertaining to the mission, the plotting gets obvious. It is no surprise that Landssdorf is going to find O'Rourke more attractive than the sultry Romy, or that the pass the general makes at O'Rourke will be answered with a punch. Nor is it particularly funny.

Perhaps the best scenes in *All The Queen's Men* are Eddie Izzard's exuberant musical numbers. Izzard is wholly captivating as he sings Marlene Dietrich or performs a cabaret show for German soldiers and officers. The film really comes alive whenever he is on-screen. Moreover, his attempt to explain his complex sexuality after reuniting with both his long-lost love Franz (Oliver Korittke) *and* his ex-wife Paloma (Sissi Perlinger) generates the film's best line, that Tony is a "bisexual lesbian in a man's body."

Unfortunately, the other supporting characters are less engaging. Running gags about Johnno's weak bladder getting the attention of the Germans—he often relieves himself in an unladylike manner—or Archie being in charge, but always kept from the action, never really amuse. This is not only a function of their characters not being fully developed, but also because they are upstaged by the other performers.

However, both David Birkin and James Cosmo acquit themselves nicely in their roles.

Ultimately, *All The Queen's Men* is cheerfully dumb, with the emphasis on dumb. It plays like a cheesy TV movie—and it is about as deep—but the movie certainly has its charms, most of which are provided by the game LeBlanc and the always wonderful Izzard. Too bad they didn't have a better vehicle than this tank.

Chapter 12
Bad Taste

Although both *Talk to Her* (2002) and *De-Lovely* (2004) have their admirers, I am not one of them. These films disappoint me, because they, respectively, push sexuality too far and not far enough. Meanwhile the little-seen *Ordinary Sinner* (2001), *Straight-Jacket* (2004), and *Love in the Time of Money* (2002) are bland films—both in content and in style.

TALK TO HER

Acclaimed Spanish director Pedro Almodóvar has had an interesting and varied career in his two decades plus of filmmaking. His early, outrageous movies, *Labyrinth of Passion* (1982), *What Have I Done to Deserve This?!* (1984), and *Law of Desire* (1987), drew hoards of gay fans with their cheeky, anarchic humor. He then pushed buttons—and the level of taste—with the scandalous *Tie Me Up! Tie Me Down!* (1990) and *Kika* (1993). And somehow, not quite overnight, Almodóvar matured and made the serious (and seriously overrated) Oscar winner *All About My Mother* (1999).

Almodovar is still in his thoughtful phase with his fourteenth feature film, *Talk to Her*, but there are moments of outrageousness—one moment in particular—that shows that the bad boy still comes out to play. The sequence in question cannot be divulged, but it must be said that Almodóvar has answered the censors who persecuted him over the rating for *Tie Me Up! Tie Me Down!* What is more, he has crafted an episode that should cause Woody Allen fits of envy.

Independent Queer Cinema: Reviews and Interviews
© 2006 by The Haworth Press, Inc. All rights reserved.
doi:10.1300/5482_13

Despite the over-the-top nature of this single vignette, the rest of *Talk to Her* is slow-going melodrama that may not raise much emotion in viewers. The convoluted story, which concerns two men, two women, and their relationships with one another, is multilayered but surprisingly unsatisfying.

Benigno (Javier Cámara) is a male nurse who cares daily for Alicia (Leonor Watling), a dancer he loves even though she has been in a coma for four years. This one-sided romance is paralleled with Marco (Darío Grandinetti), a travel writer, who falls in love with Lydia (Rosario Flores), a female bullfighter, who wants to get back at her ex. When Lydia is gored one day, she falls into a coma and is treated at the same clinic as Alicia. In the course of caring for their women, the two men meet and become close friends. It is this friendship that eventually becomes the focus of the film.

Almodóvar flips back and forth through time to tell these interlocking stories in an unusual way. (He even includes a flashback in a dream sequence.) However, this sophisticated narrative strategy dilutes rather than enhances the emotional pull of the story. When a major plot twist is subtly revealed halfway through the film, it is clever but ultimately frustrating because the viewer's sympathy is irrevocably shifted as the story goes off in a new and unexpected direction.

For viewers who choose to follow Almodóvar out there—and it is out there—they will be delighted by the director's inventiveness. For everyone else, the turn of events will wear on their benevolence.

What can be said in praise of this lukewarm film is that Almodóvar pays continuous tribute to the arts, featuring lengthy segments of music, theater, film, ballet, and bullfighting all within the same two-hour period.

Talk to Her also showcases excellent performances from the four principal actors, with Javier Cámara and Darío Grandinetti standouts as the male leads. These actors are at their best when they play against each other. They are also given strong support from Leonor Watling as the mostly comatose Alicia, Rosario Flores as the butch but femme bullfighter, and Geraldine Chaplin who appears briefly as Alicia's ballet teacher.

And like all of Almodóvar's films, *Talk to Her* is incredibly stylish, with beautiful sequences of Lydia dressing for her bullfight, or Alicia lying motionless under a bed sheet as it is being changed. While he may be playing with narrative, Almodóvar has not lost his eye for composition. Many scenes use vivid, vibrant color—red especially—to emphasize the intensity or emotion of the scene. If nothing else, this film looks dazzling.

Yet despite Almodóvar's competence, his film is really about taking chances, as he does with that one, curious sequence. Similarly, all of the characters take chances—in love, in the arena, in life—and as the story shows, they do not always pay off. The same lesson applies to viewers who take a chance on *Talk to Her*.

DE-LOVELY

A biopic of Cole Porter, *De-Lovely* presents the composer's life in the context of his music. It is a heavy three-act drama, filled with song and dance, as well as gay and straight romance—and it is a bit of a mess. Despite the noblest intentions to do justice to a fascinating, larger-than-life subject, director Irwin Winkler's film is surprisingly stifled and restrained.

Kevin Kline stars as the pleasure-seeking musician and lyricist, and the actor is perfectly cast. Kline has both the charisma and the pipes to play Cole, and his performance—even at its hammiest—keeps the film from being a total failure. The same, however, can not be said about Ashley Judd who costars as Porter's wife and muse, Linda Lee. Judd is noticeably stiff in her critical role, and while she looks smart in the film's vintage costumes, she is absolutely without appeal.

De-Lovely opens with an aged Porter sitting in a theater watching the story of his life as staged by Gabe (Jonathan Pryce). Perhaps this creaky narrative device is better suited to the theater, as it fails to work in this film. *De-Lovely* stages scenes of Porter's life in Paris, New York, and Hollywood, and the shifts back and forth to Porter watching and reacting to them. He smiles, he cringes, and he cries as the action unfolds. If only audiences watching the film smiled more and cringed less.

The story begins when Porter meets Linda at a party. He sings a song, they share some witty repartee, and they proceed to fall in love. Yet Porter leads a double life, bedding a series of beautiful men on the side. He eventually talks with Linda about his queer dalliances, and she claims to understand.

Yet every time Cole spends the night with a man, Linda sulks, and although his gay affairs are discreetly presented—a kiss here, a hug there—the film is less about his (homo)sexuality than it is his love for Linda. In fact, *De-Lovely* goes to great pains to show that most of Porter's love songs were inspired by his wife, whom he never loved enough or fairly. This may be a valid point, hit home early and often, but it comes across as being rather disingenuous. Even when Linda suggests her male decorator is a suitable companion for Porter, the relationship between the two men is glossed over.

De-Lovely could be forgiven for the poor depiction of Porter's sexuality if the show-stopping numbers had some pizzazz, but most of the musical sequences are joyless. Even with popular singers like Natalie Cole, Elvis Costello, and Sheryl Crow performing Porter's tunes, they seem canned.

There are a few exceptions. Kline's early, spirited rendition of "Did You Evah?" shows the promise the film has as a concept, which is to give meaning to Porter's lyrics. Likewise, Alanis Morissette's version of "Let's Do It (Let's Fall in Love)" is also very captivating; it has the energy the film's production of "Be a Clown" sorely lacks. The other knockout is a duet of "Night and Day," sung by Kline and an actor (John Barrowman) as part of a rehearsal for *Gay Divorce*. This sequence, which evolves into the actual theater production, is one of the film's highlights, and not just because Porter goes off into the night with the handsome actor after the show.

And perhaps this is the greatest shame of *De-Lovely*. When the film works, it can be thrilling, but more often than not, it falls flat. The fault lies squarely on Winkler's shoulders, as it appears his ambitions seem to have exceeded his talent. The director uses a variety of techniques and devices—films, stylized sets, and Porter's original music—to bring its subject to life, but *De-Lovely* just never catches fire. A simple case of this is that the costumes are terrific, but the old age makeup is terrible. Everything is uneven.

As a music tapestry, the whole production barely hangs together. *De-Lovely* is not the top, but it is not the bottom, either. It is stuck somewhere in between.

ORDINARY SINNER

The road to hell is paved with good intentions, and the well-intentioned drama *Ordinary Sinner* is, in fact, quite hellish. This extremely slow-paced film about hate crimes and gay bashing is as competent in teaching tolerance as an After-School Special—albeit one spiced up with copious uses of the F word and a brief bare ass—and about as effective.

Peter Thompson (Brendan P. Hines) is an ex-seminarian spending his summer at Pemberwick, a Vermont college. Peter, it seems, has lost his faith in God, because a skinhead boy he was counseling committed a murder. Haunted by this situation, Peter surrounds himself with friendly faces—his boyhood pal Alex (Kris Park) and Father Ed (A. Martinez), his high school priest. As he slowly readjusts to life away from the seminary, Peter is quickly seduced by Rachel (Elizabeth Banks), one of Alex's friends, and encounters a righteous Christian named Ogden (Jesse Tyler Ferguson) who follows the Bible with fervor.

All of these characters play important roles in the drama that eventually unfolds—the murder of Father Ed. After the priest announces his homosexuality to his parish one Sunday during sermon, Father Ed is killed in a local swimming quarry. In what has to be one of the most unusual murder schemes in the history of movies, it appears that someone intentionally positioned rocks into the quarry's diving area to cause Father Ed grievous bodily harm, and prevent him from interfering in his plans.

Was Father Ed killed because of his excessive pride—he sunbathed shirtless—or was it because he was queer? Actually, the answer is much more unsatisfying, and rather insulting to gays.

As a subplot to this singularly uninvolving mystery, Pemberwick is also being papered with antihomosexual flyers. Could these actions be the work of the same evildoer? Peter and his friends take it upon themselves to investigate and ferret out the killer. (Now, if these meddling kids only had a talking dog . . .)

One of the many problems with *Ordinary Sinner* is that the film takes entirely too long to get to the crime, and once it does, the resolution is hurried. Director John Henry Davis makes everything look nice—there are pretty small-town images accompanied by pretty music and pretty people—but the film lacks an overall style. The drama is padded by all the beautiful images. There is no tension in the mystery, no passion in the romance. The closest the film gets to being interesting is when Peter and Rachel move in for a kiss, and Alex tries to force a threesome.

Despite the important subject matter, nothing concrete is discussed in any depth or argued vigorously in any way. Even when Ogden quotes Leviticus 20:13 in church after Father Ed comes out, the emotions are lackluster

In the lead role, the blandly handsome Brendan P. Hines does his best with lines like "I tried running away once . . ." but nothing emphasizes a cliché more than earnestness. His solemnity is painful, and he gets only adequate support from the perky Elizabeth Banks and the lifeless Kris Park.

Equally underwritten are both A. Martinez and Peter Onorati, who plays his lover, Mike. Like the rest of the characters in this colorless film, they fail to earn any sympathy. Yet Martinez and Onorati are also unconvincing as a queer couple; they seem more like just good friends than life partners. Perhaps the only performance worth noting is Joshua Harto's brief turn as the skinhead.

Whereas *Ordinary Sinner* tries to be a sensitive meditation on crimes against gays, in reality it is just an insensitive film. That is perhaps its greatest sin.

STRAIGHT-JACKET

The phlegmatic *Straight-Jacket* tries to milk humor and social commentary from the premise of having a vain, promiscuous, gay actor in

1950s Hollywood fall in love with the man of his dreams while posing as straight to save his career. While the irony is deliberate, what should be a clever and amusing film about sexuality and the evils of conformity is, in fact, a didactic lesson about morality and being true to one's self. Written and directed by Richard Day, who also penned the play the film is based on, *Straight-Jacket* is a good idea sabotaged by lame jokes, bad pacing, and less-than-stellar performances.

Guy Stone (Matt Letscher) is a hunk who loves men for one night (if that long) and himself most of all. His fast-talking agent Jerry (Veronica Cartwright) always finds a silver lining to whatever trouble Guy gets into, but she is seriously challenged when rival actor Freddie (Jack Plotnick) photographs Guy stepping out of a gay bar.

To quell the press and quash the rumor mill—as well as to keep his contract—Guy agrees to marry Sally (Carrie Preston), the lovestruck secretary to SRO studio mogul Saul (Victor Raider-Wexler). The catch is that Sally is not aware that Guy is gay.

When *Straight-Jacket* attempts to have fun at Guy's expense—chronicling his horrified reactions to Sally's bad decorating schemes, cooking, and efforts to make love to him—hilarity does not ensue. The film is played so broadly that the only real laughs are generated by Guy's trusted queer valet, Victor (Michael Emerson), who frequently cracks wise.

There is some dramatic relief when Rick (Adam Greer) shows up as a novelist who is rewriting the script for Guy's latest film. Guy is instantly smitten with the screenwriter, but Rick is conflicted about bedding the star and "selling out" to Hollywood. Although Rick's earnestness is refreshing, it is hard to believe the men's romance because of the lack of chemistry between these attractive opposites.

Furthermore, *Straight-Jacket* uses the romance to pursue issues far greater and as far-reaching as gay bashing and the practice of naming names in the Communist era. These and a few other plot devices reinforce the main point that people should be fee to be who (and what) they are. But like Guy's career if he is outed, it all goes down in flames.

Part of the problem is that Day creates a series of throwaway gags that never build to anything substantial. Much of the humor is dead on arrival, and if not, it is quickly beaten to death. A repetitive joke about Jerry being a lesbian tires long before the payoff, and the film's various efforts at physical humor are slapstuck.

Furthermore, the main characters are one-dimensional cardboard cutouts. It is difficult to care about them and the situations, which get far-fetched without being funny. A party scene in which Sally learns the truth about her husband's homosexuality is particularly forced. In addition, the whole effort looks and feels artificial. It is supposed to be campy, but it is staged—if not performed—in the style of a Boy Scout revue.

Straight-Jacket is especially disappointing because Day's previous effort, *Girls Will Be Girls,* although flawed, showed some real comic promise. Two of the stars from *Girls*—Jack Plotnick and Clinton Leupp (aka Coco Peru)—appear in this film, but their talents are criminally wasted here. Worse yet, Veronica Cartwright is actually terrific as Jerry, but it is damning with faint praise to say she is the best thing in this wetched film.

The leads, all newcomers, simply lack charisma. Matt Letscher fails and flails at the nearly impossible task of making his unlikable character sympathetic, and his costar, Carrie Preston, is incredibly shrill throughout the film. Her deliberately hammy organ performance is not a highlight. These actors deserve better than this silly material which consists mainly of dumb double entendres. Adam Greer does his best as Rick, but he, too, overplays the underwritten role.

Straight-Jacket ultimately backs itself into a corner by trying to address too many important issues simultaneously. In the final analysis, it addresses none of them well.

LOVE IN THE TIME OF MONEY

Love in the Time of Money depicts a series of successive romantic encounters among a handful of New Yorkers, few of which are fulfilling. The film, set in the prosperous 1990s, is even more unsatisfying. This needless update of Arthur Schnitzler's *Reigen* wants to emphasize the link between sex and commerce, but it says nothing new or particularly noteworthy. (In contrast, gay filmmaker Temístocles López's

Chain of Desire [1992] was a much better contemporary version of *Reigen*—sexier, and with a higher queer quotient.)

Writer-director Peter Mattei has assembled a game cast of actors, but he gives them painfully little to do and only about ten minutes each to do it. The result is that the action moves slowly from one bland episode to the next.

The nine vignettes that unfold in *Love in the Time of Money* consist of two self-involved characters meeting and either beginning or ending a relationship (sometimes both at once). Things step and repeat in daisy-chain fashion until it all comes full circle. To wit, Greta (Vera Farmiga), a prostitute, is hired for sex one night by Eddie (Domenick Lombardozzi), a carpenter. The next day, he sleeps with Ellen (Jill Hennessy), a housewife, whose bisexual husband Robert (Malcolm Gets) is really in love with Martin (Steve Buscemi), an artist. Martin, however, is not gay, but smitten with a receptionist named Anna (Rosario Dawson), who is trying to break up with her boyfriend Nick (Adrian Grenier). Nick is consoled by Joey (Carol Kane), a phone psychic who later helps Will (Michael Imperioli), a suicidal trader who eventually seeks comfort with Greta.

Each link in the cycle has brief, sputtering moments of drama, but overall the characters are not developed well enough for viewers to care about their relationships (or lack thereof). Even the sexual hangups—Eddie's inability to climax with women, Robert's waffling sexuality—are largely unexplored. Because of the way the film is structured, it is never disclosed how Robert feels after his encounter with Martin. This question, along with others that arise during the film, are actually more interesting than what is presented on-screen. The protagonists are seen privately in scenes that mainly function as narrative segues. Had the film invested more time in its characters, *Love in the Time of Money* might have some resonance.

Perhaps Mattei is just observing the awkwardness of relationships and the nature of disconnected souls. He does this very well in a nonverbal scene in which Ellen and Robert increase the volume on the television, radio, stereo, and blender as a form of communicating what is wrong in their marriage. However, a phone-sex sequence where Joey reluctantly helps Will get off is less convincing in this respect.

More interesting is the shifting of power among the various characters. When Nick and Anna both confess their affairs to each other, there is palpable moment of despair. Had the other stories been as tense, *Love in the Time of Money* could have had some real dramatic impact. Unfortunately, too much of the film feels half-baked.

What is more, the handheld camerawork and jump-cut editing in various episodes is quite distracting. There are some nice framing devices—Mattei shoots Eddie and Greta separately in opposite sides of a car windshield—but a scene in which Anna undresses is less effective. The film is hardly stylish, and it suffers from an uneven tone.

Where Mattei does succeed is in his use of music featuring Angela McCluskey (of the Wild Colonials). Her distinctive, scratchy voice perfectly suits the film's melancholy atmosphere.

Ultimately, *Love in the Time of Money* will appeal only to viewers looking to kill time and waste money.

Chapter 13
Just Plain Offensive

Bad behavior can often be fun to watch—but not always—as some of the films in this section prove. Although I am not someone who is easily offended, I was put off by some of the features in this chapter. Bestiality is seen in *The Good Old Naughty Days* (2002), and sadomasochism is the subject of the squirm-inducing documentary *Beyond Vanilla* (2001). While *Nine Dead Gay Guys* (2002) plays amusingly with gay stereotypes, *Bulgarian Lovers* (2003), alas, did not. And the things people will stoop to doing for money, as seen in *Games People Play: New York* (2004), are pretty despicable. Then there are the bedroom activities presented in *Anatomy of Hell* (2004)—which I do not recommend people trying at home— and John Waters's naughty *A Dirty Shame* (2004), which belongs in a class by itself.

THE GOOD OLD NAUGHTY DAYS

A collection of twelve French pornographic shorts, *The Good Old Naughty Days* is more interesting as a cultural artifact than it is as an erotic pleasure. Produced between 1905 and 1930, these films—as a series of title cards indicate—were shown in brothels throughout Europe. Young men were taken by their uncles to see this kind of erotica to expose them to sex, described here by amusing euphemisms such as "getting one's crumpet" or "exercising the ferret."

The plot(s) of these features usually involves the same routine just in different settings: Women are stripped and spanked before providing oral sex to the men (and/or women) that "punish" them. The sexual intercourse on display is surprisingly quite graphic, but not unlike

Independent Queer Cinema: Reviews and Interviews
© 2006 by The Haworth Press, Inc. All rights reserved.
doi:10.1300/5482_14

today's porn, it features blow jobs, masturbation, and finger fucking in addition to rear entry. Almost all of it involves a combination of a man and two women, though sometimes there are more participants and the action gets creative. Although there is usually plenty of lesbian activity, the episodes often climax with a male orgasm.

Yet what is curious about these films is that they were made secretly on sets of actual productions, sometimes even using costumes from a film being shot on set during the day. One inter-title suggests that famous directors were responsible for making some of the erotica, though nothing can be proved.

Significantly, none of performers on display are groomed to be particularly good-looking in the way that today's porn stars are, which may suggest that these men and women were more willing and able to have sex on camera than anything else. All of the well-endowed men and curvaceous women appear comfortable sans clothes.

The same cannot be said about a dog, who shows up in the short *Devoirs de Vacances* to help a nun fellate a man. Viewers will no doubt be scratching their heads trying to figure out how the dog was coaxed to perform oral sex on both the man and woman in this strange feature as the animal looks downright uneasy.

This unexpected scene of beastiality is probably the most shocking of all the shorts. An animated film, *Buried Treasure* with Eveready Harton, which appears at the end of the program includes sex with a donkey and a cow, but the animals are drawn, so it plays more like a bad dirty joke out of *Playboy* magazine than something patently offensive.

Perhaps the most accomplished feature is an X-rated reimagining of the *Madame Butterfly* story, with a handsome officer wooing two young woman. What is more, a Chinese servant boy—though his gender is not revealed until he achieves orgasm later in the segment—services the officer before he fucks the females.

Men giving blow jobs is also part of the short *Tea Time,* which is titillating as two men and two women form same-sex couples before switching partners.

Although it is fun to see the scratches and jump cuts that are typical of silent film at first, after the third or fourth short, the novelty wears off. *The Good Old Naughty Days* features appropriate (period) piano accompaniment composed and performed by Eric Le Guen, but the silence of these silent films—like the films themselves—becomes tedious after a while.

While there is something to admire about pornography being almost 100 years old, it also proves that nothing except maybe our technical savvy has improved since the good old naughty days.

BEYOND VANILLA

There is something to offend almost everyone in Claes Lilja's extremely provocative documentary *Beyond Vanilla*. Taking its cue from "the hanky code," this fascinating to some/repulsive to others film explores how men and women, gay and straight, enjoy such activities as bondage, fisting, water sports, and scat. And despite the significant amount of explicit sexual content, this film is decidedly not erotic. Imagine HBO's *Real Sex* series taken to the *nth* and perhaps gayest degree.

The point Lilja makes—and makes both vividly and repeatedly—is that one man or woman's pain is another's pleasure. For example, dozens of talking heads on display here discuss their comfort level with being tied up and spanked, what the best flogging or caning devices are, where and how to hit the four quadrants of the buttocks, and so forth. There are also frank discussions about the rules for negotiating a "scene" and thoughts about trust and control, being safe, using power wisely, and knowing when to stop.

These are important points and they are clearly made. When one man describes the endorphin high of flogging or the rush that comes from practicing breath control (to heighten sexual pleasure) it is possible to understand the thrill, even if there is no interest in experiencing it firsthand.

In addition, it is to the filmmaker's credit that *Beyond Vanilla* never judges any of the individuals who express their fetishes, perversions, and fantasies. (Several interviewees talk about wanting to be abducted and/or raped). It is less difficult for audiences *not* to have an opinion. A very nice young man says he "enjoys a fist or two up my ass, would like to be fucked by a dog, and I drink my own urine—for fun."

Another gentleman describes the sensation of inserting a twelve-inch catheter into the head of his penis: "It's like a dildo in your dickhead," he explains, smiling. It is difficult to watch these interviews and feel indifference.

In fact, *Beyond Vanilla* contains several disturbing scenes that are likely to unsettle viewers. The filmmaker almost seems to revel in his ability to find individuals who will recount and/or show shocking sex acts. One man boasts how he inserted a knife blade completely into another man's anus, while a transgendered guy describes using a penis pump to increase the size of his female genitalia. Enacted for the camera, this latter episode is unforgettable, and for some unwatchable.

Not surprisingly, Lilja has no trouble getting these individuals to open up about their dangerous sex acts. And although the subjects are well chosen for their diversity, the film offers several interviews that produce mixed emotions. It is striking when a female claims she wants to have a gang-bang with multiple sets of twins, almost sad when a woman admits that she is into "daddy girl play," and ominous when a dominatrix warns "never say 'never' in a scene." Significantly, commentary from medical doctors, a sexologist, and gay porn star Cole Tucker flesh out the professional opinions and attitudes toward risky sexual behavior.

Beyond Vanilla may be an eye-opening look at kink, but it is likely that many less jaded viewers will find themselves shutting their eyes during some of the deviance.

NINE DEAD GAY GUYS

A high-energy, lowbrow farce, writer-director Lab Ky Mo's *Nine Dead Gay Guys* is a rude, crude, and sometimes laugh-out-loud comedy about . . . well, a specific number of homosexual gentlemen who end up murdered.

Filled with wordplay, horseplay, and foreplay, this gleefully offensive film depicts the antics of Byron (Brendan Mackey) and his best mate Kenny (Glen Mulhern), two lazy Irish lads in London. Unwilling to work a real job but in need of money to subsidize their booze intake, Byron performs blow jobs on queers—namely Jeff (Steven

Berkoff)—for money. Like Byron, Kenny, too, claims he is straight, but he soon gets into performing oral sex acts to buy "beverage breakfasts and liquid lunches."

However, when a man nicknamed "The Queen" (Michael Praed) dies from being electrocuted with a cattle prod, and his lover, Golders Green (Simon Godley), an Orthodox Jew, is left bereft, Byron and Kenny take it upon themselves to solve the mystery of whodunnit. They are also motivated by the large stash of cash that is rumored to be in Golders Green's enormous bed.

Lab Ky Mo is generally mocking—or, as the British would say, "taking the piss out of"—this situation by making the whole film a series out outrageous episodes that poke fun at sexual and ethnic stereotypes. Of course, some are more shameful than others, and a few are just altogether unfunny.

Nine Dead Gay Guys introduces a group of supporting players including Donkey-Dick Dark, a well-endowed African man, Dick-Cheese Deepak, an Indian with a nasty foreskin condition, and the Desperate Dwarf, a three and a half foot tall gentleman whom no one will fuck because they are all size queens. These colorful characters are certainly politically incorrect, but the film prides itself on being an equal opportunity offender.

In fact, one of the best jokes in *Nine Dead Gay Guys* is Golders Green's response to The Queen's death. Upon seeing his lover's corpse, the devoutly religious man utters the words "Jesus H. Christ."

Obviously, this comedy is not suitable for audiences with delicate sensibilities or even good taste.

Yet while gay viewers may laugh at the over-the-top characters and the fast-paced dialogue about really big dicks, they may be bothered by the film's not so subtle antigay attitude. Even though the film's tongue is firmly in an ass cheek—check out the sign in Margaret's bar that reads "strictly no breeders"—there is still sufficient homophobic banter to give the most forgiving queer at least a little pause. Sure, it's all a big joke, but there is truth in jest.

That said, the film's frenetic visual style is certainly appropriate for the impertinent material. Director Lab Ky Mo uses stop frame, smash cuts, and slow-motion/speed-up effects to tell his sordid story, and the quick pacing keeps things moving until the body count finally piles up. What is more, the film uses a clever musical soundtrack to comment on much of the on-screen action.

As the two lead characters, Byron and Kenny, Brendan Mackey and Glen Mulhern are engaging heroes as well as cute and charming. The pair establish a nice, easygoing rapport with each other, despite the fact that they barely share a kiss or ever fully shed their clothes.

However, the other members of the ensemble cast are perhaps more entertaining. Steven Berkoff seems to relish his turn as Jeff, a rich man who enjoys partaking in Byron (and Kenny's) services, until he can no more, and Raymond Griffiths makes a quite an impression as the Desperate Dwarf.

But it is Michael Praed as The Queen and Simon Godley as Golders Green who really steal the film. Both these actors give truly comic performances, milking their every scene for a smile, if not a genuine laugh.

Nine Dead Gay Guys may be a silly, even stupid film, but for those viewers who see it with the proper mind-set, it can be an amusing experience. Everyone else, beware.

BULGARIAN LOVERS

Bulgarian Lovers is a romantic Spanish drama about Daniel (co-writer Fernando Guillén Cuervo) a forty-something gay man who becomes hopelessly smitten with Kyril (Dritan Biba), a young Bulgarian with a bulge in his pants. Although Daniel maintains that he is a gentleman, and Kyril maintains that he is straight, the two men share some pretty passionate moments naked and in bed together. And although Daniel may fall asleep with a smile on his face, audiences may just find themselves falling asleep.

This character study with intrigue—Kyril dabbles in an illegal activity—is not intriguing at all. In fact, it is surprisingly tedious. Daniel is a patsy who ignores his friends' warnings about getting involved with Kyril, and Kyril is shameless in using sex to get what he wants from his lover. Although the point of *Bulgarian Lovers* may be to show how (Daniel's) love is blind, this does not mean it has to be boring.

Alas, Daniel is unsympathetic because he seems to *want* Kyril to take advantage of him. The reasons for this, however, are never clear, and his character is all the more frustrating because of it. As the relationship between the lovers escalates, audiences are *less* likely to be interested in the outcome of their affair.

Cowritten by actor Cuervo and director Eloy de la Iglesia, the film contains far too little drama, even though the issues of love and trust, money and sex are weighed and measured ad nauseum. When Daniel is asked to hold on to Kyril's bag, he thinks he is noble by not looking inside. This appears to be the film's idea of character development.

While *Bulgarian Lovers* is enlivened by some playful visuals—such as a melting screen or rearview mirror—the film is much better when de la Iglesia shoots a pair of nude bodies on a screen/curtain that the characters walk through during the credits. There are some notable images here, but the emphasis on surfaces only emphasizes the superficiality of the story.

For example, there is an interesting episode of magical realism, in which a Bulgarian boy leads Daniel down a railroad track, but this fantasy goes nowhere. Likewise, a recurring image of Daniel spinning in a chair fails to serve much of a purpose. If it is to show that Daniel is going round and round with Kyril, that is overstating the obvious. It is clear that Daniel acts generously to his beloved because he fears losing him, but the root of this issue is unspoken. Has he been damaged in the past? Does anyone really care? The film's ending may explain Daniel's behavior pattern, but it is not a satisfying payoff.

Maybe something is just lost in translation. The film does try to describe the screwy logic of Bulgarians, such as when they shake their heads "no," they actually mean yes. If this is meant to be a charming irony, consider Kyril's explanation that although he is straight and married to his girlfriend, it is okay for him to fuck Daniel because it is not cheating when he is with another man.

Indeed, *Bulgarian Lovers* seems to have tremendous contempt for its queer characters, and the fact that Daniel's best friend Gildo (Pepón Nieto) is a mincing overweight queen is not helpful. These men are desperate for attention from hot young studs, and are willing to sacrifice their last shreds of dignity to get laid.

For these reasons, de la Iglesia's film is very disappointing—even if it does reflect a truth about how some people live and love. Unfortunately, Fernando Guillén Cuervo should have written himself a better role. If Daniel is a doormat, though, at least he gets to spend time with Dritan Biba naked. Biba, who looks good sans clothes, actually fares pretty well playing his character, perhaps because he gets to be crafty and viewers can delight in his misbehavior. Especially since there is so little else to enjoy in *Bulgarian Lovers*.

GAMES PEOPLE PLAY: NEW YORK

Three hunky guys—one of whom is gay—and three sexy women vie for $10,000 in the new film *Games People Play: New York*. This bigscreen version of a reality show takes a half dozen contestants and puts them through seventy-two hours of sexual shenanigans. While writer/director James Ronald Whitney's film is certainly audacious, it remains to be seen if this "game show pilot" of his will take off.

What does come off, however, are the participants' clothes—and often. The six players are all asked to be "uninhibited,"—meaning they must get naked for much of the on-screen action. From the auditions, which feature two guys, two girls, or one of each improvising an erotic, three-minute love scene (one involves toe sucking) to the "games" themselves, everyone must bare their bodies.

Yet Whitney also has the cast bare their souls. Each individual meets privately with a psychologist and a celebrity publicist, where they reveal their deepest, darkest secrets. In these episodes, one contestant named David confesses that he works an escort, while another, Sarah, describes watching her father being shot when she was a teen. Other participants describe their battles with bulimia and Tourette's syndrome.

Games People Play uses these segments to uncover more about the players than the full-frontal exhibitionism. Yet most of the movie consists of the entertaining games. The women get to act out such things as "Delivery Boy's Fantasy" in which they must get a stranger naked within a specified time limit. Likewise, the guys get to do things like solicit urine samples from people on the street. It is brazen in the same way a fraternity hell week is, and for some viewers, about as much fun.

Depending on one's tolerance level for the activities depicted, some of the episodes go on a bit too long, and some are not long enough. Whitney needs to work on his editing, and the music, complete with awful lyrics, should be cut as well. Whitney's greatest achievement is to have found attractive actors who all look good sans clothes and are willing to do strange things with strangers.

If there is little suspense about who will win the big cash prize, audiences will be amazed at how the players got participation for some outrageous things shown on camera. (Much is made about getting participants to sign a release to appear.) One event, titled "Naked Trio" involves two guys and a girl getting completely nude in a hotel room—to sing. Part of the fun of the film is seeing what shameful antics Whitney has in store for them. Not all of the games work, but many of them are inventive.

Overall, the male contestants are not shy, especially Joshua, who has little trouble asking men on the street to provide him with the urine samples. (Incidentally, the blond stud Joshua was Mr. Penn, a championship bodybuilder, while he was enrolled at the University of Pennsylvania.) Likewise, David (the escort) has no reservations about being out—as when he tells a woman he's such a good kisser, he could turn her straight son gay. Scott, the third male contestant even complains that he is uncomfortable because David was coming on to him. *Games People Play* needs more of these fearless, spontaneous moments. It is perhaps the harshest criticism to say that too much of this reality show seems scripted.

In contrast, the women are not given as many opportunities to act outrageously, and this is a shame since they all appear to be such good sports.

As with any good reality program, there is a final twist that while satisfying, many viewers will see coming. *Games People Play* may not revolutionize the reality show craze as Whitney might hope, but this film will certainly have eyes popping and tongues wagging.

ANATOMY OF HELL

Viewers unfamiliar with the work of director Catherine Breillat (*A Real Young Girl* [1976], *Virgin* [1988], *Romance* [1999], and *Fat Girl* [2001]) may be unprepared for what is in store in her latest film, *Anatomy of Hell*. Simply put, Breillat does not shy away from showing graphic sexual images—from erect penises to close-ups of female genitalia—and her latest work is no exception. In fact, the visuals in this film are so intense even fans of her films may be taken aback by what is on display.

Breillat's audacious, minimalist, and pretentious film is a two-hander that explores female sexuality in unflinching detail. Anyone looking for erotic entertainment is advised to search elsewhere. As the characters are enigmatic, and the story—a "fiction" based on her novel *Pornocratie*—is ambiguous, this film is not likely to arouse anything other than questions.

Anatomy of Hell opens with a significant disclaimer that a body double was used during the film's scenes of intimacy. (This would be for the female character; the male is played by Italian porn star Rocco Siffredi in all his glory.) This announcement is followed by the image of a blow job outside a gay nightclub. Inside, a woman (Amira Casar) heads to the bathroom to commit suicide. On the way, however, she touches a gay man (Siffredi), who saves her from death. Afterward, she fellates the man, and they make a deal: she will pay him to "watch her where she's unwatchable," in an isolated house on the edge of town.

Most of *Anatomy of Hell* takes place in the woman's house over a period of several days. The woman and the man—neither are named—interact in sexually provocative ways. For starters, they dissect the woman's anatomy, discussing her body and pubic hair, and investigating her vaginal fluids and menstral blood. When a tampon is used in a nontraditional manner, audiences will get a taste of how Breillat likes to push people's buttons.

The film is nothing if not scandalous. Breillat, of course, a provocateur, would not have it any other way. The filmmaker makes sure viewers are spellbound—if they are not racing for the exits—and

Anatomy of Hell is compelling, particularly in that "where will things go next" sense.

One element that may keep viewers from leaving their seats is almost constant full-frontal nudity by both performers. Alas, despite the gorgeous bodies on display, it is not titillating watching Casar's character yield a stone dildo from her vagina, or seeing Siffredi's blood-soaked penis after intercourse. That said, both actors give incredibly brave and brazen performances.

Amira Casar has mastered the necessary facial expressions—from surprise to pleasure to amusement, sometimes during the same sexual activity—and the actress ably plays both vulnerable and in control. While Casar understands Breillat's point that women have to use their sexuality as a weapon against men, her role has its challenges, especially during a strange scene featuring a large garden implement protruding from one of her body's orifices.

In contrast, the well-endowed Rocco Siffredi is unfortunately saddled with an underdeveloped character. Siffredi tries his best with the part, but he mainly succeeds when he is asked to be emotionally naked (i.e., crying) rather than inert (i.e., staring).

Perhaps the best thing that can be said about *Anatomy of Hell* is that the images, however explicit, are all artfully composed. Much of what the characters say is ridiculous, and there are long, silent stretches of (in)action that border on boring. Breillat may be trying to deconstruct sexuality by making the intimate act of fucking clinical, but if this is the case, she has to make the characters slightly more appealing.

A DIRTY SHAME

Out filmmaker John Waters is out to shock and amuse with his latest comedy, *A Dirty Shame*. If this NC-17 rated film about a war between decency and depravity is not on par with his outrageous, outré classic *Pink Flamingos* (1972), it is still has plenty of scandalous moments. And Waters does return to fecal humor, which is a good (or bad) thing, depending on one's point of view.

The plot concerns a stressed-out housewife, Sylvia Stickles (Tracey Ullman) who becomes a sex addict after a bonk on the head. The film is less an investigation into Sylvia's libido than an excuse to hang a series of jokes about various sexual fetishes.

Sylvia is burdened with a horny husband (Chris Isaak) and a daughter named Caprice (Selma Blair), who has "criminally enlarged" breasts, which makes her transformation all the sillier. When her car runs out of gas, Sylvia is rescued by Ray Ray (Johnny Knoxville), a mechanic/sexual healer, who tunes up her automobile and turns her on. (He also gives mouth to mouth to a squashed squirrel.) Pretty soon, Sylvia is ready for action, and committing obscene acts while doing the hokey-pokey at an old age home.

Waters makes Sylvia's transformation credible, courtesy of Ullman's magnificent comic timing. Her initial expression of disgust watching a nudist take in his garbage cans is turned into bliss when she discovers the joys of an orgasm. Alas, *A Dirty Shame* keeps Ullman offscreen for long stretches so the antics of some of the other characters can be explored.

If Caprice's story, or any of the other supporting characters, were as interesting as Sylvia's, the film might have warranted the digressions, but *A Dirty Shame,* is best when it sticks to Sylvia and her efforts to satisfy her urges.

Wisely, the film showcases various sexual subgroups, from gay bears to men who want to be babies, to women who get pleasure from frottage (rubbing up against people in public places) and chronic masturbation. Waters never judges these characters, but presents all his fetishists as healthy, sexually active—if extreme—individuals. Yet there is a group of citizens, "Neuters" as they are called in the film, who are out to stop the indecency, and the film's (nonsexual) tension is depicted in the efforts waged by each of these rival factions.

Of course, during this campaign all hell breaks loose, and some of it is very funny. Waters obviously enjoyed coming up with all of the various sexual shenanigans on display, and the film is peppered with all kinds of characters getting it on in different and inventive ways and places. *A Dirty Shame* includes some wonderfully naughty sight gags, as well as some scenes that may cause viewers to gag. (For example, one character gets pleasure eating dirt and bacteria.) What is more, Waters has some hilarious euphemisms, such as "sneezing in the cabbage," for certain sexual practices.

Unfortunately, by trying to cover every possible activity—save, perhaps, incest and necrophilia, though there are suggestions—Waters waters down the film's humor. The message may be whatever turns you on is okay, but the film becomes a one-joke film that borders on boring. This may be the most shocking thing about *A Dirty Shame,* and that is the film's dirtiest shame.

Although the material may be rough, at least the cast is game. Along with the aforementioned talents of Ullman, Johnny Knoxville is sexy and engaging as Ray Ray, though he is given too little to do, and if Selma Blair manages to look ridiculous in the excessive breasts she sports, the actress seems to be having fun in the role. There are also some clever scenes featuring longtime Waters collaborators Mink Stole and Patricia Hearst.

And this is perhaps what saves *A Dirty Shame* from being just a long, fitfully funny dirty joke. The cast appears to be having such a good time, some of it will rub off onto the audience. How much, however, is up to the individual viewer. Whereas some folks are bound to be offended by the film's "pervasive sexual content," others will feel Waters has not gone far enough. This may in fact, be his point exactly.

Chapter 14
Shock and Awe

The films in this section are unnerving. *Elephant* (2003), *Carandiru* (2003), *Monster* (2003), and *The Child I Never Was* (2002) are all excellent films, and rattling for different reasons.

ELEPHANT

Gay filmmaker Gus Van Sant's *Elephant* is an astonishing cinematic experience. Daring in its execution and relentless in its tone, this disturbing but highly rewarding drama—inspired by the massacre at Columbine—is chilling and a triumph.

Van Sant evokes a palpable sense of dread in absolutely every scene as the characters, a bunch of high school students, go about their daily routines. That is, until two students, armed to the teeth, go on a shooting spree.

Elephant tracks the steps of several teenagers at Watt High School, literally, as the camera follows them as they walk through the school hallways on their way to classes, meetings, the library, or lunch. This narrative strategy allows the audience to eavesdrop on their conversations. In fact, much of the film feels informal and unscripted—so real are the dialogues between the characters that viewers may believe this is a documentary and not a fictional film. (Despite the use of a large nonprofessional cast, there is a disclaimer that *Elephant* is a work of fiction and any similarities to persons living or dead are entirely coincidental.)

Van Sant uses interesting, stylish camerawork to tell his story, which eventually forms a mosaic. Still shots and circular pans show the characters from multiple perspectives, and the editing plays with

Independent Queer Cinema: Reviews and Interviews
© 2006 by The Haworth Press, Inc. All rights reserved.
doi:10.1300/5482_15

time so that various scenes overlap, or are replayed from three different perspectives.

The director also deliberately uses sound to provide background information or cue the audience about certain events both seen and unseen. The silences in the film are especially powerful, most notably during the killers' car ride to school the morning of the massacre. Furthermore, the use of a Beethoven sonata is particularly effective in creating a stark tone.

Yes, *Elephant* is a mood piece, but it is also full of raw emotions. A sequence in which various members of a gay-straight alliance discuss being able to tell someone is queer just by how they walk down the street is fascinating, while another scene, in which Michelle (Kristen Hicks), a nerdy girl, is teased in the locker room is incredibly painful. A sequence in which Eli (Elias McConnell) develops a roll of film is tense and exciting just because of how Van Sant films it. In these brief segments, audiences will feel tremendous emotion for these characters, despite knowing so very little about them. Even a trio of haughty, vapid girls who discuss shopping and friendship earn the viewer's sympathy not because of their experiences, but because their lives will soon be changed forever.

Some people may argue that the narrative structure is manipulative, and that parts of *Elephant* are pretentious. The opening scene of clouds moving quickly—repeated again the morning of the tragedy—is a bit arty and precious, and it does fail to provide much in the way of meaning. And the film's title is also deliberately obscure, although Van Sant drops a few obtuse clues about its meaning.

Perhaps the film's only other false note is an awkward scene late in the film in which the two male killers shower together and share a kiss. It is not so much that Van Sant is ascribing his murderers a sexual identity—they embrace because one says he has never been kissed—rather, he is trying to balance their guilt with some innocence. Much more disturbing is the ease with which the killers obtain their rifles.

Ultimately, *Elephant* resonates, because even though the violent finale is expected throughout the entire film, it is still undeniably shocking when it unfolds. These promising lives cut short for some senseless reason is unsettling, and the realism with which the film depicts its events and its characters makes it all the more upsetting.

Masterfully filmed and impressively acted, *Elephant* is unforgettable.

CARANDIRU

The wedding between a sexy transvestite named Lady Di (Rodrigo Santoro) and a dwarf named No Way (Gero Camilo) is perhaps the happiest moment in Hector Babenco's *Carandiru*. This extraordinary drama—based on fact—about life in a Brazilian prison contains many vivid scenes and visceral images, and this brief moment of queer romance provides a beacon of hope among all the despair.

Carandiru, which chronicles the lives of a number of prisoners—both gay and straight—ends with a lengthy and brutal massacre, one that will leave viewers shaken to the core. Yet the film's real strength lies in the humanity on display up until the grisly finale. Despite the power of the prisoners' stories and the depiction of the riot itself, however, the parts of the film are perhaps greater than the whole.

The first two-thirds of this remarkable true story depict the various lives of the inmates, from the feuds between prisoners to the bonds that form among them. As these personal narratives segue into the devastating riot, many of the characters that viewers have started to care about are killed. Although this is undoubtedly Babenco's point—to raise awareness of the abuse of prisoners and the failure of the system to contain/control them—it takes too long to unfold, and by the time the thirty-minute massacre is over, audiences will be almost completely desensitized to the copious violence.

While the riot is undoubtedly mesmerizing, the various stories are perhaps more moving and more interesting. The film shows the efforts of a visiting doctor (Luiz Carlos Vasconcelos) to treat Carandiru's 8,000 inmates for HIV and other diseases. As he cares for the various men, he learns about their lives and why they have ended up behind bars.

These tales are captivating, and the vignettes—most of which take place outside the prison walls—are brilliantly realized by Babenco.

From Zico (Wagner Moura) and Deusdete (Caio Blat), close half brothers who become bitter rivals, to Lady Di's admission of having 2,000 sexual partners, the minidramas are absorbing and heartfelt.

Yet perhaps the most riveting story belongs to Highness (Ailton Graça), a man who has two wives, each of whom plots revenge on the other in spectacular fashion. These involving episodes give the characters real depth, and they develop sympathy that is only magnified by the film's sorrowful end.

The performances by Rodrigo Santoro and Ailton Graça, respectively, as Lady Di and Highness are remarkable. Both actors are fantastic, and they truly escape into their roles.

Babenco, who made the wonderful and tragic *Kiss of the Spider Woman* (1985) nearly two decades ago, seems to thrive at depicting fatalistic Brazilian prison films. *Carandiru* depicts both the hallucinations of a drug addict and a character whose hand is bitten by a rat in ways that are both unsetting and unforgettable. Although the filmmaker does not shy away from showing the ugliness of prison's grim reality, it becomes difficult, albeit fascinating, to watch so many wasted lives. Alas, the relentless massacre is absolutely wearying.

Carandiru makes the most of its opportunity to explore the underbelly of Latin American life in detail. Babenco truly conveys the claustrophobia of an overcrowded prison cell and his characters' desperation in a single shot. The film may be shocking and disturbing, but for those who can stomach it, *Carandiru* is magnificent.

MONSTER

In the extraordinary new film *Monster,* Charlize Theron plays famed serial killer Aileen Wuornos, the Florida prostitute who tried to turn her life around when she fell in love with a woman named Selby (Christina Ricci).

Although Wuornos's story—she was executed in 2002 after twelve years on death row—has been told before in both a 1992 documentary and TV movie-of-the-week, writer-director Patty Jenkins still manages to make this fascinating true crime drama fresh and exciting by making its subject incredibly sympathetic.

The film is also helped immeasurably by Theron's devastating performance. Under prosthetic makeup to make her look more the part, Theron brilliantly embodies Wuornos right down to the cadence of her speech and her mannerisms. Theron's Oscar-worthy performance is as mesmerizing as Hilary Swank's turn in *Boys Don't Cry* (1999).

Monster opens with a poignant look at Aileen's childhood and teenage years—when she was a dreamer who wanted "a new life where everything would be different." This overture suggests why Aileen, who wanted so desperately to be loved, may have found a romantic partner in the impressionable Selby, a young girl she meets one night in a gay bar. In one of the best scenes in the film, the young women meet at a roller rink and, as they skate to Journey's "Don't Stop Believing," Aileen seduces Selby.

After the couple agrees to run away and live together, money soon becomes tight, and Aileen hits the streets in order to make fast cash. One night, she is physically abused by a john (Lee Tergesen of TV's *Oz*) and retaliates by killing him. Getting away with the crime, Aileen feels guilt, satisfaction, and perhaps, most important, a sense of empowerment. She soon begins a violent crime spree, murdering most of her clients. Significantly, though, Aileen tries to keep her activities secret—perhaps to protect Selby—and with the hope that the police will not catch up to her.

Monster tries to explain Aileen's criminal behavior by ascribing it to her tough childhood. She was raped and abused as a young girl, and forced into prostitution at age thirteen. Yet the film also makes the point repeatedly in scenes of her interviewing for a job or fighting with a restaurant manager that she was not able to act "properly" in a normal society. If there are any parallels to be drawn here regarding Wuornos's lesbianism, none are ever audibly made. (That said, Selby's parental figure never accepts Selby's homosexuality and is more distraught by the seedy-looking Aileen as her lover.)

These facts, and a series of short, powerful voiceover narratives that pepper the film, make Aileen pitiful, and this may be the film's hook. Jenkins (and Theron, who produced *Monster*) are trying to turn this serial killer into a martyr. From the film's perspective, Wuornos selected her victims carefully and often felt justified in her actions. She lashed out—verbally or violently—at men who tried to control her, and as such, was a victim herself. As she becomes more desperate, there is more sadness than relief.

This is an interesting and provocative viewpoint, and it serves *Monster* well. The film deliberately constructs a compassionate portrait, but it is also quite eerie when Aileen makes an effort to convince Selby not to return to her family in Ohio. "You'll never meet someone like me again," she says, lovingly and without a trace of irony, unlike the platitudes she repeats from time to time.

Jenkins gets the grittiness of the story absolutely right, and she perfectly captures the texture of Aileen's sordid life, which often includes washing up in truck stop restrooms.

As good as it is, however, *Monster* falls short of being a true masterpiece because Jenkins telegraph's some of the action. The killings are denoted by creepy music on the soundtrack, and Wuornos's capture is clumsily handled.

These flaws aside, the film is an unforgettable and haunting portrait of a damaged woman, brought to life by Theron's powerhouse performance.

THE CHILD I NEVER WAS

The Child I Never Was is a chilling look into the mind of a gay teenage serial killer. Based on the true life of Jürgen Bartsch, this difficult film features two actors playing the lead role. Tobias Schenke is the twentysomething Jürgen, who tells his story to the camera in prison, while Sebastian Urzendowsky plays Bartsch as a teenager, committing the heinous sex crimes that ultimately land him in jail.

This highly stylized drama, directed by German filmmaker Kai S. Pieck, is frequently unsettling, especially as it tries to explain what motivated Bartsch to seduce and murder several boys his age in Langenberg between 1962 and 1966. The film ascribes Jürgen's actions to his "sexual desire for power." Not only does Jürgen enjoy dominating these boys he seeks out and captures, but he also finds erotic pleasure in the naked skin of the boys *after* he has killed them.

Jürgen's sickness is deep-set, and he himself is aware of his mental illness. As he seeks absolution or tries to control his actions, he eventually admits that it was easier to repress his homosexuality than to stop his thirst to murder. Although audiences may feel some sympathy for Jürgen at these revelations, as with the magic tricks he likes to perform, there is no explanation for his actions.

Pieck, however, does try to present several possible reasons for Jürgen's aberrant behavior—most obviously, a lack of love from his parents and a bad relationship with the church. One of the more disturbing sequences in the film involves Jürgen under the care of a sadistic priest who molests him. (Not surprisingly, the adult Jürgen is reluctant to discuss this episode of his life.) This abuse is as horrifying as the manner in which his parents treated him—even as a teenager, his mother still bathes him like a young child. In addition, Jürgen, who struggles with his longing for boys, discovers something about his life that also impacts him significantly. Although these factors may explain why he needs to dominate his peers—paying them to play dead so he can explore their young bodies—it certainly does not excuse his actions.

Yet *The Child I Never Was* is most shocking when it examines the crimes themselves. As the older Jürgen calmly recounts how he stripped a boy naked, and bound and gagged him before killing him, the film shows nothing but the older killer, sitting at a table, talking to the camera. With one exception, none of the murders are depicted on-screen. Yet they are described so intensely, viewers may swear later that they have seen the killings for real. Such is the impact of this film, which culminates with a powerful, extended sequence in the cave where Jürgen committed most of his crimes.

Likewise, the sexual activity is all discussed and never shown. The film distinctly treats Jürgen's extreme sexuality—fetishizing corpses to the point of reaching orgasm—as deviant behavior. While his crushes on various boys and a kiss he shares with another male youth are portrayed, these sexual escapades are discreet and not salacious. Hearing that Jürgen masturbated at the sight of the naked buttocks of a rotting victim is disquieting enough.

Given the way in which he films these sequences—with jump cuts and a certain amount of ironic detachment—there is no denying that Pieck is an original storyteller. Not only is he using Jürgen's life as a way of commenting on European attitudes toward homosexuality in the early 1960s, but the film provides insights into the mind of a serial killer with the same unsparing tone as the recent film *Monster*. This is an impressive achievement, notwithstanding the gruesome subject matter.

Pieck also coaxes outstanding performances from his two leads. Both Sebastian Urzendowsky and Tobias Schenke are brave actors, and they exceed the demands of their tough roles.

The Child I Never Was is certainly not for all tastes, but adventurous cinephiles should seek out this worthwhile film. The film ends with a coda about Jürgen's post-1966 life that is as stunning as the story that proceeded it.

Chapter 15
Passions

The films in this section all reveal characters that dream of different lives. *Facing Windows* (2003), *Far from Heaven* (2002), *My Mother Likes Women* (2002), *Suddenly* (2002), *Latter Days* (2003), and *Km. O* (2000) all present endearing characters who are lost in, confused about, or frantically searching for love.

FACING WINDOWS

Ferzan Ozpetek, the queer, Turkish writer-director who lives and works in Italy, seems to be carving a niche for himself making what Hollywood used to call "women's pictures." His bittersweet film *His Secret Life* (2001) concerned a widow who upon discovering her late husband's male lover befriended him. In his equally extraordinary new drama *Facing Windows*, Ozpetek tells the story of a young woman named Giovanna (Giovanna Mezzogiorno) who also reexamines her life with the help of a male stranger.

Facing Windows opens during World War II when a young man flees an incident at the bakery where he works. He is shown, literally, at a crossroad in Rome when the scene dissolves into the same intersection sixty years later. In the present day, Simone (Massimo Girotti) is in his eighties, wandering the city streets and suffering from hallucinations and a form of amnesia in which he can recall little more than his name.

Simone is picked up and taken home by Filippo (Filippo Nigro), the ruggedly handsome husband of Giovanna. Giovanna is perturbed by her husband's decision to help this old man, and she tries to get rid of Simone, whom she sees as another problem she does not need.

Independent Queer Cinema: Reviews and Interviews
© 2006 by The Haworth Press, Inc. All rights reserved.
doi:10.1300/5482_16

Giovanna's life is full of frustration. She is unhappy with her work and dreams of being a professional baker. Her marriage has become routine, and she spies lustfully on the sexy Lorenzo (Raoul Bova, from *Under the Tuscan Sun*, 2003), who lives in the apartment facing her window.

Giovanna at first appears to be a selfish woman, one who is stuck in a rut of her own making, and unable to do anything about it. However, as she cares for Simone, and unravels the mysteries of his life and former love, Giovanna is inspired to make some changes of her own.

And, as Lorenzo comes to assist in Giovanna's efforts to help Simone, the two neighbors are forced to confront their attraction to each other. Of course, there are parallels to be drawn between Giovanna's story and Simone's, but they are not necessarily the ones viewers might expect. The meaning of love, if not life itself, Ozpetek seems to suggest in this striking film, is in the connections we make and miss.

Facing Windows is considerably more intelligent than its soapy plot may suggest, and although the story features some contrivances, the film has some very important things to say about finding love and happiness. Ozpetek and his coscreenwriter Gianni Romoli have created an absorbing tale, and they offer some candid insights about loss and regret.

Audiences will be easily sucked into the characters' lives, especially as Simone and Lorenzo reveal their true selves to Giovanna. Each man's romantic disclosure prompts Giovanna to make a decision about how she should behave. The screenplay masterfully ties the three characters together, and although Ozpetek and Romoli have created characters that are initially enigmatic or unlikable, by the end they are sympathetic and/or exposed.

The characters are not only beautifully realized but are brought to life by a fine cast. Giovanna Mezzogiorno is captivating as Giovanna, and her transformation from frustrated wife to empowered woman is tremendous. Mezzogiorno conveys Giovanna's desires and her decisions superbly, and her reactions to Simone's and Lorenzo's revelations are entirely credible.

Massimo Girotti lends a gravity to his role as the elderly Simone, playing his part with appropriate conviction and intensity, and the very good-looking Raoul Bova is suitably engaging as Lorenzo. In addition, Filippo Nigro is compelling as Giovanna's well-meaning husband, and Ozpetek regular Serra Yilmaz lends strong support as Giovanna's best friend, Eminé.

Facing Windows also features some lovely scenes of Giovanna baking, as she and Simone bond over pastry making, and the film, shot on location in Rome, includes some gorgeous images of the Eternal City.

Ultimately, Ozpetek has crafted a startling, multilayered melodrama, one that is memorable as well as provocative and passionate.

FAR FROM HEAVEN

Writer/director Todd Haynes's *Far from Heaven* is a brilliant homage to 1950s domestic melodramas. Every detail—from the language and the costumes, to the furniture and the cars—is absolutely spot-on perfect. The film is a remarkable achievement in the period re-creation alone.

Yet Haynes does more, much more, than simply pay tribute to a long-dormant genre; he twists it—introducing such forbidden things as the F word and a same-sex kiss that would never have been seen in films of the bygone era. *Far from Heaven* soon becomes less of a resurrection of a cinematic style than a very profound examination of race and sexuality.

Significantly, the film is not striving for irony, although the dialogue is frequently corny. Characters say things such as "jeepers," "jiminy," and "aw, shucks," which underscore their real emotions, and this is precisely the point. *Far from Heaven* gets deep under the surface of its characters and explores their hidden lives and the consequences of their desires.

Cathy and Frank Whitaker (Julianne Moore and Dennis Quaid) are known in suburban Hartford, Connecticut, as the perfect "modern" couple. Cathy is even profiled in the town's society column. But these happy suburbanites have secrets. Although he seems to be the ideal father and husband, Frank is first seen calling from the police station, where he has been unjustly arrested. He spikes his morning coffee with liquor and finds himself ordering drinks in all-male bars. One fateful night, Frank is caught by his wife kissing another man, when she stops by the office with his dinner. Soon Frank is seeing a doctor twice a week about his "problem," which he hopes to cure.

While coping with her husband's troubles, Cathy finds herself spending time with Raymond Deagan (Dennis Haysbert), a black gardener who offers her solace. She encounters him at an art show, and appreciates his views on Miró. This causes some ladies' tongues to wag, but the whole town starts talking when Cathy and Raymond are seen together by the local gossip on the road one afternoon. Soon there are serious repercussions for both Cathy's and Raymond's families.

Far from Heaven traces these parallel stories within the confines of the 1950s melodrama and yields surprisingly powerful results. Not only do the Frank and Cathy try to suppress their "inappropriate" desires and return to "normalcy" and conformity, but they find the difficulties of living a lie.

Furthermore, the Whitakers must also contend with the hypocrisy and judgment of their friends and social peers. The dynamic of this is summed up beautifully in a scene in which a partygoer makes a comment about there being "no Negroes in Hartford," as the camera fixes on the black waiter offering him a drink.

Haynes shrewdly alludes to other topics that were "taboo" back in the day, such as the prominent—but invisible—issues of alcoholism, abuse, and divorce. The filmmaker takes painstaking care to question these social issues in the very context where they were being denied. The result is quite telling.

Although the intentions of the film are ambitious, *Far from Heaven* succeeds admirably thanks to the tremendous contributions of its talented cast. Julianne Moore is a revelation in the lead role, and her portrait of a housewife awakened by feeling of love and sacrifice is equal to the excellence of her last collaboration with Haynes, the criminally neglected *Safe* (1995). Likewise, Dennis Quaid turns in a moving performance as a man nearly torn apart by his homosexuality. Perhaps Quaid's most heartfelt moment is the melodrama's most atypical—when he actually breaks down and cries. Dennis Haysbert lends outstanding support as Raymond, and Patricia Clarkson, as Cathy's best friend and confidant, is exceptional in her important role.

Fabulously made—like everything else, the music and cinematography are top-notch—*Far from Heaven* is an extraordinary achievement.

MY MOTHER LIKES WOMEN

Not another serious coming out drama about gay/lesbian children facing disapproving parents, the enjoyable Spanish comedy *My Mother Likes Women* features three sisters who are ashamed of their *mother's* newfound lesbianism. This lightweight, likeable farce, written and directed by Inés París and Daniela Fejerman, may have the depth of a TV sitcom, but the film has charm to spare and there are plenty of humorous moments.

The story opens at Sofía's (Rosa María Sardà) birthday party where her three daughters are shocked to discover that mom is in love with a Czech woman twenty years her junior named Eliska (Eliska Sirová). The children's initial reactions are telling. Sol (Silvia Abascal) is pleased, Jimena (María Pujalte) is pissed off, and Elvira (Leonor Watling) is perplexed.

While the three sisters try to accept their mother's new lifestyle, each one struggles with her feelings toward Eliska. Sol, a pop singer, is inspired, and she writes the catchy title tune—which infuriates the family when it is publicly performed. Jimena is all for keeping up appearances, and she wants the affair ended at once, and Elvira worries that Eliska is taking advantage of their mother financially. The siblings hatch a plan to break off the relationship—"for mom's good," they insist—however, in true sitcom fashion, complications ensue.

Most of *My Mother Likes Women* is told from the perspective of Elvira, who is plenty neurotic before Sofía's disclosure, and completely off balance after mom comes out. Elvira, a would-be novelist, has a publishing job that she hates and a psychiatrist helping her with her self-esteem. When she meets Miguel (Chisco Amado), an author who flirts with her shamelessly, Elvira sabotages the relationship at every opportunity, blaming her confusion on the "crisis" in her family. Making matters worse, Elvira truly bonds with Eliska, and this calls into question not only her feelings about mom's lover but also her own sexuality. And if that is not enough, Elvira finds herself with that fear of fears—she worries that she is becoming like her mother!

Of course, the lesbian couple is the sanest and most stable in the family, and *My Mother Likes Women* has fun at the expense of its scheming characters. A running gag shows that only Sofía's daughters take issue with her sexuality—nobody else cares. The idea behind this is that Elvira, Jimena, and Sol—named after the characters in *El Cid* (1961)—are jealous of their mother's love for another woman. Sibling rivalry is not the issue, the film suggests, it is rivalry for mom's affections!

This point comes across well during one of the many occasions when Elvira screws up her chances with Miguel. Upset with her own bad behavior, Elvira rushes to her mother—on a date at the same restaurant with Eliska—for comfort. The idea that mother knows best is echoed in the fact that all of her daughters need to grow up and find the right partner to make them happy. This message may not be novel, but it goes down easier than a pitcher of sangria.

One reason *My Mother Likes Women* is so captivating is courtesy of Leonor Watling's superb performance as Elvira. The lovely actress—who will be familiar to most viewers as the comatose patient in gay director Pedro Almodóvar's *Talk to Her* (2002)—gets the chance to really perform here, and she is an exquisite comedienne. Playing up her character's amusing frustrations with great aplomb, Watling is absolutely enchanting. She expertly handles the story's demands to be self-destructive with Miguel and sensitive with Eliska, and she makes her character likeable even at her most selfish.

Although *My Mother Likes Women* may at times get a bit silly, it is endearing, nonetheless. París and Fejerman have created a very sweet and satisfying film that should please everyone—mother and daughters, women and men, gay and straight alike.

SUDDENLY

The arty Argentine drama *Suddenly (Tan de Repente)* is an engrossing road movie about a trio of would-be lesbians searching for love or something like it. Shot in luminous black and white, this low-budget film, directed and cowritten by Diego Lerman, features gorgeous imagery and excels in capturing the complex emotional arcs of its central characters.

Although not much happens as the film's three young women travel from Buenos Aires to the countryside town of Rosario, their personalities slowly emerge and transform. *Suddenly* may not be a film of great action, but it is an outstanding character study of three very lost women.

Marcia (Tatiana Saphir) is a lonely salesgirl who works in an underwear store in the city. One afternoon, Mao (Carla Crespo) and Lenin (Veronica Hassan) stop her on the street. Mao declares that she fell in love with Marcia at first sight and asks her bluntly, "Do you want to fuck?" Marcia is appalled by this proposition, but she cannot escape. Suddenly, Mao and Lenin kidnap her, steal a taxi, and set off for adventure.

Lerman creates a nice tension between the characters in these initial scenes, and it percolates throughout the film. However, the relationship between Mao and Lenin—they claim to be lovers, but not girlfriends—is never addressed. Instead, the story concentrates on the burgeoning affair between Mao and Marcia. Although neither woman claims to be a lesbian, they both seem to find an uneasy comfort in the other.

Mao does eventually fuck Marcia in Rosario, when the travelers stop at Lenin's aunt Blanca's (Beatriz Thibaudin) house. Curiously, the women's intimacy does not bring them any closer. Marcia seeks out Blanca's boarder Delia (María Merlino) for friendship, and Mao gravitates to Felipe (Marcos Ferrante), another housemate. Meanwhile, Lenin bonds with her aunt, whom she has not seen in at least a decade.

It is this second half of *Suddenly* where Lerman really hits his stride as a filmmaker. Not only does the director show off his terrific eye for composition—shots of an old woman sitting at an empty table or Blanca's face in the sun are fantastic—but he mines each scene for the characters' genuine emotions. As the characters pair off with one another, a kind of symmetry develops, and each young woman finds an outlet for finding her self-respect.

Although Marcia reveals her thoughts in her conversations with Delia, she is equally thoughtful just looking in a mirror or sitting quietly on a bed. Likewise, when Lenin tucks Blanca into bed and they talk about Lenin's mother, what is not said is quite telling. Lerman wisely uses these unspoken moments to allow audiences to fill in the blanks about the characters.

In contrast, Mao is more of an enigma, masking her insecurity with a hard exterior. But her actions, which include stealing Marcia's clothes and shoplifting food from a bodega, speak volumes.

Suddenly never reaches any big narrative crescendo—the most significant event happens offscreen—but the film excels in creating a distinctive mood and atmosphere. The only dramatic misstep is an episode involving a trucker who gives the girls a ride. This sequence contains an incident that is freighted with importance, and yet surprisingly unmoving.

Lerman coaxes wonderful performances from his entire ensemble cast, but Tatiana Saphir and Beatriz Thibaudin are the two standouts. Saphir is lovingly filmed in close-ups, and the strength of her expressive performance is enhanced by Lerman's attention to her. Thibaudin is also memorable in her role. The elderly actress not only injects the film with some humor, but she is especially charismatic performing a bolero. As Mao and Lenin, both Carla Crespo and Veronica Hassan are enjoyable to watch, particularly when they misbehave.

Suddenly may not be riveting drama, but it is an absorbing film. The characters are not always likable, and still Lerman makes them sympathetic. And, best of all, he films it beautifully.

LATTER DAYS

Latter Days portrays the relationship between a straight-arrow Mormon missionary named Elder Davis (Steve Sandvoss) and Christian

(Wes Ramsey), a promiscuous LA party boy/waiter. Written and directed by C. Jay Cox (who wrote *Sweet Home Alabama*, 2002) this sexy romance benefits from a pair of fine performances from the attractive screen newcomers.

The story has Elder Davis moving into the same apartment complex Christian shares with his roommate and co-worker, Julie (Rebekah Johnson), an aspiring singer. At the restaurant one night, Christian accepts a bet that he can sleep with the hunky Elder Davis. Given the sexual sparks between the two good-looking young men, this should not be too much of a challenge, especially for someone like Christian, who keeps a Palm Pilot with data on everyone he ever bedded.

As the two guys bond over laundry and movie quotes, a real chemistry develops, yet Elder Davis resists temptation. Of course, when Christian scrapes his side and drops his skintight pants for his potential new boyfriend—it as much as a tease as a ploy. And Elder Davis, tending to the wound on Christian's ass, slowly confronts his sexuality, even if he stops short of an actual kiss. The sexual tension between these two characters is palpable, and it makes the film compelling during its enjoyable first half.

Although *Latter Days* could have simply chronicled Christian's seduction of Elder Davis, Cox introduces a spiritual component that has Christian questioning his shallowness. When he realizes that caring about people is more important than just fucking them (well, duh!), Christian makes a pact to be a better person, and begins by delivering food to an AIDS patient. This point about "equating sex with a handshake" is driven home when Christian, naked and bent over, stops a very intimate encounter with a stranger to talk. Even if audiences gag at the simplicity of the message, the sight of one gorgeous naked man going down on another makes it go down easy.

It will come as no surprise that Christian does get to "convert" Elder Davis, and their erotic encounter will probably generate the film's most enthusiastic response. The leads are attractive, and they both look good in bed together sans clothes. However, as fate would have it, the lovers are torn apart, and it would spoil the film to explain more about what happens.

That said, Cox is perhaps too ambitious in his plotting after this midpoint in the film, and the coincidences pile up like cars in a bad traffic accident. *Latter Days,* which opens with witty lines about sex, wannabe careers, and failed relationships, soon becomes incredibly heavy-handed. From the religious imagery—scenes of Christian, shirtless and with his arms outstretched on the dance floor looking Christlike, or a woman, dressed with angel wings, smoking, waiting for a bus—to all the Mormon shame and dishonor, it is all a bit too much.

Alas, the film also introduces a third act subplot about Julie's recording career that ties the many plot strands together. Unfortunately, it is way too contrived to be convincing. But maybe a romance—particularly one about a Mormon missionary discovering his homosexuality—does not need much in the way of credibility.

Nevertheless, both Sandvoss and Ramsey fit comfortably in their roles, and each has an engaging screen presence. (It would be interesting to see the film had the actors played the opposite roles.) Likewise, Rebekah Johnson impresses as Julie, and she does her own singing, as well.

In support, the excellent (and reliable) character actress Mary Kay Place plays Elder Davis's mother, while Jacqueline Bisset lends her magnificent talent as Lila, the owner of the restaurant where Christian and Julie work. Despite having awful crying scenes, Place and Bisset are wonderful in their respective roles.

Cox does bite off more than he can chew, but he makes *Latter Days* appealing, even if it is a sermon served up with a side of sex.

KM. 0

The sunny Spanish film *Km. 0* is an easygoing ensemble piece about fourteen characters that form various love connections on a hot summer's day. Most of the film's various couples meet cute at Kilometer 0, the point of origin of arterial roads in the Puerto del Sol in Madrid. And more often than not, they meet by accident. Love, as writers/directors Yolanda García Serrano and Juan Luis Iborra, seem to insist, should involve destiny, not determination.

And such is the case with Marga (Concha Velesco) who arranges a liaison with a male escort (Jesús Cabrero) that has consequences she never imagined. Meanwhile, Tatiana (Elisa Matilla), a hooker, misses her intended rendezvous with a virgin named Sergio (Alberto San Juan) looking to be deflowered, and instead meets adorable aspiring filmmaker Pedro (Carlos Fuentes).

Concurrently, Bruno (Víctor Ullate Jr.), a flamenco dancer, mistakenly comes on to Benjamín (Miguel García), believing him to be the guy he met online moments before, while aspiring actress Silvia (Mercè Pons) literally throws herself in front of theater director Gerardo (Georges Corraface) to get his attention. In addition, Amor (Silke) is a naive young woman who keeps getting robbed trying to buy her fiancé a birthday present. Rounding out the cast are a handful of individuals who become involved sexually or emotionally with these main players.

Although *Km. 0* is fast-paced and fun to watch, it never quite rises above the level of a TV movie or sitcom. (Given the brief flashes of nudity and the film's significant queer content, this would be a cable-TV program.) The episodic structure of the film works well, but the mistaken identity/chance encounter stories are all a bit forced. To the film's credit, the episodes are never confusing, or overlong as sometimes happens with ensemble pieces. However, during the film's weaker passages, it could be entertaining to reimagine *Km. 0* had the characters that were originally supposed to meet gone off together.

The best episodes are the ones that have some depth, such as the one depicting the gay couple, Bruno and Benjamín. The energy between these two cute guys will make viewers wish for them to have more screen time. Amor's storyline is stupid at first, but it turns sweet in the end, which redeems it. Less successful is the sequence in which Silvia attempts to woo Gerardo. Their interaction includes Silvia performing a musical number, which should be a showstopper—but instead, it stops the film in its tracks. Likewise, the scenes involving the virgin, Sergio, and a gay man he meets who helps him overcome his fears about sex are unsatisfying. The unevenness of all the plots is perhaps the film's biggest drawback.

The casting is also a delicate balance. Whereas the ensemble performers are all well suited to their roles, several actors seem to have been cast more for their good looks than their acting talents. That said, Concha Velesco easily gives the best performace as Marga, and this may be because she gets to show off her range with the fleshiest part. Carlos Fuentes is extremely engaging as Pedro, and Alberto San Juan makes the most of his role as Sergio. San Juan has an impressive scene waiting for his date and fumbling with his sport coat and cigarette.

Km. 0 may be undemanding, but it is not unlikable. It is a pleasant diversion for a hot summer afternoon. There are worse ways to spend 105 minutes than with a bunch of sexy and sex-crazed Spaniards.

Chapter 16
Family Redefined

The comedies in this section—*Hush!* (2001), *Mambo Italiano* (2003), *Touch of Pink* (2004), and *Sordid Lives* (2000)—all show how characters create the families they want when the ones they have won't do. And they do it with humor.

HUSH!

The heartfelt Japanese comedy-drama *Hush!*, written and directed by Ryosuke Hashiguchi, is an absorbing film about redefining family. Both episodic and deliberately paced, this affecting character study about two gay men and the woman that wants to have a child with one of them is frequently poignant and at times quite powerful.

The film opens by introducing the three main protagonists individually, allowing viewers to understand where they are in their respective lives and relationships. The adorable Naoya (Kazuya Takahashi) works in a pet shop and wants a steady boyfriend, not a one-night stand; Katsuhiro (Seiichi Tanabe), is a handsome and closeted engineer who is kind to everyone he meets; and Asako (Reiko Kataoka) is an insecure young woman who fits dental crowns and makes bad decisions when it comes to men. Establishing the rhythms of each of these characters' lives, Hashiguchi eventually introduces them to one another.

After spending the night together, Naoya and Katsuhiro tentatively begin a relationship. While they are still getting used to being with each other, a complication arises. Asako, a woman they meet in a noodle house one afternoon, tells Katsuhiro that she would like him to father her child. Although Katsuhiro considers this unexpected proposal, Naoya wants to have nothing to do with this stranger. However, Katsuhiro thinks quite seriously about Asako's request. "Just because I'm gay," he tells his new boyfriend, "doesn't mean I have to live a certain way."

Hush! mostly explores how Asako acts as a catalyst for the gay couple, forcing each of them to determine how to get what they want out of their relationship. Their unusual circumstance also makes the two men decide if (and how exactly) they will stay together. This storyline unfolds naturally, and when Naoya accuses Katsuhiro of lying about his discussions with Asako about having a baby, their arguments are realistic and well staged. The main characters in the film are not stereotypes or symbols, and this is largely why viewers will care about them.

Yet as Katsuhiro struggles with his sexuality and tries to make the right decision about the baby, he encounters another problem. Nagata (Tsugumi), a co-worker who is in love with him, is determined to marry Katsuhiro, and her actions—which provoke a serious confrontation with Naoya's and Katsuhiro's family members—upset the already fragile balance among the three protagonists. This explosive scene, in which Asako justifies wanting to have a child with Katsuhiro to complete strangers, is perhaps the film's most remarkable, devastating moment.

Although the film is a bit long, it is nevertheless always engaging, especially when the storyline shifts gears slightly and the characters form an easygoing rapport with one another. Scenes of Asako, Naoya and Katsuhiro going bowling, shopping for baby clothes, and sharing meals form an enjoyable sequence, and this paves the way for the heroes to grapple with a tragedy that befalls one of the characters late in the film.

Hashiguchi secures uniformly excellent performances from his three leads, giving each actor a plum role. Seiichi Tanabe is outstanding, always making Katsuhiro sympathetic, and never pathetic. Likewise Reiko Kataoka as Asako beautifully conveys her character's transformation, while Kazuya Takahashi is continuously likeable as Naoya.

Ultimately, *Hush!* is about how each character develops his or her self- respect with the help of the others. While Naoya learns to be less selfish, and Asako finds a ray of hope in Katsuhiro, Katsuhiro himself becomes more assertive. Hashigushi treats these emotional arcs with sensitivity, and the film's lack of sentimentality or mawkisness is refreshing.

MAMBO ITALIANO

Mambo Italiano is an over-the-top but frequently laugh-out-loud comedy about being gay and Italian—which according to several of the film's characters is a fate in which "there's nothing worse!" In fact, it seems that at any given moment, one member of the Barberini family in Montreal's "Little Italy" is yelling to someone about something—usually having to do with being an "omosessuale." At least they get in a large number of funny one-liners in the process.

In this very broad comedy, nimbly directed by Émile Gaudreault (who co-wrote the script with Steve Galluccio, whose play the film is based on), Angelo (Luke Kirby) is struggling with both his sexual and his Italian identity. On the phone to a gay help line, he decides he must do something about his stifled life—he must move out of his family home. Of course, his overbearing parents (Paul Sorvino and Ginette Reno) prefer he stay in with them until he gets married, or dies. What they do not know, though—and what may hurt them more than his leaving home—is that their son is gay.

When his apartment is robbed, however, things improve for Angelo. Not only is he reunited with Nino (Peter Miller), a hunky cop he was quite close to as a kid, but Nino soon moves in with Angelo. Unfortunately, the couple's domestic harmony is also a closeted one, and it is short-lived. Angelo eventually comes out to his parents. But when Nino's mother Lina (Mary Walsh) learns the truth about her son, a plan is hatched to put an end to Nino and Angelo's relationship.

Mambo Italiano uses this setup to comically and dramatically explore how the two male characters (and their families) deal differently with their homosexuality. Whereas Angelo wants to live an openly gay life, Nino prefers to conceal his sexuality. What happens will not necessarily please all gay viewers, but at least it will provide them with some laughs.

Although the film deals with some pretty serious issues, it does so in a very silly and even shrill way. Gaudreault takes such an unsubtle approach to the material, queer audiences may feel slapped upside the head with the messages "be yourself" and "it's okay to be gay." This is not necessarily a bad thing—self-acceptance sometimes bears repeating—but *Mambo Italiano* may find its best audience in the parents of gay and lesbian children who need the message reinforced.

Gay viewers will no doubt be disappointed that the film features minimal sexual contact between Angelo and Nino. The good-looking couple share only one brief kiss and have almost little or no on-screen tenderness.

The filmmakers take such great pains to make the lead characters nonstereotypical homosexuals that they sometimes fail to convince. Angelo's discomfort around gays is almost off-putting, yet he wears his sexuality on the sleeve of his very loud shirts. His clothes are deliberately used to scream "I'm different," but they really just prove he lacks style. In contrast, Nino's character heads in the opposite direction after being outed, and he starts dating a woman. Gaudreault and Galluccio seem to wants to queer the queerness, which is, well, pretty queer, for a pro-gay love story.

That said, Luke Kirby is rather endearing as Angelo, although obviously an alter ego for screenwriter Steve Galluccio. Kirby displays some teriffic comic timing and he has some great expressions of disbelief. As his lover, Nino, Peter Miller is quite engaging, but unfortunately, he is not given enough to do.

The film's best performances come from the talented supporting cast. As Angelo's father, Paul Sorvino is very amusing, and he emotes profusely. He is nicely upstaged by his on-screen wife Ginette Reno, whose deadpan delivery of almost all of her lines is priceless. Likewise, as the neurotic, pill-popping daughter in the Barberini family, Claudia Ferri steals every scene she is in. Only Mary Walsh, who plays Nino's mother, is a bit of an Italian ham.

If Gaudreault keeps things at too high a pitch, so be it. *Mambo Italiano* is an affectionate portrayal of Italian life, right down to the garish wallpaper that adorns the family home.

TOUCH OF PINK

Although it traverses the same territory as *The Wedding Banquet* (1993) and *Mambo Italino,* the queer multicultural comedy *Touch of Pink* is a lightweight and extremely likeable romantic comedy. The story is yet another variation on a gay son masquerading as straight to gain approval/acceptance from a domineering parent.

Writer-director Ian Iqbal Rashid distinguishes his gossamer fantasy version by making it a throwback to the romantic comedies of yesteryear that often starred Cary Grant. What is more, the ghost of Grant (played here by Kyle MacLachlan) advises the film's hero Alim (Jimi Mistry) about life, love, and family.

The story unfolds like this: the closeted Alim lives with his boyfriend Giles (Kristen Holden-Reid) in London. Meanwhile, in Toronto, Alim's mother Nuru (Suleka Mathew) watches as her nephew Khaled (Raoul Bhaneja) makes plans for his big wedding. Like her sister Dolly (Veena Sood), Nuru wants grandchildren from a successful son, and so, to keep up appearances, Nuru lies to her friends and family about Alim having a fiancée.

The fabrications prompt Nuru to pay a visit to her Alim who "straightens up" his apartment—removing the nude photos he took of Giles—and messes up his life, deceiving his mother by telling her that he is heterosexual. Of course, the relationship between the disapproving mother and her independent son—which was never great to begin with—is further strained by all these lies.

As Alim and Nuru try to navigate pleasing the other, they each seek outlets for their unhappiness. In an episode that pays homage to old Hollywood films, Nuru allows Giles to take her shopping and to sip champagne, while Alim looks to his "invisible friend" Grant and the actor's old movies to help him sort out his conflicting emotions. However, as Alim screws up his courage to be honest with his mother,

Giles becomes frustrated with his lover, and their relationship starts to fall apart.

Although other complications arise, the film has very few surprises. Cynics, especially, will be unamused by *Touch of Pink,* which is really just another predictable coming out tale. But despite all of the characters' pretending, the film is thankfully free of pretension. Viewers who give themselves over completely to the fantasy elements—and a few moments do strain credibility—will wholly enjoy this modest film.

And although the message by be trite, it is hard not to be moved by the poignant moments in which the characters are honest with one another. Alas, the big coming out scene may the subtlest moment in this broad comedy.

One reason why the film succeeds is the first-rate performances by the lead actors. The adorable Jimi Mistry (*East Is East,* 1999, and *The Guru,* 2002) is charming and utterly captivating as Alim, and audiences will share his struggle for self-identity. Mistry exudes star quality here, and hopefully his role will get him the notice he deserves as an actor so he can start making Hollywood films like Cary Grant. Likewise, Suleka Mathews is fantastic as Nuru, and the film is as much her story as it is Alim's. Mathews is wonderful and expressive—when she smiles, the actress is absolutely radiant.

In support, Kyle MacLachlan plays the thankless Cary Grant role with noticeable aplomb, and his character's acerbic comments to Alim about Nuru or Giles are often very witty. The ghost angle may be a creaky plot device, but surprisingly, it mostly works.

Ultimately, *Touch of Pink* may be all about how people escape from an unpleasant truth, but this familiar tale makes for an agreeable piece of escapism.

SORDID LIVES

"Ain't it a bitch, sortin' out our sordid lives," sings the lesbian ex-con Bitsy Mae Harling (Olivia Newton-John) in the opening of Del Shores's *Sordid Lives*. It is a bitch, awright—but it's plenty of fun, too.

This Southern-fried family comedy, based on Shores's play, may be a mess, but it's often very amusing.

Viewers, however, might need a score card to keep track of all the crazy characters. Here goes:

G. W. Nethercott (Beau Bridges), who is married to the high-strung Noleta (Delta Burke), is unintentionally responsible for causing the death of his mistress Peggy when she fatally tripped over his wooden legs in a motel room and suffered a brain hemorrhage. Peggy's sister Sissy (Beth Grant), who lives next door to Noleta, has two very different nieces—the earthy LaVonda (Ann Walker) and the uptight Latrelle (Bonnie Bedelia)—both of whom are fighting about Peggy's funeral arrangements.

Meanwhile, Latrelle's son Ty (Kirk Geiger), a closeted actor out in Los Angeles, is talking to his twenty-seventh shrink about returning home to attend his grandma's funeral and coming out to his mother. In another therapy session back in Texas, Peggy's sibling, Brother Boy (Leslie Jordan) is meeting with the esteemed Dr. Eve Bolinger (Rosemary Alexander), who hopes to cure him of his penchant for dressing up as female country music stars. (He lip-synchs to Tammy Wynette records for the other patients in the institution he has been in for twenty years.)

Sordid Lives mines the humor in all of these situations by carrying things to the extreme as often as possible. Brother Boy's "recovery" involves a wildly unexpected seduction, and the pitch-perfect performance by veteran character actor Jordan makes these scenes sparkle like his sequined red dress.

Less successful is an episode in which Noleta exacts her revenge on G. W. by humiliating him and his bar buddies with the help of LaVonda. Watching Bridges and his pals strip to their boxers and don makeup and a bra is, however, more enjoyable for the women in the film than the audience watching it. At least there is some pleasure seeing Delta Burke act up. Bridges's good ol' boy is just being a good sport.

These scenes prove that Shores is a better writer than he is a director. The film's staging is pretty flat and uninspired, but he generously provides the excellent ensemble cast with terrific dialogue. In addition, there are some absolutely hilarious one-liners—even from characters, such as a female prisoner, who have only one line.

Although *Sordid Lives* is often quite funny, the film's comic rhythm is interrupted by Ty's dramatic segments. The hunky Geiger is given some fantastic monologues, but most of these scenes are out of place with the otherwise outlandish comedy. Although there is a purpose to Ty's character in the scheme of things, his storyline is easily the film's weakest.

In contrast, Beth Grant's Sissy is a stitch in her every scene, and she is the best reason to see the film. Sissy may be a stereotype with her wagging tongue, her addiction to cigarettes, and her back-combed hair, but Grant makes the most out of this priceless character.

Likewise, Bonnie Bedelia is equally impressive as the rigid Latrelle, and her episodes at Peggy's "one and only funeral" are a highlight. Bedelia has a field day with the material, confirming once again that she is a terribly underemployed actress.

Rounding out the unusual cast is Olivia Newton-John, who scores with her singing. Unfortunately, she is not given much more to do other than pluck a guitar and find a place for her gum—a shame, because the Australian is obviously is having fun trashing it up Texas style in this role.

Offbeat and outrageous, *Sordid Lives* is a seriously funny cult film.

Chapter 17
Artistic Temperaments

The films in this section depict models (*Chop Suey,* 2001), writers (*Borstal Boy,* 2000, and *Bright Young Things,* 2003), and musicians (*Prey for Rock & Roll,* 2003) to show different forms of queer representation.

CHOP SUEY

Bruce Weber's documentary *Chop Suey* is a wonderful mélange of the celebrated photographer's favorite people and images. From his "muse" Peter Johnson to musician Frances Faye and her longtime companion/manager Teri Shepherd—this scrapbook of memories is alternately poignant and provocative.

In a sentimental voiceover, Weber recounts the photographs he has both created and collected, offering viewers a personal tour of his studio. There are several interesting stories of Weber getting his first camera, or talking about "photographing things we can never be," and his observations about the famous photographs on his walls are worth the price of admission.

Yet *Chop Suey* is chock-full of fantastic images. Peter Johnson frequently models unusual costumes—and sometimes nothing at all—for Weber's infatuated camera. These scenes, which are beautifully filmed, lend the documentary its romantic glow. It doesn't hurt that Johnson has a naturalness in front of the camera that is truly captivating.

Likewise, archival footage of Frances Faye on Ed Sullivan and other TV shows showcases her powerhouse performances, and audiences unfamiliar with the late entertainer will becomes instant fans. Meanwhile, Shepherd fondly recalls anecdotes about their relationship,

Independent Queer Cinema: Reviews and Interviews
© 2006 by The Haworth Press, Inc. All rights reserved.
doi:10.1300/5482_18

allowing a full-fledged portrait of this lesser-known artist to come to life.

Yet Weber also focuses on his photo shoots with Jan-Michael Vincent, Robert Mitchum (seen singing here, with Dr. John), and the explorer/author Sir Wilfred Thesiger. These scenes are terrific time capsules, and it is great to hear Weber reminisce about the subjects that have long held appeal for him.

There are some fascinating interviews with the legendary Diana Vreeland, who talks candidly about many topics, including her interest in surfing and skateboarding; however, this segment is followed by a portrait of the Fletcher family, best known as "Nixon's neighbors." Although this particular digression is easily the weakest segment of the film, Weber soon returns to form with a moving story about the athlete-turned-model Jeff Aquilon.

Ultimately, *Chop Suey* is an outstanding pop culture memory piece, paying tribute not only to the artists, models, musicians, actors, writers, and designers that shaped Weber's world, but also the fleeting nature of fame and celebrity. There is a tinge of sadness to almost all of the images that flash across the screen, for they are of people caught forever in a specific moment in time. But perhaps this is what makes Weber's photographs—both still and moving—all the more powerful.

BORSTAL BOY

Lovingly made in that *Masterpiece Theatre* kind of way, *Borstal Boy* is a sensitive coming-of-age/getting-of-wisdom film about the troubled teenage years of Irish playwright Brendan Behan. This modest drama, directed by Peter Sheridan (brother of *My Left Foot*, 1989, director Jim Sheridan), is inspired by Behan's jail journal in which the young man learns life lessons and develops an appreciation for Oscar Wilde.

Set in the 1940s, this handsomely mounted production opens with the sixteen-year-old Brendan (American actor Shawn Hatosy, doing a reasonably good Irish accent) carrying a bomb from Ireland to Liverpool in the name of the IRA. Caught by the authorities, Brendan is imprisoned and sent to the Borstal, a boy's reformatory in East Anglia, for four years.

Before he is tried for his crime, however, Brendan is beaten up for his anti-English politics, and haunted by a nightmare. He is comforted by his cellmate Charlie Milwall (the adorable Danny Dyer), a sailor who is also being sent to the Borstal. Charlie is queer, though, and Brendan does not take kindly to Charlie's compassionate kiss.

Although there is considerable tension between the boys at first, they come to respect each other after a boxing match in the Borstal, and soon develop an ever-deepening friendship. Meanwhile, a caring librarian (Arthur Riordan) tries to get Brendan to read the works of Oscar Wilde, another jailed Irish rebel, but Brendan refuses, preferring instead to do research on how to escape.

The escape attempt—a beautifully executed sequence—unfortunately ends badly, and Brendan, Charlie, and another boy are brought forth to the kindly headmaster, Mr. Joyce (Michael York), who tells them to "make a new start."

This episode gets Brendan to thinking, and he decides to mount a production of *The Importance of Being Earnest,* which features Charlie and the librarian in the female roles. Under the guise of the play, Brendan and Charlie share another kiss, which further strengthens the bond between them.

Although *Borstal Boy* quietly pursues the affection between Brendan and Charlie, but surprisingly little is made of it. Brendan's attraction to Liz (Eva Birthistle), Joyce's daughter, seems to have a greater positive effect on him, but the tug-of-war for Brendan's heart is never fully waged. There is, however, a nice scene in which Liz confides in Charlie as she helps him get into drag for the play.

In fact, the limited drama in *Borstal Boy* is perhaps its greatest weakness. The film unfolds episodically, and some of it feels patched together. There is an energetic rugby game, and a touching, private scene in which Brendan gives Charlie his medallion for the patron saint of sailors, but such fine moments are few and far between. Director Sheridan allows the film to go off in too many directions for the subdued narrative to have any real impact. A portrait of Behan emerges, but it is too broadly painted.

Despite this flaw, the performances are lively. Shawn Hatosy—who proves here that he is able to carry a serious film—is commendable as Brendan, and he ably shows his character's transformation from confused youth to confident young man. Likewise, Danny Dyer is quite winning as Charlie. Dyer exudes charisma throughout *Borstal Boy,* and he is easily the film's most engaging character. It should be noted, though, that Dyer's accent (as well as some of the others in the film) is at times hard to make out for untrained ears.

Borstal Boy is ultimately a good period piece, and for viewers unfamiliar with Brendan Behan, the film can be quite satisfying. Moviegoers looking for something with more depth are advised to read the book instead.

BRIGHT YOUNG THINGS

Bright Young Things, queer writer-director Stephen Fry's outstanding directorial debut, is one of the year's finest films. A faithful adaptation of Evelyn Waugh's novel *Vile Bodies,* this fabulous period piece is impeccably written and skillfully performed by a cast of both fantastic newcomers and reliable character actors.

The main plot concerns Adam Fenwick-Symes (Stephen Campbell Moore) trying to marry his longtime (and long-suffering) girlfriend Nina (Emily Mortimer). Their romantic status is dependent upon his bank account, and the film has fun depicting Adam's various reversals of fortune at the hands of such characters as a drunken Major (Jim Broadbent) and Nina's father (Peter O'Toole).

However, it is the satiric jabs at London's smart set that really propel the story. Adam and Nina's mischievous friends include Agatha (Fenella Woolgar), a goofy and impulsive young party girl, and Miles Malpractice (Michael Sheen) a flamboyant and indiscreet queer boy. As they move from party to party, each one more decadent than the last, Agatha and Miles can always be relied upon for providing wit and amusement.

And it is precisely their foolishness that creates good copy for the Fleet Street newspapers that seek to "tear the lid off the young idle and rich." Publisher Lord Monomark (Dan Aykroyd) runs a column by his society snoop, "Mr. Chatterbox," which exposes the wrong-doings of the well-to-do. Things come to a head, however, when the current "Mr. Chatterbox" goes too far. Adam eventually lands the job with comic results.

As Adam tries to gain perspective on his friends and his world, things start to change, and pretty soon, it is every man for himself. Suddenly, Agatha, Miles, and even Adam find themselves facing personal crises that alter the world they once knew and loved. Parallels can be drawn to today, for those who care to look for them.

Fry makes *Bright Young Things* compelling because audiences will care about these characters from the very start. Even though Adam is continuously broke, there is hope that he will succeed with Nina. Likewise, Agatha is endearing in spite of her folly, and Miles deserves to find happiness with a hunky racecar driver (Alec Newman) he meets. However, such dreams do not always come true, and when the film shifts it tone in the second half, the story is especially riveting. Even though some viewers may quibble with the uneven story structure, the film follows the book exactly.

The film's commentary on how society allows—or prevents—certain behavior is especially telling. The voices of reason are unapologetic, and even silenced. This idea is most effectively conveyed in a single moment, at a party when "Mr. Chatterbox" defiantly tells the prime minister (Bill Paterson), among others, that he is not at all sorry for the content in his column.

Fry's screenplay captures not only the meaning of Waugh's satire, but also the exact language of the characters; Agatha, in particular speaks in an almost code. The writer is also a remarkably astute director, making his film visually exciting as well. From the glamorous, stylized parties, to the terrific period details and set design, Fry seems to have worked wonders on a modest budget.

The filmmaker also coaxes terrific performances from his entire ensemble cast. Stephen Campbell Moore is perfect as Adam, and Emily Mortimer is fragile and lovely as Nina. The chemistry between this pair is what makes their romance believable. Both Fenella Woolgar and Michael Sheen steal every scene they are in as Agatha and Miles, respectively, and the cast of supporting actors are excellent as well.

Dan Aykroyd continues to show what a great actor he can be as Lord Monomark, and Peter O'Toole is priceless in his big scene. Jim Broadbent and Stockard Channing also make memorable appearances throughout the film.

Ultimately, *Bright Young Things* is a brilliant film, and one that speaks volumes about society's fascination with scandal. What is more, it is as timely today as when it was written seventy-five years ago.

PREY FOR ROCK & ROLL

As the bisexual rock star wannabe Jacki, in *Prey for Rock & Roll*, Gina Gershon has found a role that is absolutely perfect for her. Covered in tattoos, swathed in black leather, and her dark hair highlighted blonde in places, Jacki is one tough and sexy woman. Yet Jacki is also vulnerable. Turning forty, she and her band, Clam Dandy, have not "made it" yet, and if she does not get a recording contract soon, she says she will hang up her guitar.

Being a rock star—famous or not—is what *Prey for Rock & Roll* is all about. Directed by Alex Steyermark, this gritty musical drama is a testament to those people who believe that if they dream it, they can be it. (The film is based on the stage play by Cheri Lovedog, who co-wrote the script, penned many of the Clam Dandy songs, and even designed the tattoos for the character named Animal.)

The band, which doubles as Jacki's friends and surrogate family, includes Tracy (Drea de Matteo), the bassist with a skeevy boyfriend named Nick (Ivan Martin), perky lead guitarist Faith (Lori Petty), and Sally (Shelly Cole), the drummer who is also Faith's girlfriend.

Jacki is often seen as the group's den mother, and she keeps things together—or at least she tries to. When Tracy's boyfriend rapes Sally, Jacki exacts punishment with the help of Sally's hunky brother, Animal (Marc Blucas), who recently turned up fresh out of prison. Meanwhile, Tracy tries to control her drug addiction and show up on time for gigs. This is pretty much the extent of the band's sex, drugs, and rock-and-roll lifestyle. And it is not pretty.

Unfortunately, neither is *Prey for Rock & Roll*. Although it is a film about alternative and unconventional lifestyles, the story follows a rather traditional path. All of the expected clichés abound. The characters suffer, the band threatens to break apart, ultimately, the music matters.

But before the film veers completely into melodrama, *Prey for Rock & Roll* features many enjoyable scenes of Clam Dandy jamming. The songs "Punk Rock Girl," "Every Six Minutes," and the title track—which plays during the end credits—are all catchy tunes. (It should be noted that Stephen Trask of *Hedwig and the Angry Inch* [2001] fame arranged the music.)

Gershon, who coproduced this low-budget rocker girl flick, sings all her character's songs, and does so dazzlingly. She also does a mean—in both senses of the word—impersonation of Cher. Gershon's concert performances are so good that were she not such an accomplished actress, Gershon could conceivably make her living as a rock star. She exhibits the talent other actors who are part-time rockers (e.g., Keanu Reeves) only *think* they have.

Gershon's acting is equally noteworthy. Her Jacki spits out her thoughts with attitude, determination, and a bit of righteous outrage. Just check out her response in the tattoo parlor she operates when two prissy teens consider getting a rose inked on one's ankle. Even a scene of Jacki alone in her bathroom, jumping around and dancing happily after a producer gives her the promise of good news, is a memorable moment.

It is a good thing that Gershon makes such a positive impression, because the film's supporting characters are not given enough depth or time to develop. For example, Faith and Sally have little more than a chaste kiss, while Jacki has a pretty erotic encounter with a temporary girlfriend.

As a result, the cast does their best with the limited material. The talented Lori Petty is mostly underused in an underwritten part, and newcomer Shelly Cole is saddled playing the thankless victim role. Alas, Drea de Matteo, who has the juiciest character as the junkie, tries too hard to make Tracy convincing. In support, Marc Blucas does little more than stand around watching everyone else.

Regardless of the film's shortcomings, *Prey for Rock & Roll* does have one thing going for it—it allows Gina Gershon to rock and roll.

And she is riveting and cool while doing it.

Chapter 18
Coming of Age

It is almost impossible to find a quality coming-of-age film that is not preachy or stupid. Some of the films in this chapter handle this oft-told story better than others, but *Swimming* (2000) and *The Mudge Boy* (2003), *Gypsy 83* (2001), *Saved!* (2004), the short film collection *Boys Life 4: Four Play* (2003), and *You'll Get Over It* (2002) include a few of the finest films of this genre.

SWIMMING

Often, an actor's success means that films they made before they were famous get exhumed from the vault. This is not always a good thing but there are happy exceptions to this rule, and one of them is director Robert J. Siegel's marvelous film *Swimming,* starring Lauren Ambrose.

Ambrose, as viewers of HBO's *Six Feet Under* know, is the artsy, wise-beyond-her-years teenager who has a caustic attitude toward life. Before she took on the role of Claire Fisher, Ambrose made this impressive low-budget film. (Queer moviegoers may also remember Ambrose playing Chicklet in the little-seen film version of Charles Busch's *Psycho Beach Party,* 2000.)

Swimming, which was made when the redheaded Ambrose still had some baby fat, is notable not only because the young actress is on screen 95 percent of the film's ninety eight minutes, but also because Ambrose has to play many of her scenes without dialogue. Her facial expressions are masterful here, and they—like the film—resonate long after *Swimming* is over.

Independent Queer Cinema: Reviews and Interviews
© 2006 by The Haworth Press, Inc. All rights reserved.
doi:10.1300/5482_19

With her pale skin, tomboy looks, and baggy overalls, Frankie Wheeler (Ambrose) stands out in Myrtle Beach, South Carolina—and not in a good way. At a beach resort where everyone else sports a beautiful tan and a skimpy bikini, she is the reluctant heroine who wants nothing more than a car to literally get her out of town and away from everything.

Frankie's life—depicted here in lovely, leisurely paced scenes that are a pleasure to watch—is pretty much one of routine. Working tirelessly all day waiting tables at the burger joint she co-owns with her much older brother, Neil (Josh Pais), Frankie is more put upon than in charge. She also lives with Neil, his wife, and their two kids, and cares for Neil's small boys probably more than he does.

When Frankie does have time for herself, she and her spitfire best friend Nicola (Jennifer Dundas Lowe), who owns a tattoo parlor next door to the Wheeler's restaurant, hang out and ask each other, "What do you want to do?"

The lifelong friendship between Frankie and Nicola is tested with the arrival of Josee (Joelle Carter), a knockout who gets a job in the Wheeler's diner through her hunky lifeguard boyfriend Brad (James Villemaire). Neil is sufficiently enamored with Josee that he cares more about her looks than her skill, and this irks Frankie.

However, after a few days together, Josee seems to have a positive effect on Frankie, and when the girls are together, Frankie's whole face brightens up—as if this goddess with her self-assurance can offer her the escape from her mundane life that a car cannot.

Frankie's growing attraction to her gorgeous co-worker further deepens when she and Josee dance with each other at a nightclub, or fall asleep together on the beach. Of course, Nicola takes to Josee like oil to water, and *Swimming* beautifully plays out the escalating rivalry between Frankie's oldest and newest friends, especially when Josee breaks up with Brad and seeks comfort with Frankie. Nicola, in a quest for attention, begins a heated relationship with a Kalani (Anthony Ruivivar), a cute Marine with an imaginary best friend.

Yet while Frankie is figuring out how to deal with Nicola's jealousy and her own crush on Josee—which culminates with a kiss—another entanglement arises. Heath (Jamie Harrold), a stoner dude who sells tie-dyed shirts out of his van, begins to romance Frankie, and with some encouragement from Josee, Frankie finds herself tentatively embarking on a relationship with him.

While *Swimming* concentrates mostly on Frankie's budding sexuality, the film is much more notable for its realistic depiction of the ebb and flow of emotions among the three young women. Rarely does a film present the shifting of loyalties between teens with the sensitivity displayed here, and director Robert J. Siegel deftly handles the emotional bonds that forge and break between these all-too-real characters.

If *Swimming* falters, it is only briefly, when the focus shifts from Frankie's dilemmas to those of the other characters whose intense affairs threaten to upset the preciousness of the rest of this unassuming film.

In the lead role, Lauren Ambrose shines, perfectly capturing Frankie's longing, and her gradual steps toward independence. *Swimming* proves that her success is no accident, and Siegel provides an excellent showcase for this gifted young actress.

The film also features excellent support from the scene-stealing Lowe, and the lovely and talented Carter—both of whom make their characters come alive, flaws and all.

One of those rare exhumed films that deserves the attention—and the audience—it seeks, *Swimming* is a real find.

THE MUDGE BOY

A sensitive and moving drama, *The Mudge Boy* deals with a young man in the heartland coming to terms with both his homosexuality and his grief for his recently deceased mother. This heartfelt film, written and directed by Michael Burke, is an unexpected gem—filled with fine performances and artfully composed images. What is more, this quietly observed character study packs an emotional wallop.

Emile Hirsch stars as Duncan, a gawky teenager whose best friend is his pet chicken. He is derided by other kids as "The Chicken Boy," and has few friends in his rural community. He also has trouble connecting with his strict father (Richard Jenkins). This tension between the two grieving men is complicated by Duncan's efforts to keep the memory of his mother alive—by wearing her robes. His father shames him for this behavior.

Meanwhile, Duncan strikes up a friendship with Perry (Thomas Guiry), a strapping young farmhand who has an overactive sex drive and an abusive father. As the boys bond swimming in the local river, or talking in the fields and farms, Perry helps the timid Duncan come out of his shell.

At one point, Duncan shows Perry a secret—how he can calm a chicken by putting its head in his mouth. The sexual imagery of this is not lost on Perry, who later uses his innocent friend's unspoken attraction to him as a means to an end. When Perry is interrupted with getting a blow job from a local girl, he enlists Duncan—who spied this activity—to later finish him off. It is in this riveting scene that *The Mudge Boy* is particularly astonishing. Burke fully explores his story's themes about masculinity, sexuality, and desire to remarkable effect.

Significantly, Perry, who acts as the catalyst for Duncan's transformation, seems to have as many demons as Duncan does. One of the film's strengths is the way these two very different young men seem to be coping with their respective crises of masculinity. While Perry overcompensates for his insecurities by protecting Duncan when he is teased—beating up a guy who insults his friend—Duncan is quiet and effeminate, unable to fully comprehend or express his thoughts and feelings as his sexuality blossoms.

Furthermore, Duncan's slow maturation is poignantly expressed when he succumbs to the peer pressure of Perry friends. These boys use Duncan's money to buy beer and then proceed to get him drunk and make him act foolish for their amusement. Burke captures these moments without sentimentality, making them painful, if astutely observed, episodes.

The Mudge Boy benefits tremendously from Emile Hirsch's magnificent portrayal of Duncan. It is perhaps the young actor's best screen role to date. Hirsch communicates the pain and confusion Duncan faces without making him seem pathetic. Hirsch's every gesture—from his wide-eyed innocence and hesitant speech to his awkward way of running and overall gawkiness are extraordinary. The smile he has when he thinks he belongs is as powerful as the look of terror in his eyes when his pet chicken is threatened.

Hirsch is ably supported by Richard Jenkins, who proves yet again how underrated an actor he is. With few words, Jenkins expertly conveys the anger and rage his character feels seeing Duncan in his wife's clothes—and the realization that his son may be gay.

Likewise, Thomas Guiry is sexy and impressive as Perry. Guiry, who adopts a cocky swagger to match his macho personality, is alluring when he delivers a speech about having sex with a woman, and frightening when his pent-up anger explodes in an act of violence.

Featuring unusual, realistic characters, *The Mudge Boy* is an outstanding coming-of-age drama.

GYPSY 83

Todd Stephens penned the wonderful, semi-autobiographical coming out drama *Edge of Seventeen* (1998). His latest film, *Gypsy 83*, which he both wrote and directed, is an unofficial companion film to *Seventeen*, continuing the emotional narrative of a gay small-town boy dreaming of a better life in New York. This modest road movie may not be as affecting as his previous, more personal film, but Stephens's quasi-sequel is pretty enjoyable all by itself.

The film begins in Sandusky, Ohio (the same town as *Seventeen*) where Clive (Kett Turton) dresses like the Cure's Robert Smith and hangs out with his best friend Gypsy (Sara Rue), a Stevie Nicks wannabe. With their offbeat fashion and musical sensibilities, it does not take much for this pair to raise more than a few eyebrows in town. Treated as "freaks and losers" by their peers, both Gypsy and Clive are looking to belong. What is more, Gypsy hopes to reunite with her long-lost mother, Velvet, while Clive wants to lose his virginity to another man.

The odd couple get their chance when Clive learns about a "Night of 1,000 Stevies" concert event in New York City. Hitting the road, they begin a journey that, of course, transforms them.

The road movie narrative is as old as *The Wizard of Oz* (1939), but *Gypsy 83* accepts this fact and tries to introduce interesting characters to distinguish its story. The problem is that the supporting players are actually more interesting than the leads.

Bambi LeBleau (Karen Black) is an "International Recording Artist and Karaoke Hostest Extraordinaire" who teaches Gypsy about the price of fame. Zechariah (Anson Scoville) is a studly Amish guy the travelers pick up, and they have fun guessing if he is straight or gay. Then there is the frat boy (Paulo Costanzo from *Road Trip,* 2000) who secretly catches the eye of Clive, away from the judgment of his college buddies.

Yet as Gypsy and Clive learn more about their new friends, their luster begins to wear off, and things are a bit less special than they originally thought.

So too with *Gypsy 83*. The film, which starts out well enough, loses some of its steam along the way. As the characters eventually arrive in New York, a bit more jaded, a bit more self-aware, they are forced to confront some harsh truths. But these scenes do not have quite the impact they should. Even when Stephens gets the awkward moments right—such as an early bit when Gypsy performs a Stevie Nicks song to a group of strangers in a Pennsylvania bar—he serves his story much better when the characters are carefree.

Although the material peters out by the time of the "Night of the 1,000 Stevies," the performers are perfectly cast. Sara Rue makes a great Gypsy, and she displays the right amount of energy for the role. Her impersonation of Stevie Nicks is brave—as is her nude scene in a truck stop restroom. As her coconspirator and confidante, Kett Turton does not have the acting chops of *Edge of Seventeen*'s lead actor Chris Stafford (who was originally slated to play the role), but he is an adequate replacement.

The supporting cast members, however, are more impressive—perhaps because their roles are smaller and more tightly written. Karen Black is quietly powerful as Bambi LeBleau, and perhaps the most fascinating character in the film. (Despite being a karaoke hostess, Black actually performs a tune or two, and she is fantastic.) Anson Scoville is both very sexy and very engaging as Zechariah, the Amish boy searching for his freedom. Rounding out the unusual ensemble, there is a fun cameo by John Doe (of the punk band X) who plays Gypsy's dad in Ohio.

Gypsy 83 is certainly likeable, and the story should resonate with queer moviegoers. The film also boasts a great soundtrack and costumes. Stephens does not lack for talent, but his film could use a little bit more heart.

SAVED!

A sweet teen comedy with a queer twist, *Saved!* dramatizes—and also satirizes—life at a Christian high school. Although the tone of this amusing farce moves back and forth between spoof and slapstick, as well as seriousness and mean-spiritedness, it does so mostly with grace.

Mary (Jena Malone) is a Jesus-worshiping teen whose boyfriend Dean (Chad Faust) announces, underwater no less, that he thinks he is gay. Shocked, but not quite convinced, Mary believes that by sleeping with him, she can "save" Dean. Her plan, however, backfires badly. Dean not only remains gay—his parents ship him off to Mercy House to be "straightened" out—but Mary also discovers that she is pregnant.

Forced to hide her conception from her Jesus-loving mom (Mary-Louise Parker), Mary finds that her problems are multiplying. Her haughty best friend, Hilary Faye (Mandy Moore), soon casts her out of their clique, The Christian Jewels. Mary finds some support in the form of Cassandra (Eva Amurri), the school's troublemaker and token Jewish girl. Adding injury to insult, Mary finds herself attracted to Pastor Skip's son Patrick (Patrick Fugit) who recently joined the student body after doing a year of missionary work in South America.

Directed and cowritten by Brian Dannelly, *Saved!* walks a very fine line between silliness and savagery, which is, perhaps, the film's blessing and its curse. *Saved!* contains only small doses of saccharine and strychnine, but some viewers may feel uncomfortable laughing at some of the darker humor.

The tone of the film is also a little uneven. The jokes about Mary praying her home pregnancy test are negative—she repeats the mantra

"I hope I get cancer"—scenes of Pastor Skip (Martin Donovan) rapping about religion pale a bit in comparison. The film's best moments arguably feature the outspoken Cassandra—who really knows how to misbehave—pushing Hilary Faye's buttons by shouting obscene things in assembly as if she was experiencing Jesus' rapture. The tensions between the good Christian girl and the bad Jewish one are hilarious, if slightly disrespectful.

Yet despite the erratic and unashamed sense of humor, *Saved!* has a very positive message about thinking for oneself and the dangers of conformity. Even though these ideas are hit home with a sledgehammer, they still resonate. Dannelly is not the subtlest of filmmakers, but given the ripe topic at hand, it would be hard not to take broad aim.

The director is in fact subversive in his own way—for he gets to address issues of teen pregnancy and homosexuality wisely, and in a teenpic without being condescending. Dean even gets to consider taking his boyfriend to the obligatory prom.

What makes *Saved!* work, though, is Dannelly's tremendous affection for his characters. He makes Mary and her friends easy to care about. Even Tia (Heather Matarazzo), the scheming girl looking to replace Mary as a popular girl, is someone worth rooting for because her lust for power is so naked.

Dannelly benefits from having a perfect ensemble cast for the roles. Jena Malone acquits herself nicely to the role of Mary, and she makes a compelling, complex heroine. But the supporting players are the memorable ones. Especially good is Mandy Moore as the shrill Hilary Faye. Moore, who puts her pipes to use singing "God Only Knows" during the credits, excels at being bitchy. As her nemesis, Cassandra, Eva Amurri is also wickedly funny. Chad Faust is irresistible as the queer Dean, but sadly he has only a few scenes. Likewise, Patrick Fugit and Heather Matarazzo, along with Mary-Louise Parker and Martin Donovan, could have had more screen time.

Saved! tackles a provocative subject pretty well. Dannelly deserves to be commended for making an entertaining teen film that features positive messages.

BOYS LIFE 4: FOUR PLAY

Short films, which are often calling cards for a director's chance at feature work, barely get theatrical release outside of the festival circuit. So it is exciting that the *Boys Life* shorts program comes around every few years to allow audiences to view the work of up-and-coming queer directors.

Boys Life (the original, 1995) included a short film, *Pool Days* by Brian Sloan, who went on to direct the inferior gay romantic comedy *I Think I Do* (1997). One of Sloan's recent shorts, *Bumping Heads* appears third in *Boys Life 4: Four Play*, the latest installment of shorts.

Unfortunately, this story about two guys whose relationship comes to a crossroads one evening at a disco is not Sloan's sharpest work. Although it showcases nice performances by Craig Chester (*Grief*, 1993; *Swoon*, 1992) and Andersen Gabrych (*Edge of Seventeen*, 1998)—Gabrych is sexy and terrific here; hopefully this hottie will get more film roles—the material is subpar. Sloan's concept is to examine what makes relationships work (trust) and why they fall apart (failure to communicate). This not the problem; it is his weak script. The dialogue is pretty stupid, especially when it comes out of the mouths of established performers. Furthermore, the emotions of the characters seem forced. There is a good idea here; it is just poorly executed.

The opposite it true with the last entry in the program, Eric Mueller's *This Car Up*, in which a lawyer (Michael Booth) and a bike messenger (Brent Doyle) flirt and think about each other as they go through their daily routines. The beauty of this film is its presentation, which is done in four split screens. The two main characters' thoughts spiral on the screen above while their actions are depicted in the space below. Yet this gimmick eventually becomes distracting, and even tedious, for viewers. The boys take too long to meet, and little of interest happens until that point.

Split screens are employed much more effectively in the best short in the program, Alan Brown's *O Beautiful*. A story about a gay-bashed teen and the young man who tries to help him, this dramatic tale is incredibly heartfelt and powerful. Told simultaneously from the viewpoints of the two characters, the narrative structure is riveting. In thirty minutes, Brown has audiences caring about these young men (David Rogers and Jay Gillespie) as they come to terms with their lives. The performances by both the unknown actors are excellent. It is a shame this short was not made into a feature—the ending will likely leave viewers wanting more.

It should also be noted that *O Beautiful* is the only entry that features any nudity (and given the context, it is not sexy). Despite several attractive actors throughout, *Boys Life 4: Four Play* is surprisingly lacking on the sex and skin content.

Rounding out the quartet is the first entry, *L.T.R.*, an amusing mockumentary by Phillip Bartell about a teenage couple's relationship. As the filmmaker gauges the compatibility of Weston Mueller and Cole Williams over the course of two weeks, this winning little film makes great fun of the characters it depicts.

Although "reality"-TV is getting increasingly tired, in small doses (as is the case here) it can provide the basis for good satire. *L.T.R.* is clever for talking to the fact that there are many unsuitable gay matches, and immature men—and they are not always teenagers.

Ultimately, *Boys Life 4: Four Play* is a mixed bag. Each entry has its moments of pleasure—either verbal or visual—and the empowering messages come across clearly. The problem is that the parts are better than the whole.

This is not to say that there is not talent on display here. Rather, that there is a hope for better work in the future from these filmmakers, some of whom show outstanding promise.

YOU'LL GET OVER IT

One of the best portraits of gay teen life on-screen, *You'll Get Over It* was originally produced for French television. Given the frank depiction of teenage sexuality—and frequent full-frontal nudity—it is unimaginable that anything like this, much less of this quality, would ever be made for American television, even cable. (The theatrical film *Edge of Seventeen*, 1998, comes closest in caliber.) For this reason alone, audiences should rush out at once to this fantastic coming-of-age drama.

Seventeen-year-old Vincent (Julien Baumgartner) has a perfect high school life—he gets good grades, excels on the swim team, and has a beautiful girlfriend, Noémie (Julia Maraval). His parents, friends, teachers, and coaches respect him. In fact, all the kids on the swim team and in the school look up to Vincent as a role model. What everyone does not know—and what Vincent is terrified to tell them—is that he is gay.

When another student, Benjamin (Jérémie Elkaïm of *Come Undone*, 2000) arrives in school, however, Vincent finds himself drawn to the stranger. The two young men talk and flirt, and eventually, Vincent makes a pass at Benjamin. Benjamin dismisses this kiss, but he later says something to some other students that prompts someone to pen graffiti "outing" Vincent to his classmates. Within moments, the school star becomes ostracized by his teammates and harshly criticized by his girlfriend.

The ramifications of the graffiti comprise the crux of this tender, heartfelt film, and *You'll Get Over It* handles Vincent's crisis with great aplomb. Whereas he is reluctant to tell his parents about his troubles at school, Vincent's shiftless older brother Régis (Antoine Michel) happily blurts it out to their folks over dinner. The reaction of the parents—concerned and mystified—is terrific and helps set the stage for Vincent's own self-acceptance.

The film makes its best points about how other people react to Vincent's personal situation. One of his teachers may be reluctant to hold out a hand for Vincent, who is in noticeable despair, but his swimming coach provides Vincent with the support he needs. In the film's most gratifying scene, the coach tells Vincent why he must continue to fight against adversity and work at breaking stereotypes.

If this appears preachy, or if *You'll Get Over It* sounds like an After-School Special, it is anything but. The film raises interesting issues and questions about teenagers and the choices they face and make in life. Vincent's relationship with Bruno (Nils Ohlund), his quasi-boyfriend, is presented especially well. The change in the dynamic between the two lovers before and after Vincent's outing is pretty satisfying. It shows Vincent's transformation, and expresses his mixed feelings about being gay and coming to terms with his sexuality on his own terms.

Likewise, Vincent's friendship with Noémie is beautifully handled. Noémie is pretty selfish about how Vincent's homosexuality affects *her,* and yet he relies on her like a sister. These reactions are realistic, and *You'll Get Over It* deserves praise for treating its characters fairly and without patronizing them or the audience.

Director Fabrice Cazeneuve shoots much of the film's action in close-up, and with a handheld camera, which lends an added intimacy to the story. If the film has a flaw, it is that it ends a bit too neatly and abruptly. Viewers may find themselves wanting to spend more time with the characters.

The performances are also first-rate. Julien Baumgartner is excellent as Vincent, and his expressions—from masking the pain he feels inside to trying to suppress a smile—are wonderful. Jérémie Elkaïm is also notable in the pivotal role of Benjamin, and Julia Maraval lends fine support as Noémie.

Ultimately, *You'll Get Over It* may tell a familiar story, but it does so very eloquently. Never sentimental or sappy, this is a life-affirming queer film. Don't miss it.

Name Index

Abascal, Silvia, 205
Accorsi, Stefano, 12-14, 141-142
Aïnouz, Karim, 34-36, 122-124
Akers, Michael, 89-91
Alexander, Rosemary, 219
Alig, Michael, 31-34
Almodóvar, Pedro, 120-121, 169-171, 206
Allen, Nancy, 31
Allen, Woody, 169
Allyson, June, 46
Altman, Robert, 43
Amado, Chisco, 205
Ambrose, Lauren, 60-62, 229-231
Amurri, Eva, 53, 235-236
Aquilon, Jeff, 222
Arcand, Denys, 56-58, 94
Arden, Eve, 93
Arenas, Reinaldo, 2, 73-75
Arizmendi, Diego, 130
Avary, Roger, 149-150
Aykroyd, Dan, 224, 226

Babenco, Hector, 195-196
Bailey, Fenton, 31-34
Baldwin, Stephen, 104
Baker, James Robert, 153
Baker, Josephine, 123
Bancroft, Cameron, 46
Banks, Elizabeth, 173-174
Barbato, Randy, 31-34
Bardem, Javier, 2, 73-77

Barrowman, John, 172
Bartell, Phillip, 238
Bartsch, Jürgen, 198-200
Baumgartner, Julien, 239-240
Baur, Gabriel, 164-166
Bauraqui, Flávio, 123
Bazadona, Lisa, 61
Béart, Emmanuelle, 144-145
Bedelia, Bonnie, 219-220
Behan, Brendan, 222-224
Bell, Richard, 85-89
Bengolea, Cecilia, 129-130
Benza, A.J., 64
Berg, Sandon, 89-90
Berkoff, Steven, 182-184
Bernal, Gael García, 120-122
Bernhard, Sandra, 109
Bhaneja, Raoul, 217
Biba, Dritan, 184, 186
Biel, Jessica, 150
Birkin, David, 166, 168
Birthistle Eva, 223
Bishop, Kevin, 20-22
Bisset, Jacqueline, 210
Black, Karen, 234
Blair, Selma, 190-191
Blank, Claas, 36-40
Blat, Caio, 196
Blechman, Jonah, 147
Blucas, Marc, 226-227
Bobbitt, Sean, 152
Bohringer, Richard, 159, 161
Boira, Francisco, 122

Independent Queer Cinema: Reviews and Interviews
© 2006 by The Haworth Press, Inc. All rights reserved.
doi:10.1300/5482_20

Title Index

Order a copy of this book with this form or online at:
http://www.haworthpress.com/store/product.asp?sku=5482

INDEPENDENT QUEER CINEMA
Reviews and Interviews

_____in softbound at $16.95 (ISBN-13: 978-1-56023-343-5; ISBN-10: 1-56023-343-5)

Or order online and use special offer code HEC25 in the shopping cart.

COST OF BOOKS_____

☐ **BILL ME LATER:** (Bill-me option is good on US/Canada/Mexico orders only; not good to jobbers, wholesalers, or subscription agencies.)

☐ Check here if billing address is different from shipping address and attach purchase order and billing address information.

POSTAGE & HANDLING_____
(US: $4.00 for first book & $1.50 for each additional book)
(Outside US: $5.00 for first book & $2.00 for each additional book)

Signature_____

SUBTOTAL_____

☐ **PAYMENT ENCLOSED: $_____**

IN CANADA: ADD 7% GST_____

☐ **PLEASE CHARGE TO MY CREDIT CARD.**

STATE TAX_____
(NJ, NY, OH, MN, CA, IL, IN, PA, & SD residents, add appropriate local sales tax)

☐ Visa ☐ MasterCard ☐ AmEx ☐ Discover
☐ Diner's Club ☐ Eurocard ☐ JCB

Account # _____

FINAL TOTAL_____
(If paying in Canadian funds, convert using the current exchange rate, UNESCO coupons welcome)

Exp. Date_____

Signature_____

Prices in US dollars and subject to change without notice.

NAME_____

INSTITUTION_____

ADDRESS_____

CITY_____

STATE/ZIP_____

COUNTRY_____ COUNTY (NY residents only)_____

TEL_____ FAX_____

E-MAIL_____

May we use your e-mail address for confirmations and other types of information? ☐ Yes ☐ No
We appreciate receiving your e-mail address and fax number. Haworth would like to e-mail or fax special discount offers to you, as a preferred customer. **We will never share, rent, or exchange your e-mail address or fax number.** We regard such actions as an invasion of your privacy.

Order From Your Local Bookstore or Directly From
The Haworth Press, Inc.
10 Alice Street, Binghamton, New York 13904-1580 • USA
TELEPHONE: 1-800-HAWORTH (1-800-429-6784) / Outside US/Canada: (607) 722-5857
FAX: 1-800-895-0582 / Outside US/Canada: (607) 771-0012
E-mail to: orders@haworthpress.com

For orders outside US and Canada, you may wish to order through your local sales representative, distributor, or bookseller.
For information, see http://haworthpress.com/distributors

(Discounts are available for individual orders in US and Canada only, not booksellers/distributors.)
PLEASE PHOTOCOPY THIS FORM FOR YOUR PERSONAL USE.
http://www.HaworthPress.com

BOF06